Ius Gentium: Comparative Perspectives on Law and Justice

Volume 114

Ius Gentium is a book series which discusses the central questions of law and justice from a comparative perspective. The books in this series collect the contrasting and overlapping perspectives of lawyers, judges, philosophers and scholars of law from the world's many different jurisdictions for the purposes of comparison, harmonisation, and the progressive development of law and legal institutions. Each volume makes a new comparative study of an important area of law. This book series continues the work of the well-known journal of the same name and provides the basis for a better understanding of all areas of legal science.

The *Ius Gentium* series provides a valuable resource for lawyers, judges, legislators, scholars, and both graduate students and researchers in globalisation, comparative law, legal theory and legal practice. The series has a special focus on the development of international legal standards and transnational legal cooperation.

Edyta Hadrowicz
Editor

Polish Entrepreneurial Law in the Era of the COVID-19 Pandemic

Problems and Challenges

Springer

Editor
Edyta Hadrowicz
Mazovia Academy
University of Business and Applied Sciences "Varsovia"
Warsaw, Poland

Institute of Law and Administration
University of Business and Applied Sciences "Varsovia"
Warsaw, Poland

ISSN 1534-6781 ISSN 2214-9902 (electronic)
Ius Gentium: Comparative Perspectives on Law and Justice
ISBN 978-3-031-57479-5 ISBN 978-3-031-57480-1 (eBook)
https://doi.org/10.1007/978-3-031-57480-1

This Springer imprint is published by the registered company Springer Nature Switzerland AG
The registered company address is: Gewerbestrasse 11, 6330 Cham, Switzerland

Preface

The COVID-19 pandemic, caused by the Severe Acute Respiratory Syndrome Coronavirus 2 (SARS-CoV-2) and emerging around the turn of 2019 and 2020, posed a significant global challenge, deeply affecting social and economic structures worldwide. Poland was no exception. The pandemic's effects permeated various life aspects, notably within the private law sector. In Poland, the ensuing social chaos, largely due to restrictive measures like lockdowns, was accompanied by a surge of legislative initiatives. These initiatives, both in their duration and content, were not always directly linked to the pandemic. This "mixed" legislative content deviated from the principles of "good law" or, more specifically, bona lex. In many instances, the COVID-19 crisis provided a pretext for public authorities to implement legal changes that had previously encountered legislative barriers or sparked legal debates. Furthermore, the sheer volume of these changes hindered effective monitoring, leading to unprecedented restrictions on human and civil rights and freedoms. The sudden and violent outbreak of the Covid-19 pandemic presented the Polish legislator with many legal dilemmas, which resulted in numerous legislative changes. A significant part of these relates to the law of entrepreneurs,[1] who were among the main entities affected by the consequences of the pandemic. However, the situation caused by the Covid-19 pandemic had a much more serious dimension. It has led to the introduction of unique solutions which have become the global norm. In such conditions, the measures of the public authorities that took various forms (restrictions, limitations or lockdowns), as well as extra-legal activities, have given rise to many doubts and became the subject of various opinions in Poland. The public debate, filled with uncertainties, has sparked a scientific examination of the legal circumstances facing entrepreneurs during the COVID-19 pandemic. This examination particularly focuses on the statutory changes and new regulations introduced during this period. These include laws widely known as "covid laws"

[1] Article 43^1 of 23.04.1964 the Polish Civil Code (Journal of Laws of 2023, item 1610, as amended) states: "An entrepreneur is a natural person, a legal person or an organizational unit referred to in article 33^1 § 1 conducting business or professional activity on its own behalf."

and "anti-covid shields" in public discourse.[2] Each of these laws introduced during the pandemic primarily served to amend existing legal statutes in Poland. In a notable deviation from the standard legal principle of "lex retro non agit"—which stipulates that laws should not apply retroactively—the Polish legislator also enacted some of these provisions with retroactive effect.

The idea of this book was inspired by a scientific discussion that took place during the Nationwide Scientific Conference "Entrepreneurs' law in the era of the Covid-19 pandemic—problems and challenges," held at Collegium Humanum in Warsaw on 27.5.2022. The book contains a collection of selected, most important issues—from the point of view of legal theorists and practitioners—related to the effects of Covid-19 on the law of entrepreneurs. It aims to familiarize the reader with selected legal aspects concerning the situation of entrepreneurs, drastically affected by the effects of the Covid-19 pandemic.

The subject of the book is divided into three thematic areas:

1. an assessment of the constitutionality of the Covid-19 legislation;
2. an assessment of the Polish legislation process and the effectiveness of the legal solutions adopted by the legislator in order to counteract the threats posed by the Covid-19 pandemic;
3. an attempt to assess the application of post-Covid law in terms of whether constitutional bodies have effectively provided legal protection to entrepreneurs in the era of the Covid-19 pandemic, especially when it comes to state-entrepreneur relations.

The changes introduced into the Polish legal system due to the COVID-19 pandemic, including both legislative and non-legislative actions, are open to varied assessments. However, it is broadly acknowledged that few entrepreneurs escaped the pandemic's negative impact. While the restriction of economic liberty during the pandemic, lasting over 2 years, hasn't faced major objections—given that economic freedom isn't absolute and can be legally limited as per the Polish Constitution (Article 22, Article 31(3)) and the Law on Entrepreneurs (Article 8)—the form of these restrictions has sparked debate. These restrictions, especially in the areas of economic and personal freedoms, were unprecedented in post-1989 Polish legal history.

The Polish government's lockdown measures, which severely limited or even halted business activities, faced significant criticism, including from constitutional experts. The legal foundation for these extensive restrictions, contrary to Article 31(3) of the Polish Constitution, was not through statutes but via regulations of the Council of Ministers. This approach, particularly the added Article 46b point 2 in

[2] In connection with the state of threat posed by the COVID-19 pandemic, a series of laws, referred to as "special acts," have been introduced into the Polish legal system. Act of 31.3.2020 amending the Act on special solutions related to the prevention, counteracting, and combating of COVID-19, other infectious diseases and crisis situations caused by them, as well as some other acts (Journal of Laws of 2020, item 568, as amended); Act of 31.3.2020 r. *amending* the *Act* on the *system* of *development* of *institutions* (Journal of Laws of 2020, item 569); Act of 31.3.2020 r. Act of 31.3.2020 on amending certain laws in the field of the health care system related to the prevention, prevention and combating of COVID-19 (Journal of Laws of 2020, item 567, as amended).

the Act on preventing and combating infections, clashed with constitutional standards. The Constitution, in Articles 22, 31(3), and 64(3), emphasizes the primacy of statutory law, thereby limiting the scope for regulation.

In the absence of a constitutional state of emergency, the "covidium" law's assessment should hinge on the general provision of Article 31(3) of the Constitution. This article states that limitations on constitutional freedoms and rights should be imposed only by statute and only when necessary in a democratic state for protecting certain values, including health, without violating the essence of freedoms and rights. However, some restrictions on entrepreneurs were not only introduced through ordinances but also fundamentally breached the essence of the constitutional right in question. This led to public allegations that the lack of a declared state of emergency (martial law, state of emergency, or natural disaster) was a violation of the Polish Constitution. Despite the ongoing pandemic, none of these states was formally declared, even though such institutions are established mechanisms for addressing threats.

The absence of a declared state of emergency resulted in a dispersion of regulations across laws and ordinances, rendering the legal landscape difficult to navigate. This scenario underscores the problematic nature of Poland's COVID-19 legislation, which is explored in detail in the subsequent chapters of this book. It raises questions about whether the Polish authorities acted in accordance with emergency procedures, whether their response was appropriate to the evolving situation, and whether the Council of Ministers' interventions were excessively intrusive. Highlighting these issues, it's important to recognize that economic freedom is a public subjective right. The state's responsibilities include not only enacting laws to enable this freedom but also avoiding excessive interference and creating conditions conducive to economic activity.

The Polish government, aware of potential unconstitutionality accusations regarding the lockdown, attempted to limit citizens' ability to hold the state accountable for damages and losses incurred by entrepreneurs due to business disruption. This situation raises further questions about the viability of compensation claims in Poland and whether the anti-covid legislation has effectively restricted the application of compensation law for unlawful state actions. These topics are only an exemplary catalogue of the issues that have been legally assessed within the scope of the book, especially as more than 3 years have passed since the first Covid laws were enacted. At the most general level, all articles included in this study answer the following questions: **(1)** whether the Polish regulations achieved the objectives intended by the legislator and **(2)** whether the Polish practice of applying the law during the Covid-19 pandemic made it easier or more difficult to do business. In this context, the book has a groundbreaking character, because it presents in a comprehensive manner both the issues identified by practitioners and the scientific achievements of legal theorists.

In this regard, the book holds a pioneering position within the realm of Polish law. It uniquely strives to present a comprehensive analysis that bridges the gap between practical challenges and the theoretical advancements of legal dogmatics. This balanced approach, giving equal weight to real-world issues and scholarly legal achievements, sets it apart as a significant contribution to the field. It was the intention of the editor of the book to structure the articles in such a way as to provide the reader with a full picture of the fact that no matter how perfect and "anticipatory" the legislation might have been, the pandemic has, as a rule, exposed the "inherent delay" of the law. This pattern manifests itself in the fact that, during the pandemic, the legislator was not regulating events yet to occur in the future, but rather was forced to respond to a series of emerging problems. This implied the creation of new, often completely incidental, regulations.

Therefore, the authors draw attention to the practice of enacting provisions contrary to the Constitution of the Republic of Poland (e.g. with regard to the approach to the so-called states of emergency), the level of legislative technique (in the light of fundamental freedoms and rights of man and citizen) and the issues of substantive law, formulating *de lege ferenda* postulates in this respect.

The aim of this book is therefore to assess legal solutions and the level of legislative technique in the area of broadly understood entrepreneurs' law during the pandemic. For this reason, the solutions introduced by the Polish legislator have been analyzed, in terms of an attempt to answer the question: To what extent have the relevant public authorities realistically responded to the threats caused by the Covid-19 pandemic, and whether they have effectively provided legal protection to entrepreneurs. The basis for the adoption of such an objective is theoretical and practical knowledge supported by the expertise of authors of the book. The authors of individual chapters are well-known authorities in the field of legal theory and practice (law professors and university lecturers, and at the same time Judges of the Supreme Court, former Presidents and Counsels at the General Counsel to the Republic of Poland, directors of Law Institutes, heads and employees of departments of Civil Law, Civil Procedure as well as doctoral students at the University of Warsaw).

In conclusion, it is hoped that this publication will not only familiarize readers with the developments and changes in Polish law in response to the COVID-19 pandemic but also inspire further research in this critical area. By delving into the intricate legal landscape shaped by the pandemic, readers are invited to deepen their understanding and contribute to ongoing scholarly discourse. This is justified in particular by the fact that the Polish practice during the Covid-19 pandemic—in contrast to Germany or France—was often characterized by chaos and accusations of unconstitutionality of the adopted solutions.

***

We would like to extend our heartfelt gratitude and appreciation to the rectorial authorities in Warsaw, as well as to the esteemed academic community, for their invaluable support and kindness throughout the process. Without their assistance, the publication of this monograph would not have been possible. Furthermore, equal acknowledgment is due to the authors of the chapters for their innovative contributions to the development of this monograph.

Warsaw, Poland
January 2024

Edyta Hadrowicz

Contents

Editor and Contributors

About the Editor

Edyta Hadrowicz Professor at Mazovia Academy, University of Business and Applied Sciences "Varsovia", legal adviser, Director of the Law Institute at University of Business and Applied Sciences "Varsovia" in Warsaw, author of over 150 scientific works on civil law and the borderline between private and public law.

The basic area of my professional activity was and is the scientific and research activity related to the nature of the work performed. Since the beginning of my work, I have concentrated my research primarily in the area of substantive civil law (and directly related issues) and public law (particularly in the area of association law issues)—trying to link these matters together. However, I consider it crucial to combine theory and practice. For many years, as a legal adviser (and since 2021 as a legal adviser), I have provided legal services (currently also legal aid) to public (state) sector entities, the economic sector and *non-profit* organizations. I have also represented leading state institutions (former Office of the President of the Republic of Poland, the lower chamber of the Polish Parliament and the Senate of the Republic of Poland).

List of Contributors

Leszek Bosek Faculty of Law and Administration, University of Warsaw, Warsaw, Poland

Marcin Dziurda Faculty of Law and Administration, University of Warsaw, Warsaw, Poland

Izabella Gil University of Wrocław, Wrocław, Poland

Edyta Hadrowicz Mazovia Academy, University of Business and Applied Sciences "Varsovia", Warsaw, Poland

Institute of Law and Administration, University of Business and Applied Sciences "Varsovia", Warsaw, Poland

Sandra Hadrowicz Faculty of Law and Administration, University of Warsaw, Warsaw, Poland

Dariusz Kowalski SWPS University of Social Sciences and Humanities, Faculty of Law, Warsaw, Poland

Krzysztof Koźmiński Faculty of Law and Administration, University of Warsaw, Warsaw, Poland

Angelika Kozyra Trigon Orthopedia Clinic and Softmed-Laser Clinic, Warsaw, Poland

Ryszard Piotrowski Faculty of Law and Administration, University of Warsaw, Warsaw, Poland

Piotr Ratusznik Faculty of Law and Administration, University of Warsaw, Warsaw, Poland

Tadeusz Zembrzuski Faculty of Law and Administration, University of Warsaw, Warsaw, Poland

Possible Liability of the State Treasury for the Restriction of Economic Activities During the Pandemic of COVID-19

Edyta Hadrowicz

Abstract In connection with numerous restrictions on civil rights and freedoms, in particular on the freedom to conduct business activity during the SARS-CoV-2 virus, the question arises whether entrepreneurs who suffered damage due to these restrictions may seek compensation from the State Treasury. Thus, the subject of this study is an attempt to answer the question of the possibility to effectively pursue claims for compensation from the State Treasury for damage caused to entrepreneurs as a result of the implementation of bans or restrictions in certain areas of economic activity in connection with the COVID-19 pandemic. Lawsuits for compensation for such damage are currently being announced in the public space, and their legal basis is provided by the provisions of Article 417 et seq. Polish Civil Code.

The study analyses two possible bases for the State Treasury's liability for damages. The first of them is Article 417[1] §1 of the Polish Civil Code concerning—as it is accepted in the literature—normative (legislative) unlawfulness. This regulation is applicable in the case of claims by entrepreneurs based on the allegation of illegality of regulations introducing bans or restrictions on business activity during the COVID-19 pandemic, while the second one is the provision of Article 417[1] § 4 of the Polish Civil Code regulating liability for damage caused due to the so-called legislative omission. This norm, in turn, can be the basis for claims in a situation where entrepreneurs do not question the legality of restrictions or prohibitions. However, they argue that their introduction should be a consequence of the proclamation of a state of emergency, which is a universal instrument for combating threats in the form of a statute issued on the basis of the provisions of Chapter XI of the Constitution of the Republic of Poland—the Act of 18.4.2002 concerning the state of natural disaster.

The author's intention was to structure this chapter in such a way that the reader would obtain an answer to the questions: **1)** whether it is possible for entrepreneurs to pursue compensation claims in Poland and **2)** whether the anti-covid law has in

E. Hadrowicz (✉)
Mazovia Academy, University of Business and Applied Sciences "Varsovia", Warsaw, Poland

Institute of Law and Administration, University of Business and Applied Sciences "Varsovia", Warsaw, Poland

E. Hadrowicz (ed.), *Polish Entrepreneurial Law in the Era of the COVID-19 Pandemic*, Ius Gentium: Comparative Perspectives on Law and Justice 114,
https://doi.org/10.1007/978-3-031-57480-1_1

practice limited or even prevented the application of compensation provisions for so-called "legislative unlawfulness" (Polish: "*bezprawie legislacyjne*")?

1 Introductory Remarks

The COVID-19 pandemic, which broke out in the first half of 2020, prompted authorities in many countries to take extraordinary measures to prevent the spread of the new disease. These have covered many areas of social life, including the private sector. However, the COVID-19 pandemic and the fight against it above all revolutionized the relationship between state and citizen—in a way that most people of our generation have never experienced. With the continuing threat of the SARS-CoV-2 virus, the sphere in which the state is accountable, acts within its imperium and influences its citizens has expanded significantly. At the same time, the scope of matters over which citizens are free to decide and can act for themselves, such as freedom of business, has shrunk to unprecedented level.

With the Act of 2.3.2020 on special solutions related to preventing, counteracting and combating COVID-19, other infectious diseases and emergencies caused by them,[1] a series of laws was initiated that were intended to create special legal conditions for the time of the COVID-19 pandemic. However, the laws that were intended to prevent and counteract the pandemic, and its consequences, also contained provisions that can hardly be considered, as *bona lex* norms.

The introduction of numerous bans or restrictions in connection with the declaration of an epidemic emergency and then an epidemic state, reaching up to lockdown, has also had an impact on business activities carried out by entrepreneurs. The discretionary powers accompanying these unusual phenomena, which cannot be fully verified by a court,[2] as well as the numerous legislative changes and the method of regulation adopted therein, can be judged differently. However, few entrepreneurs were not negatively affected by the pandemic. Despite the fact that quite a number of forms of assistance were directed to entrepreneurs, many of them have suffered serious property (material) damage since the beginning of the pandemic. The frequent restrictions on civil rights and freedoms during the COVID-19 pandemic and, in particular, the restrictions and bans on various types of business activity raise the question—can those who suffered damages claim compensation from the State Treasury?

Undoubtedly, the lack of well-established jurisprudence determining the existence or non-existence of State Treasury liability for damage caused to entrepreneurs during the pandemic means that we will still have to wait for unambiguous solutions to this issue. One thing, however, has to be agreed with: the growing avalanche of potential lawsuits from entrepreneurs who intend to file claims for

[1] Polish Journal of Laws 2021, item 2095, as amended.

[2] See: against the background of German case law, judgment of the BGH from 17.3.2022, III ZR 79/21, NJW 2022, 2252.

damages against the State Treasury does not remain only in the realm of prognosis, which justifies taking a stand.[3] The subject of this consideration is therefore an attempt to answer the question of the possibility of pursuing possible claims for damages from the State Treasury for damage caused to entrepreneurs as a result of the implementation of prohibitions limiting the freedom of economic activity in connection with the COVID-19 pandemic.

In this respect the legal basis is provided in particular by the provisions of Article 417 § 1 of the Polish Civil Code. Claims under Article 417^1 of the Polish Civil Code cannot be excluded either. In view of the premise of damage caused by the issuance of a normative act indicated in this provision in § 1, it is necessary to speak in this respect of both normative[4] and legislative[5] unlawfulness. Moreover, liability for damages may also be connected with the so-called legislative omission mentioned in Article 417^1 § 4 of the Polish Civil Code. For this reason, the issue of possible liability of the State Treasury for damage to entrepreneurs caused by the SARS-CoV-2 virus pandemic was analyzed taking into account these two legal grounds. The first concerns claims based on the allegation of illegality of regulations introducing restrictions during the pandemic (Article 417^1 §1 of the Polish Civil Code). The second, on the other hand, relates to claims based on the allegation of a legislative omission in connection with the failure to introduce a state of emergency in Poland, recognized by the doctrine[6] as a legislative tort (Article 228 section 4 of the Constitution of the Republic of Poland in conjunction with Article 417^1 § 4 of the Polish Civil Code) consisting in the failure to issue a normative act, the obligation to issue which is provided for by a legal provision on the basis of Article 417^1 § 4 of the Polish Civil Code.

The present study is also an attempt to formulate *de lege ferenda* postulates regarding selected problems of the analyzed matter with simultaneous reference to German legal solutions.

2 Damage Caused by Business Restrictions and Bans in Connection with the COVID-19 Pandemic Against the Background of Polish and Foreign Legal Orders. Did COVID Lockdowns Harm Entrepreneurship?

Lawsuits for damages caused to entrepreneurs as a result of the implementation of bans or restrictions in certain areas of business activity (such as the retail, sports or service industries) in connection with the COVID-19 pandemic are not only a Polish

[3] Łukasik (2020), https://msp.money.pl/wiadomosci/pozew-za-koronawirusa-zaniechanie-wprowadzenia-stanu-nadzwyczajnego-wywolalo-chaos-6510051753949313a.html.

[4] Banaszczyk (2009), p. 814; Safjan and Matuszyk (2009), p. 50; Safjan (2005), pp. 13–17.

[5] Kremis (2014), art. 417^1 CC, Rn 3; Kuźmicka-Sulikowska (2021), art. 417^1 CC, Rn 1.

[6] See: Zoll et al. (2021), p. 12; Koralewski (2020), Lex/el.; Dudek (2020), https://konstytucyjny.pl/pawel-m-dudek-odszkodowanie-dla-przedsiebiorcow-z-powodu-wprowadzenia-stanu-zagrozenia-epidemicznego/.

practice.[7] As a matter of fact, lawsuits for compensation of such damages are commonly announced in the public space on a global scale. Similar attempts by entrepreneurs to compensate property (material) damage caused by the COVID-19 pandemic through claims against states have also occurred in foreign jurisdictions (e.g. Germany). In Germany, the first court rulings dismissed pandemic compensation claims against the state.[8] This was justified by the complex nature of the state's liability to compensate the aggrieved entrepreneur. Currently, the judicial review of the COVID regulations has entered a second phase in Germany. This means that the first judgements on the merits are being made and the courts[9] are finding (after careful examination of the facts) that the provisions of the COVID regulations were unlawful in whole or in part.[10]

The vast majority of these claims are based on allegations made in relation to the legal measures applied by public authorities to mitigate the negative effects of the pandemic. Three types of such actions can therefore be identified. The first group is made up of lawsuits in which entrepreneurs claim compensation for damage caused by the failure to take appropriate legislative action (the so-called legislative omission). The second group is composed of claims in which entrepreneurs link the damage they suffered to the fact that the state introduced legal measures resulting in significant limitations and bans on their business activity. The last group of claims, on the other hand, identifies the source of damage suffered by entrepreneurs in preventive restrictions on "healthy" (German: *gesund*) economic activity or temporary bans on such activity (e.g. preventive closure of hairdressing and beauty salons, hotels, bars, restaurants, gyms, or premises in shopping centers).

The widespread assumption that the state has the legitimacy to manage the risk of abnormal phenomena such as a pandemic makes it legitimate to conclude that the public authority is the natural addressee of compensation claims. On the other hand, it is also difficult to expect the State Treasury to bear full responsibility for the property damage to entrepreneurs caused by a pandemic. Therefore, the essence of the analyzed issue lies in the extent to which the Polish state has introduced instruments

---

[7] Cf. Larenz and Canaris (1994), p. 351; Fikentscher and Heinemann (2017), p. 365.

[8] See: Heilbronn Regional Court, judgment of 29.4.2020 – I 4 O 82/20; Berlin Regional Court, judgment of 13.10.2020 – 2 O 247/20 (no compensation due to closure of hair salon). Cf. Hofstätter (2021).

[9] In the German public space, a major stir was caused by several court rulings in which the administrative courts declared the regulations of the earlier COVID regulations to be unlawful. For example, the VGH, in its ruling of 4.10.2021. (At: 20 N 20.767), indicated that the "curfew" (in the formal legal sense: a time restriction) imposed in the first "lockout" in spring 2020 was disproportionate and therefore unlawful.

[10] German entrepreneurs who were harmed by the closure or restriction of their business activities on the basis of unlawful COVID regulations could have claims against the state under the liability for damages of public authorities on the basis of § 839 BGB in conjunction with Article 34 GG. See, e.g. § 39 (1)(b) OBG NRW (German Law Enforcement Agencies Act; hereinafter: OBG - of the 13.5.1980) according to which, "damages suffered by persons as a result of actions taken by public authorities shall be compensated if they are damages resulting from unlawful actions, regardless of whether the public authorities are at fault or not".

that violate the law and the principles of correct legislation, which has resulted in chaos and legal uncertainty. The relevant bodies will therefore have to assess the legitimacy of claims brought in this respect, which may be difficult for at least several reasons:

(1) it is not clear whether the damage in the form of lost earnings (profit) of entrepreneurs suffered as a result of the introduction of temporary bans or restrictions in certain spheres of economic activity can be considered as an unlawful act within the meaning of the provisions of Articles 417 et seq. of the Polish Civil Code. What has occurred is an atypical destructive phenomenon that has hit the whole of society and a large part of the economy. At the same time, a socially acceptable distribution of the burden of the pandemic is not the matter of protecting property or general fundamental rights, but primarily the task of the welfare state (e.g. through various aid programs).
(2) In this context, further hurdles arise, such as proving the occurrence of damage, establishing the amount of damage actually suffered (to prevent unjustified enrichment) and proving the existence of an adequate causal link.

3 The State Treasure's Liability for Damages Against the Background of Article 417[1] § 1 of the Polish Civil Code

In the Polish public space, from the beginning of the pandemic there was a lively discussion on whether its outbreak justified the introduction of one of the three constitutional states of emergency. To a certain extent, this was legitimate, as such states are immanently linked to the specific regulation of State Treasury liability for damage caused by the introduction of one of them. This regime is provided for by the Act of 22 November 2002 on *compensation* of *losses resulting* from *limitation* of *freedom, human* and citizen *rights in* the *state* of *emergency.*[11]

The liability stipulated therein differs from the provisions of the Polish Civil Code (Articles 417 et seq. of the Polish Civil Code), because it serves to compensate only legal damages. Thus, unlike the Code regime (Articles 417 et seq. of the Polish Civil Code), it does not cover damage caused by unlawful action of public authorities. This means that the State Treasury's obligation to pay damages is connected only with lawful action of the public authority, i.e. **1)** introduction of one of the three states of emergency in circumstances exhausting the prerequisites for its introduction and **2)** entry into force of provisions interfering with constitutional rights and freedoms justified in a particular state of emergency. Unfortunately, none of the states of emergency has been established in Poland, therefore it is not possible for the aggrieved entrepreneurs to invoke the provision of Article 2 of the Act of 22 November 2002.

[11] Journal of Laws, No. 233, item 1955, as amended, hereinafter: the Act of 22 November 2002.

Thus, the basis for the claims formulated by them in the current legal state remains the code regulation and the right to compensation under the administrative procedure. As far as the Code regulation is concerned, the provision of Article 417[1] § 1 of the Polish Civil Code is of key importance. However, liability under this provision is based solely on the premise of unlawfulness. This provision stipulates the possibility to claim compensation from the State Treasury for damage caused by the issuance of a normative act. Nevertheless, the condition for claiming reparation of damage is the prior determination, in an appropriate proceedings, of the incompatibility of such an act with the provisions of the Constitution of the Republic of Poland, a ratified international agreement or a statute. This means that obtaining compensation, on the basis of Article 417[1] § 1 of the Polish Civil Code, for damage caused by a pandemic will depend, in each case, on the entrepreneur proving that the regulations introducing restrictions or prohibitions on conducting business activity are inconsistent with the Constitution of the Republic of Poland or another legal act hierarchically higher than the legal act containing the questioned regulations. In addition to unlawfulness understood in this manner, further prerequisites of the State Treasury's liability (liability ex delicto) include damage (within the meaning of Article 361 § 2 of the Polish Civil Code) suffered by the aggrieved entrepreneur[12] and proof of an adequate causal link (Article 361 §1 of the Polish Civil Code), i.e. a link between the damage and the entry into force of the questioned restrictive regulations.

On the other hand, with regard to the right to compensation under the administrative procedure, it is granted on the basis of a decision issued at the request of the injured party submitted to the competent voivode.[13] However, the possibility of pursuing claims under the liability for damages relates only to the compensation of the material damage actually suffered, without the right to compensation for the lost profits that the aggrieved entrepreneur could have achieved if the prohibitions or restrictions had not been introduced. This implies that it will be necessary for entrepreneurs to pursue claims for damages against the State Treasury only under general rules.

---

[12] It should be noted that in Poland, despite the prevailing pandemic, the civil law obligation to compensate for damage has not changed its form and covers the repair of damage in two forms: actual damage (*damnum emergens*) and lost benefits (*lucrum cessans*). It is assumed that the loss is that which has gone out of the assets and would have remained therein if the event causing the damage had not occurred. Lost benefits, on the other hand, are those which did not enter the assets of the injured party, but would have entered if the damage had not occurred (see: judgment of the SN (Supreme Court of Poland) from 10.7.2008, III CZP 62/08, Legalis). Damage related to lost benefits is therefore hypothetical in nature and generally occurs in addition to the loss actually suffered. A claim relating to lost benefits can therefore only be granted if the injured party proves beyond a degree of certainty that, had the event leading to the obligation to pay damages not occurred, he or she would have obtained that benefit. Cf. judgment of the SN (Supreme Court of Poland) from of 22.3.2019, IV CNP 43/17, Legalis.

[13] See: Article 4 of the Act of 22 November 2002 (the application should include, inter alia, the amount of the property damage suffered, when and where it occurred and the limitation from which it arose) and Article 6(1) of the Act of 22 November 2002, according to which "an aggrieved party dissatisfied with a decision on compensation may, within thirty days of delivery of the decision on the matter, bring an action before the ordinary courts".

4 The Premise of Unlawfulness in the Context of a COVID Regulation Instead of a Statute

In the Polish public space, it is generally accepted that the illegality[14] of regulations introducing COVID-19-related bans or restrictions is connected with the fact that they were incorporated into the legal order in the form of basic legislative measures, i.e. regulations. This position is also shared in Polish judicature.[15] The above is justified by the fact that a regulation would constitute a permissible juridical instrument for the introduction of restrictions on freedoms or human rights related to the prevention, counteraction and combating of COVID-19 only in the event of the introduction of one of the three constitutional states of emergency.[16] In view of the fact that none of these states has been established in Poland, the restrictions remain exclusively a statutory matter, which may possibly be further specified in regulations. As it is known, regulations may be issued only based on a clear authorization contained in a statute and only for the purpose of implementing it (Article 92 of the Constitution of the Republic of Poland). The Act of 5 December 2008 in force in Poland on preventing and combating infections and infectious diseases in humans,[17] authorises inter alia, the establishment in a regulation of a "temporary limitation of the activity of certain scopes of activity of entrepreneurs" (Article 46b (2) of the aforementioned Act). Such a statutory authorization, however, does not make it permissible to completely prohibit business activities for a specific period. Accordingly, it should be considered unlawful within the meaning of the Code regulation of Article 417^1 § 1 of the Polish Civil Code. Irrespective of the assessment made in this respect, it should be noted that the allegation of unauthorized application of the form of the regulation seems irrelevant for entrepreneurs. This is due to the fact that there is no causal connection between the unlawfulness of these prohibitions, understood as the fact that they were introduced by means of a sub-statutory act (regulation) and the damage for which the entrepreneurs are seeking redress, which is a necessary prerequisite for State Treasury liability. In this case, it is reasonable to believe that the construction of legal alternative behavior (rechtmäßigem Alternativverhalten) may apply here.

This refers to situations in which the debtor—despite the unlawfulness of his conduct causing the damage—invokes the fact that the damage would also have occurred if he had acted in a lawful manner.[18] This means that the damage suffered

---

[14] As to the concept of illegality see: Banaszczyk (2018), art. 417^1 CC, Rn 31; Skoczylas (2005), p. 110. Cf. judgment of the TK (Polish Constitutional Tribunal) from 4.12.2001, SK 18/00, Legalis, p. 3. Differently, with a broad understanding of illegality, including, for example, non-compliance with ethical obligations, see Bagińska (2006), p. 334.

[15] See: Article 31(3) of the Constitution of the Republic of Poland (Polish Journal of Laws, No. 78, item 483 as amended)—hereinafter: the Constitution of the Republic of Poland.

[16] See: Florczak-Wątor (2020), p. 9; Kardas (2020), pp. 10–11.

[17] Journal of Laws of 2022, item 1657, as amended.

[18] Kaliński (2018), pp. 163 et seq.

by entrepreneurs (in the form of loss of profits) would also have arisen if their activities had been temporarily prohibited in a lawful manner. This in turn means that the damage would also have arisen in the absence of the injurious event.

5 Constitutional Guarantee of Freedom of Economic Activity and Breach of the Equal Justice Under Law by COVID Regulations

Irrespective of objections of a procedural nature with regard to regulations introduced into the Polish legal system in connection with the COVID-19 pandemic, further reservations—of a constitutional nature—may be raised. Against this background, it is necessary to raise the allegation that the so-called COVID provisions violated the essence of the restrictions on freedoms and rights, contrary to the provision of Article 31(3) of the Constitution of the Republic of Poland. Legal acts enacted during the epidemic, in particular the Regulation of the Minister of Health of the 20 March 2020 regarding the announcement of the state of epidemic in the territory of the Republic of Poland,[19] contained a number of restrictions on conducting economic activity. However, while constitutional rights and freedoms are not absolute and may be subject to certain limitations, these rights and freedoms cannot be completely suspended or excluded. There is also a view in the literature that the suspension or exclusion of constitutional rights and freedoms is only possible in the event of the introduction of one of the states of emergency. In any other case, it must be considered to be incompatible with Article 31(3) of the Polish Constitution.[20] It appears, however, that the introduction of a limitation on the exercise of constitutional rights and freedoms is permissible not only during a state of emergency. This is because Article 31(3) of the Constitution of the Republic of Poland unequivocally establishes the possibility for the legislator to restrict constitutional rights and civil freedoms, provided that the restriction does not violate the essence of the restricted right or freedom. This means that a possible claim for damages would require a prior determination that a specific limitation of a constitutional right or freedom did not fall within the scope of limitations permissible under Article 31(3) of the Constitution of the Republic of Poland.[21] In the absence of the declaration of a constitutional state of emergency, the provisions introducing restrictions in specific areas of economic activity should therefore be deemed inconsistent with the Constitution of the Republic of Poland, and thus unlawful within the meaning of Article 417^1 §1 of the Polish Civil Code.

---

[19] Polish Journal of Laws, item 491.

[20] See: Tuleja (2022), https://www.youtube.com/watch?v=3Tr3U-T08RY; Tuleja (2020), pp. 5–21; Nawrot (2020), p. D4.

[21] Sobolewski (2022), art. 417^1 CC, Rn 87.

A similar position should be presented with regard to the allegation that the COVID provisions violate the constitutional principle of equality before the law (Article 32 of the Constitution of the Republic of Poland). This principle also refers to the process of lawmaking,[22] stipulating the necessity to shape legal norms in such a way as not to differentiate the legal situation of entities belonging to the same class (i.e. entrepreneurs), distinguished due to a specific relevant feature (type of business activity).[23] The degree of risk of transmission of the SARS-CoV-2 virus, which characterizes a certain type of activity, should be regarded as such a feature. Doubts concerning the compliance of these regulations with the principle expressed in Article 32 of the Constitution of the Republic of Poland may arise from the selective character of prohibitions and restrictions on the conduct of business activities. Such epidemiological restrictions or prohibitions did not cover all types of activities. Against this background, the criterion which guided the selection of restricted areas of activity may raise reservations. I believe that it is highly questionable whether the choice was based on the degree of risk of transmission of the SARS-CoV-2 virus. This leads to the conclusion that behind the introduction of COVID restrictions, after the initial acute phase of combating the pandemic, there was rather an intention to globally restrict the mobility of citizens (such as closure of cinemas, bars, restaurants, hotels, entry and exit restrictions affecting tourist traffic etc.).[24]

Confirmation of the validity of this thesis could constitute a further argument to claim that the indicated prohibitions constitute a violation of Article 32 of the Constitution of the Republic of Poland.[25] In the light of this provision, unequal treatment of entrepreneurs through selective areas of activity covered by restrictions seems justified as long as certain types of activity do not share a similar degree of risk of virus transmission. Meanwhile, the provisions of the Covid Regulations also failed to respect the principle of proportionality.[26] In fact, the introduced restrictions were not adequate to achieve the intended objective, which was the legitimate protection of life and health. Ultimately, the inadequacy of these provisions can be questioned. For instance, the protection of life and health was disproportionate to the restrictions concerning provision of food to the population. However, given the special situation during the pandemic and the resulting pressure on the legislature to take action against the spread of the SARS-CoV-2 virus[27]—there is good reason to argue that the differentiation of restrictions in specific areas of economic activity

[22] See: judgment of the TK (Polish Constitutional Tribunal) from 24.10.2001, SK 10/01, OTK 2001/7, item 225.

[23] See: inter alia, judgment of the TK (Polish Constitutional Tribunal) from 15.7.2010, K 63/07, OTK-A 2010/6, item 60.

[24] Cf. Zoll et al. (2021), p. 14.

[25] Compare: judgment of the TK (Polish Constitutional Tribunal): from 15.7.2010, K 63/07, OTK-A 2010/6, item 60; from 30.3.2004, K 32/03, OTK-A 2004/3, item 22; from 2.12.2009, U 10/07, OTK-A 2009/11, item 163 and 2.4.2003, K 13/02, OTK-A 2003/4, item 28.

[26] Brzeziński (2007), pp. 173–174; Prokop (2005), p. 31.

[27] For example, measures to temporarily reduce the number of customers in the market in the service, retail or catering sectors.

inherent in the issued COVID regulations can ultimately be considered to be objectively justified.

The German judicature takes a similar view. It articulates that, in view of the dynamic development of the pandemic and the associated threats to existential legal assets (such as life and health), the introduction of the SARS-CoV-2 regulations raises difficult legal questions which are the subject of controversial discussions.[28] And this means that the competent public authorities should be able to intervene effectively in order to combat infectious diseases. Especially since the regulation criticized here was temporary and quite short-term.

6 Liability for Damages and Ascertainment of Unlawfulness of Legal Acts

Establishing the unlawfulness of legal acts constituting a source of prohibitions or restrictions on business activity is not the only difficulty that is associated with entrepreneurs' claims for damages against the State Treasury. Other complications concern proving the occurrence of damage and its amount in cases where entrepreneurs file claims for compensation for lost profit caused by the introduction of numerous restrictions limiting the freedom of economic activity. Determining the extent of the damage by comparing the entrepreneur's current profits (lack of profits) with the profits the entrepreneur made before the pandemic outbreak does not seem applicable here. The differential method requires a comparison of the economic situation of the entrepreneur existing after the event giving rise to the damage with the hypothetical state of the assets that would have existed if that event had not occurred.[29] It seems that it will be difficult to establish to what extent, the loss of profits through a general decrease in the number of customers was the real reason for the losses resulting from the introduction of numerous restrictions.[30] In addition, the lack of data on the impact of the occurrence of the pandemic customers' behavior and thus on the company's profits may make it difficult to establish the extent of the damage in the form of lost profits.[31] The power granted to the court in Article

[28] See: judgment of the OVG from 21.12.2020, 3 EN 812/20, http://www.thovg.thueringen.de/webthfj/webthfj.nsf/BFDE4E67AFAFDE2CC12586470031B3ED/$File/20-3EN-00812-B-A.pdf?OpenElement.

[29] "The level of probability of a fictitious course of events must be so high that it dictates, in the light of the state of knowledge and taking into account the rules of life experience, to exclude possible alternative models and to consider that the accidents would most probably have occurred in accordance with the adopted hypothesis". See judgment of the SN (Supreme Court of Poland) from 11.4.2014, I CSK 291/13, Legalis; similarly judgment of the SN (Supreme Court of Poland) from 12.2.2016, II CSK 172/15, Legalis. This is also the case in the doctrine of Kaliński (2018), Rn 121.

[30] Cf. Wandt (2017), p. 463; Lange and Schiemann (2003), p. 27.

[31] It may therefore be helpful to compare the financial results from the time of the COVID-19 epidemic during the period without restrictions and during the COVID-19 epidemic when restrictions

322 of the Polish Code Civil Procedure[32] to estimate the amount of damages based on all the circumstances of the case may also be a certain limitation.

Another difficulty in this respect is connected with the question of whether, when determining the amount of compensation due to an entrepreneur,[33] one should also take into account reliefs, exemptions or subsidies which, following the introduced restrictions and prohibitions on conducting business activity, were provided for by successive so-called governmental "anti-crisis shields".[34]

The State Treasury's liability is linked to the introduction of restrictions during an epidemic state. However, it must be assumed that the attribution of aid solutions from the so-called anti-crisis shields to the damage (*compensatio lucri cum damno*) would require the proof that this aid remained in a sine qua non causal link with the introduced restrictions.[35] The construction of *compensatio lucri cum damno* would therefore not be applicable. It is reasonable to conclude that the financial support provided by the public authority was a result of the pandemic crisis in general, as reflected in the provisions introducing the aid instruments. In such a situation, however, it can be argued that there is no causal link between the harmful event and the benefit as required under *compensatio lucri cum damno.* On the other hand, a different conclusion would have to be drawn if it was possible to link a specific aid instrument to the type of activity to which the restrictions apply.[36]

Notwithstanding the above, a real challenge for entrepreneurs pursuing claims for damages under Article 417^1§1 of the Polish Civil Code will be the necessity to obtain the prejudicature referred to in this provision. In fact, this provision makes the possibility of claiming damages before a civil court conditional on the prior

were in place.

[32] Act of 17.11.1964. - Code of Civil Procedure (Polish Journal of Laws 2021, item 1805, as amended).

[33] The extent of this damage has also been influenced by legal regulations to limit the impact of the state of the COVID-19 epidemic on business, such as the statutory regulation concerning the suspension of certain rents.

[34] See: the Act of 31.3.2020 an amendment to the Act on specific solutions related to the preventing, counteracting and combating COVID-19, other infectious diseases and crisis situations caused by them, together with other acts (Polish Journal of Laws, item 568, as amended), which entered into force on 31.3.2020; the Act of 3.4.2020 on special solutions supporting the implementation of operational programs following the occurrence of COVID-19 (consolidated text, Polish Journal of Laws 2021, item 986, as amended); the Act of 16.4.2020 on special support instruments in connection with the spread of the SARS-CoV-2 virus (consolidated text Polish Journal of Laws 2021, item 737 as amended), which entered into force on 18.4.2020; the Act of 14.5.2020 on amending some acts in the field of protective activities in connection with the spread of the SARS-CoV-2 virus (Polish Journal of Laws, item 875 as amended), which entered into force on 16.5.2020; the Act of 19.6.2020 on interest subsidies for bank loans granted to entrepreneurs affected by the effects of Covid-19 and on simplified proceedings for approval of an arrangement in connection with the occurrence of Covid-19 (consolidated text Polish Journal of Laws 2021, item 1072 as amended). Cf.: Dobosz (2020), p. 122.

[35] See: Kaliński (2018), pp. 163 et seq.

[36] However, a different position is also presented in the doctrine, emphasizing the link between the aid arrangements and the imposed restrictions.

determination, in appropriate proceedings, of the incompatibility of the normative act, the illegality of which is deemed to be the source of the damage, with the Constitution of the Republic of Poland, a ratified international agreement or a statute. However, it is not within the competence of the civil court adjudicating on the issue of damages to declare such incompatibility, as it is necessary to first issue a prejudicial ruling that the regulation or statute introducing the restrictions is incompatible with a hierarchically higher legal act.

In practice, this means that the claim for damages under Article 417[1] §1 of the Polish Civil Code depends on the Polish Constitutional Tribunal declaring the incompatibility of the provisions introducing the restrictions,[37] which will certainly be a time-consuming procedure and its outcome will be uncertain,[38] due to the discretionary power of the Polish Constitutional Tribunal in this regard. As a consequence, this may result in the practical impossibility of realizing the right to a court.

7 Introduction of a State of Emergency as a "Legislative Omission" (Article 417[1] § 4 of the Polish Civil Code) and Possible Liability for Damages (Article 2 of the Act of 22 November 2002)

With regard to the claim for damages against the State Treasury, another solution may also be considered alternatively. However, it will only apply to those entrepreneurs who rest their claims on the allegation that the introduction of COVID restrictions should have been preceded by the declaration of one of the states of emergency. Recognizing the accuracy of this position would open the way for entrepreneurs to claim damages on the ground of Article 417[1] § 4 of the Polish Civil Code, which is

---

[37] Cf. In a judgement of the TK (Polish Constitutional Tribunal) from 3.12.1996 it was stated that "the Constitutional Tribunal is not competent to adjudicate on omissions of the legislator consisting of the failure to issue an act, even if the obligation to issue such an act results from constitutional norms. However, in the case of a legislative act that has been passed and is in force, the Constitutional Tribunal is also competent to assess its constitutionality from the point of view of whether its provisions lack normative provisions, without which, due to the nature of the regulation covered by the act, it might raise doubts of a constitutional nature. The allegation of unconstitutionality may therefore concern both what the legislator has regulated in a particular act, as well as what he omitted in the act, despite the fact that, acting in compliance with the Constitution, he should have regulated it" (K 25/95, OTK ZU No 6/1996, item 52). This position has found a continuation in further jurisprudence, under the currently binding Constitution of the Republic of Poland (cf. judgments TK from: 6.5.1998, K 37/97, OTK ZU No 3/1998, item 33; 30.5.2000, K 37/98, OTK ZU No 4/2000, item 112; 2412.2000, SK 7/00, OTK ZU No 7/2000, item 256). In the latter, the Tribunal stated that "while the Parliament has a very broad field of decision as to which matters it chooses to regulate by way of laws, once such a decision has been taken, the regulation of the matter in question must be done in compliance with the constitutional requirements".

[38] See: e.g. Sobolewski (2022), art. 417[1] CC, Rn. 82; Kuźmicka-Sulikowska (2019), pp. 906 et seq. Cf. Zoll and Wortham (2019), p. 875 and 881–882.

the legal basis for liability for so-called "legislative omission" (Polish: "*zaniechanie legislacyjne*").[39]

Cases of legislative omission are similar to cases of issuance of an unlawful normative act and therefore constitute a special kind of normative (legislative) unlawfulness (Polish: "*bezprawie normatywne/legislacyjne*") in which a public authority, despite being obliged to issue a normative act, fails to perform a legally required act.[40]

However, unlike compensation for damage caused by the issuance of an unlawful normative act (Article 417^1 §1 of the Polish Civil Code), the pursuit of compensation claims for damage caused by legislative lawlessness does not depend on the prior obtaining of prejudgment.[41] It follows from the fact that Polish law does not provide for a procedure for ascertaining legislative omissions.[42] This means that the court hearing the case for damages has the power to decide on its own whether the omission of the legislative body was unlawful. For this reason, it should be considered that the lack of a requirement to obtain a prejudgment is a faster path to claiming damages.[43] Nevertheless, such facilitation is accompanied by significant limitations concerning the amount of damages that could be awarded to entrepreneurs who would indicate Article 417^1 § 4 of the Polish Civil Code as the legal basis for their claims. These limitations are a consequence of the solutions adopted in the Act on Compensation of Property Losses Resulting from Restriction during a State of Emergency of Freedom and Rights of Man and Citizen. Pursuant to Article 2 of the Act of 22 November 2002, anyone who has suffered a property loss due to the restriction of human and civil rights and freedoms during a state of emergency is entitled to claim compensation. This compensation includes compensation for the *damnum emergens*.[44] By contrast, it does not cover the lost benefits that the injured party could have achieved if the loss had not occurred (*lucrum cessans*).[45] The key question is therefore whether only the formal declaration of a state of emergency justifies a claim for damages under Article 2 of the Act of 22 November 2002. It is undoubtedly not permissible to interpret the provisions on states of emergency in such a way that they could not fulfil their purposes, including the protection of the individual also in the event of a legislative omission. The regime under the Law of

---

39 See: Banaszczyk (2015), p. 223; judgment of the SN (Supreme Court of Poland) from 24.9.2003 r., I CK 143/03, OSNC 2004, No 11, item 179; judgment of the SN (Supreme Court of Poland) from z 24.9.2003 r., I CK 143/03, OSNC 2004, No 11, item 179. Otherwise: Bosek (2003), pp. 14 et seq.

40 See: Banaszczyk (2020), art. 417^1 CC, Rn. 51; Skoczylas (2005), p. 233; Bosek (2006), pp. 237 et seq.; Bieniek (2009), p. 419.

41 The notion of a prejudicature should be understood as a judgement of a common or administrative court or, in the case of legislative unlawfulness, of the Polish Constitutional Tribunal (TK), which declares a normative act unconstitutional pursuant to Article 188 of the Constitution of the Republic of Poland - judgment of the SA (Polish Court of Appeal) in Warsaw from 27.6.2001, I ACa 8/01, unpublished). Adamczyk (2019), pp. 124 et seq.; Stefanicki (2004), p. 41.

42 See: Sobolewski (2022), art. 417^1 CC, Rn 83, Legalis; Strugała (2021), p. 30.

43 See: Sobolewski (2022), art. 417^1 CC, Rn 86, Legalis; Strugała (2021), p. 30.

44 See: Zoll et al. (2021), pp. 14–20.

45 See: Zoll et al. (2021), pp. 14 and 20–22.

22 November 2002 rejects the possibility of claiming damages, as the condition for a claim under Article 2 of the Law of 22 November 2002 is the introduction of one of the constitutional states of emergency, none of which were declared during the COVID epidemic in Poland.[46]

However, regardless of the assessment of the legal situation,[47] it should be agreed that the introduction of one of the three states of emergency should be a reaction of public authorities to a sudden and unexpected change in the factual situation in the country, which could constitute a possible basis for compensation for the damage suffered by the entrepreneur in terms of *damnum emergens*. On the basis of Article 228(1) of the Constitution of the Republic of Poland, there are no grounds for the assumption of an 'implied' state of emergency. As it is argued in the literature, "the Constitution does not provide for any automatism regarding the necessity of establishing such a state, which is not obligatory but optional".[48] Therefore, it is crucial to consider whether the failure to impose a state of emergency in a pandemic can be regarded as a failure to fulfil a constitutional obligation. According to the wording of Article 228 (1) of the Constitution of the Republic of Poland, in situations of special threat, if ordinary constitutional measures are insufficient, an appropriate state of emergency may be imposed: martial law, state of emergency or state of natural disaster. Against this background, therefore, a doubt arises as to whether an organ of the state is free to exercise the competence set out in Article 228 of the Polish Constitution. In other words, the question is: if there are grounds for imposing a state of emergency that can be objectified, does the obligation to impose a state of emergency become valid?

The term "may" used in Article 228 (1) of the Constitution of the Republic of Poland means that the introduction of a state of emergency is not mandatory, but constitutes only the competence of the responsible body (in the case of a state of natural disaster—the Council of Ministers). In addition, it should be noted that Article 228 (4) of the Constitution of the Republic of Poland also provides that the legislator "may" define the grounds, scope and manner of compensation for property losses resulting from the restriction during the state of emergency of freedoms as well as human and civil rights.[49] Therefore, it follows *a contrario* from the wording of Article 228 (4) of the Constitution of the Republic of Poland that even under the hypothetical assumption of the introduction of a state of emergency, the legislator does not have to grant compensation for the restriction of human and civil freedoms and rights.[50]

---

[46] See: Sobolewski (2022), art. 417^1 CC, Rn 83, Legalis; Strugała (2021), p. 30.

[47] Cf. Bosek (2022), Legalis.

[48] Karpiuk (2013), p. 97; Zoll et al. (2021), p. 12; Dobrzeniecki (2020), https://www.rp.pl/Rzecz-o-prawie/303319986-Karol-Dobrzeniecki-Stan-nadzwyczajny-w-krzywym-zwierciadle.html (dostęp: 17.1.2023); Sobolewski (2020), art. 417^1 CC, Rn 85; Miemiec (2016), p. 24. See: Judgment of the Warsaw SO (District courts) from 24.3.2022, IV C 1835/20, Legalis.

[49] Steinborn (2016), p. 1612.

[50] See: Sobolewski (2022), art. 417^1 CC, Rn 83, Legalis.

Therefore, the entrepreneur pursuing a claim under Article 417^1 § 4 of the Polish Civil Code who considers the failure to declare a state of emergency to be unlawful, but at the same time who does not challenge the legality of the restrictions imposed on business activity, still bears the burden of proving before the court that the failure to declare a state of emergency caused losses resulting from the failure to apply the provisions of the Damages Act to the extent of the damnum emergens. In addition, it should be noted that pursuant to Article 2(3) of the Act of 22 November 2002, the provisions of the Polish Civil Code, with the exclusion of Articles 415–420 of the Polish Civil Code, shall apply to damages claimed on this basis. In turn, the provisions of Articles 361–363 of the Polish Civil Code and the differential method shall apply to determine the emergence of the duty to compensate and its scope. This means that additional costs of the entrepreneur related to adaptation of the conducted activity to the regulations introducing restrictions in connection with the pandemic (such as costs related to a justified reorganisation of the conducted activity, the costs of maintaining or utilizing of equipment not used as a result of the restrictions, or the costs of procuring disinfectants and equipment) may also be considered as compensable losses. However, not all expenses, such as those incurred prior to the introduction of covid restrictions, can be included in these costs. Consequently, it must be concluded that the mere fact that a restriction has been imposed does not, in principle, constitute a premise for liability.[51]

It results from the lack of an adequate causal link between the injurious event and the damage. Therefore, such expenses cannot be considered as a loss that would generate an obligation to compensate for the damage on the basis of Article 2 of the Act of 22 November 2002, as this act is limited to damnum emergens only. As a consequence, it does not seem possible that damages in the form of "unproductive expenditure" can be compensated by bringing an action based on the allegation of a legislative omission in the form of a failure to declare a state of emergency.

8 Liability of Public Authority for Damages Against the Background of German Legal Solutions

On the other hand, in German law the liability of a public authority is governed by Article 34 GG[52] and §839 BGB, which define the prerequisites for a claim for damages. Article 34, sentence 1, GG provides that if someone in the exercise of the public office entrusted to him breaches an official duty towards a third party, the state or the corporation under public law in whose service the official remains shall,

[51] For example, *Kaliński* indicates that the loss can only be such an obligation which has arisen in the assets of the debtor and has actually been satisfied by him. Otherwise, there is no certainty that the obligation will actually be fulfilled, which means it is unknown whether the loss resulting from the creation of such an obligation is not only of an abstract nature. See: Kaliński (2018), Rn 92.

[52] German Constitutional Law of 23.5.1949, Grundgesetz, hereafter: GG. See: Fuchs and Pauker (2012), p. 203.

as a general rule, be liable.[53] It should be noted that this regulation constitutes a significant limitation of the scope of protection and guarantees of individual rights. In fact, it amounts to proving that the legal norm violated by the entity carrying out the public duty is addressed exclusively to the aggrieved entity, to whom it confers certain rights. However, this limitation is mitigated by the concept of self-sacrifice remedy (Aufopferungsanspruch) which has its origin in the natural law implemented in the Prussian Landrecht of 1794. It relies on the fact that compensation is due in all situations where the damage results from an individual fulfilling a duty to tolerate an infringement of his or her rights by a public authority acting in the general interest.[54] Notwithstanding the limitation by the construction of the protective purpose of the legal norm (Schutzzweck der Norm), German liability of a public authority is also limited by the subsidiarity clause in § 839 (1) sentence 2 BGB. This provision stipulates that, in the event of a breach of a legal duty by an official through mere negligence, damages may only be awarded if there is no possibility of redress by any other means. In addition, § 839 (3) BGB excludes official liability (German: *Amtshaftung*) if the injured party through his or her own fault failed to prevent the damage when exercising his or her legal remedies. In fact, the institution of Amtshaftung does not provide for direct personal liability of a public official. In addition, a characteristic feature of the German institution of liability of public authority for damages is the form of compensation. On the basis of the § 839 BGB in conjunction with Article 34 GG, ordinary courts can only award monetary compensation to public law entities.

The regulation of liability for normative illegality also deserves special attention. German law adopts the principle of the subsidiarity of the action for damages, emphasising the connection between unlawfulness and the construction of the invalidity of normative acts. Thus, as in the Polish legal order, it is only when this invalidity is established in the relevant proceedings that damages can be claimed. As a matter of principle, however, the Federal Supreme Court considers that there are no grounds for accepting state liability for damage caused by legislative acts. With reference to the wording of § 839 BGB, it must be assumed that if the legislative activity is an action in the general interest, the issuance of an unconstitutional provision, regardless of the common assessment of this fact, does not infringe the interests of the injured party. For a different interpretation would open the way to unlimited liability and thus threaten the fiscal stability of the state.[55]

---

[53] Medicus and Lorenz (2010), p. 488.

[54] Enneccerus and Lehmann (1958), p. 922; judgment of the BGH from 19.2.1953, BGHZ, vol. 9, p. 83.

[55] Judgment of the BGH from 12.3.1987 r., III ZR 216/85, Juristen Zeitung 1987, p. 1026.

9 Conclusions

The conducted analysis leads to the following conclusions:

(1) The State Treasury (as well as other entities exercising public authority)—may be liable for damage caused to entrepreneurs in connection with a pandemic. Significantly, for this it is not necessary to have first introduced one of the three constitutional states of emergency. This means that the lack of introduction of a constitutional state of emergency in Poland does not exclude the State Treasury's liability for the so-called actual losses (*damnum emergens*) and lost profits (*lucrum cessans*). On the other hand, this factor makes it significantly more difficult to seek redress for such damages in court.

(2) In the current state of the law, it may be assumed that the general provisions of the Polish Civil Code allow for seeking damages from the State Treasury. Each time, however, a thorough analysis of the facts and legal prerequisites of the case is required. Therefore, with a view to open prospects of success in claiming damages, it is important to generally balance the consequences (proportionality principle), i.e. the losses that would have arisen if the temporary restrictions on business activity had not been introduced and the losses that would have arisen regardless of their introduction.

(3) Since ex delicto liability of the State Treasury can be triggered by damage caused "in the exercise of public authority", it should be said that it is also the unlawful issuance of a regulation that can lead to possible liability for damages. However, the Constitutional Tribunal would first have to declare the COVID regulation unlawful, which has not happened in Poland so far. In contrast, it should be noted that this practice is not an isolated case in German jurisprudence. And this, in turn, would mean that the first obstacle on the way to claiming liability for damages (the premise of illegality) is removed. A prejudgment stating the illegality of these regulations would determine the possibility of claiming damages on the basis of Article 417^1 § 1 of the Polish Civil Code. On the other hand, it should be pointed out that even the alternative legal basis for claims for damages, i.e. Article 417^1 § 4 of the Polish Civil Code, is fraught with considerable uncertainty as to whether the civil court deciding the case would consider that the prerequisites for the introduction of a state of emergency have been met. For example, BGH, in assessing whether there is a risk of the spread of a dangerous infectious disease (§ 2 section 3a IfSG[56]), explicitly pointed out that the legal protection authorities have a discretionary power which, however, cannot be fully verified by the court.[57] In addition, obstacles to causation, as well as difficulties in proving the existence of damage, may *in casu* determine the disallowance of a number of actions by entrepreneurs.

---

[56] Act on the Prevention and Control of Infectious Diseases in Humans of 20.7.2000, Federal Law Gazette I, p. 1045.

[57] Judgment of the BGH from 17.3.2022 r., III ZR 79/21, NJW 2022, 2252.

With the above in mind, it must be said that the process of balancing the interests of the parties to the lawsuit regarding possible state liability in connection with the COVID 19 pandemic has only just begun. With the increasing number of lawsuits alleging the illegality of pandemic containment measures, the question will become increasingly relevant—whether and to what extent tangible (financial) consequences for the state can be drawn from this illegality. The Code regulation of Articles 417–417[2] of the Polish Civil Code could provide a basis for attributing liability to the public authority for serious violations of fundamental rights that have occurred since spring 2020. Furthermore, since this has been achieved (albeit insufficiently) in some cases before the German administrative courts, the declaration of illegality is now not only of ideological importance, but is already able to mitigate the negative effects that have occurred in this respect. In conclusion, it is possible to assume a "hypothetical" liability of the State Treasury for damage caused during the pandemic. However, what is particularly relevant for the subject under consideration and amid the inconsistency of European law, is the scope of acceptable compensation in connection with the introduction of Covid restrictions or limitations.

Nevertheless, no matter how perfect and "anticipatory" the legislation might have been, as a general rule, the pandemic exposed the "inherent delay" of the law. This pattern manifests itself in the fact that, during the pandemic, the legislator was not regulating events yet to occur in the future, but rather was forced to respond to a series of emerging problems. This implied the creation of new, often completely incidental, regulations.

References

Adamczyk M (2019) Niezgodność z prawem działania lub zaniechania organu władzy publicznej jako przesłanka odpowiedzialności odszkodowawczej Skarbu Państwa, Warszawa

Bagińska E (2006) Odpowiedzialność odszkodowawcza za wykonywanie władzy publicznej, Warszawa

Banaszczyk Z (2009) Odpowiedzialność za szkodę wyrządzoną przy wykonywaniu władzy publicznej. In: Olejniczak A (ed) System Prawa Prywatnego. Prawo zobowiązań – część ogólna, t. 6, Warszawa

Banaszczyk Z (2015) Odpowiedzialność za szkody wyrządzone przy wykonywaniu władzy publicznej, Warszawa

Banaszczyk Z (2018) In: Pietrzykowski K (ed) Kodeks cywilny. Komentarz. Art. 1–449[10], vol I, Legalis

Banaszczyk Z (2020) In: Pietrzykowski K (ed) Kodeks cywilny. Komentarz. Art. 1–449[10], vol I, Legalis

Bieniek G (2009) In: Bieniek G (ed) Kodeks cywilny. Komentarz, tom I, Warszawa

Bosek L (2003) Odpowiedzialność państwa za legislacyjne bezprawie w prawie niemieckim. Państwo i Prawo 1:14

Bosek L (2006) Bezprawie legislacyjne, Warszawa

Bosek L (2022) Stan epidemii. Konstrukcja prawna, Warszawa

Brzeziński M (2007) Stany nadzwyczajne w polskich konstytucjach, Warszawa 2007

Dobosz D (2020) Wpływ ustawy antykryzysowej na niektóre zobowiązania umowne. Transformacje Prawa Prywatnego 2:122

Dobrzeniecki K (2020) Stan nadzwyczajny w krzywym zwierciadle, Rzeczpospolita 31.3.2020 r. https://www.rp.pl/Rzecz-o-prawie/303319986-Karol-Dobrzeniecki-Stan-nadzwyczajny-w-krzywym-zwierciadle.html
Dudek P (2020) Odszkodowanie dla przedsiębiorców z powodu wprowadzenia stanu zagrożenia epidemicznego, Konstytucyjny.pl, z 20.3.2020 r., https://konstytucyjny.pl/pawel-m-dudek-odszkodowanie-dla-przedsiebiorcow-z-powodu-wprowadzenia-stanu-zagrozenia-epidemicznego/
Enneccerus L, Lehmann H (1958) Lehrbuch des Schuldrechts. Recht der Schuldverhältnisse Tübingen
Fikentscher W, Heinemann A (2017) Schuldrecht Allgemeiner und Besonderer Teil, Berlin
Florczak-Wątor M (2020) Niekonstytucyjność ograniczeń praw i wolności jednostki wprowadzonych w związku z epidemią COVID-19 jako przesłanka odpowiedzialności odszkodowawczej państwa. Państwo i Prawo 12:9
Fuchs M, Pauker W (2012) Delikts- und Schadenserstazrecht, Heidelberg-Dordrecht-London-New York
Hofstätter C (2021) Amtshaftung bei rechtswidriger COVID-19-Verordnungserlassung. ZfV 57:4
Kaliński M (2018) In: Olejniczak A (ed) System Prawa Prywatnego. Prawo zobowiązań – część ogólna, vol 6. Warszawa
Kardas P (2020) Konstytucyjne podstawy rozstrzygania kolizji obowiązków i konfliktów dóbr w czasie epidemii. Palestra 6:10–11
Karpiuk M (2013) Kształtowanie się instytucji stanów nadzwyczajnych w Polsce, Warszawa
Koralewski M (2020) Odpowiedzialność Skarbu Państwa za szkody w trakcie epidemii, Warszawa
Kremis J (2014) In: Gniewek E, Machnikowski P (eds) Kodeks cywilny. Komentarz, Warsaw: art. 417^1 KC. Legalis
Kuźmicka-Sulikowska J (2019) In: Gniewek E, Machnikowski P (eds) Kodeks cywilny. Komentarz, Warszawa
Kuźmicka-Sulikowska (2021) In: Gniewek E, Machnikowski P (eds) Kodeks cywilny. Komentarz, Warsaw Legalis
Lange H, Schiemann G (2003) Schadensersatz, Tübingen
Larenz K, Canaris C (1994) Lehrbuch des Schuldrecht. Band II: Besonderer Teil 2. Halbband, Munchen
Łukasik M (2020) Pozew za koronawirusa. "Zaniechanie wprowadzenia stanu nadzwyczajnego wywołało chaos" (Money.pl z 13.5.2020 r., https://msp.money.pl/wiadomosci/pozew-za-koronawirusa-zaniechanie-wprowadzenia-stanu-nadzwyczajnego-wywolalo-chaos-6510051753949313a.html
Medicus D, Lorenz S (2010) Schuldrecht II, Besonderer Teil, Ein Studienbuch, Munchen
Miemiec M (2016) Stany nadzwyczajne (stan wojenny, stan wyjątkowy, stan klęski żywiołowej) w Konstytucji Rzeczypospolitej Polskiej, Acta Universitatis Wratislaviensis, No 3738: 24
Nawrot RA (2020) Po odszkodowanie do Skarbu Państwa, Dziennik Gazeta Prawna z 26.5. 2020, No 10: D4
Prokop K (2005) Stany nadzwyczajne w Konstytucji Rzeczypospolitej Polskiej z dnia 2 kwietnia 1997 r., Białystok
Safjan M (2005) Odpowiedzialność odszkodowawcza z tytułu bezprawia normatywnego. Ruch Prawniczy, Ekonomiczny i Socjologiczny 1:13–17
Safjan M, Matuszyk KJ (2009) Odpowiedzialność odszkodowawcza władzy publicznej, Warszawa: 50
Skoczylas JJ (2005) Odpowiedzialność za szkody wyrządzone przez władzę publiczną, Warszawa
Sobolewski P (2020) In: Osajda K (ed) Kodeks cywilny. Komentarz, Warszawa
Sobolewski P (2022) In: Osajda K, Borysiak W (eds) Kodeks cywilny. Komentarz, t. 2, Warszawa
Stefanicki R (2004) Odpowiedzialność odszkodowawcza państwa wobec jednostki z tytułu niewypełniania prawa wspólnotowego. Państwo i Prawo 4:41
Steinborn S (2016) In: Safjan M, Bosek L (eds) Konstytucja RP. Komentarz, t. II, Warszawa

Strugała R (2021) Odpowiedzialność Skarbu Państwa za szkody wynikające z zakazów prowadzenia działalności gospodarczej w okresie pandemii Covid-19. Przegląd Prawa Handlowego 5:26–32
Tuleja P (2020) Pandemia COVID-19 a konstytucyjne stany nadzwyczajne. Palestra 9:5–21
Tuleja P (2022) Stany nadzwyczajne – Perspektywa Konstytucyjna Q&A, https://www.youtube.com/watch?v=3Tr3U-T08RY (accessed: 27.12.2022)
Wandt M (2017) Gesetzliche Schuldverhaltnisse, Frankfut am Main
Zoll F, Wortham L (2019) Judicial independence and accountability: withstanding political stress in Poland. Fordham Int Law J 42(3):875 and 881–882
Zoll F, Południak-Gierz K, Bańczyk W (2021) Zakres odpowiedzialności odszkodowawczej Skarbu Państwa za szkody majątkowe spowodowane ograniczeniami wprowadzonymi w związku z COVID-19. Studia Prawa Prywatnego 3–4:7–25, Legalis

Edyta Hadrowicz Professor at Mazovia Academy and Collegium Humanum, legal adviser, Director of the Law Institute at Collegium Humanum in Warsaw, author of over 140 scientific works on civil law and the borderline between private and public law.

Between Necessity and Constitutionality. Evaluating Covid-Related Legislation in Poland

Ryszard Piotrowski

Abstract The pandemic encourages authoritarian arrangements that restrict basic rights. The Constitution of Poland allows for restricting the rights of the individual, both in normal times, when such restrictions come as ordinary constitutional measures, and, where these measures fail, also in state of emergency. The COVID-19 legislation provides an example of constitutional circumvention: while no state of natural disaster was actually imposed, the legal arrangements were being introduced which could only be acceptable under such state. The authorities introduced a peculiar state of pandemic which served as a vehicle to push for changes that otherwise would, probably, have not been adopted so easily and so effectively.

1 The Consequences of Pandemic for Human Rights and Freedoms

The Covid-19 pandemic, while posing major threats to human health and life on a scale comparable, perhaps, with only the consequences of a war, has also entailed the risk of limitation of human rights and liberties. As it happens, these rights and liberties have been subjected to a certain hierarchization, reflecting the persuasive power of the argument that the necessity of saving human lives implies an acceptance of a number of restrictions. Consequently, when faced with this necessity, the imperative of respecting the constitutional principles of a democratic state ruled by law loses its previous importance as a criterion to assess governments that follow the maxim *salus rei publice suprema lex esto*.

The pandemic has deepened crisis developments, by providing new justifications to doubt the effectiveness of democratic governments, guided as they are by the rule of law, non-arbitrariness and respect for the dignity of the human person. In addition

R. Piotrowski (✉)
Faculty of Law and Administration, University of Warsaw, Warsaw, Poland
e-mail: r.j.j.piotrowski@uw.edu.pl

E. Hadrowicz (ed.), *Polish Entrepreneurial Law in the Era of the COVID-19 Pandemic*, Ius Gentium: Comparative Perspectives on Law and Justice 114,
https://doi.org/10.1007/978-3-031-57480-1_2

to widening inequalities, the pandemic encourages authoritarian arrangements that restrict basic rights, including the right to privacy and the freedom to move—and even, to a certain extent, it enforces such arrangements, by providing justifications to view the state as such a common good that exceeds (and mutualizes) the good of the individual in the name of survival of the community.

The legitimacy of a democratic government stems from the optimistic assumption that it is capable of delivering a safe future. Democratic institutions lose their legitimacy when they fail to tackle problems which they themselves help create or which pop up suddenly and unexpectedly as a kind of "black swans".[1] The emergence of the black swan of pandemic has rendered the world of democratic rules still more fragile than before.[2]

2 Constitution and the Limitations of Rights and Freedoms

The Constitution of the Republic of Poland, though, is by no means hamstrung vis-a-vis extraordinary situations such as the pandemic, and it allows for restricting the rights of the individual, both in normal times, when such restrictions come as ordinary constitutional measures, and, where these measures fail, also in a state of emergency.

Among the ordinary constitutional remedies are those provided in Article 31.3 of the Constitution, which allows for limitations upon the exercise of constitutional freedoms and rights where this is necessary for the protection of public health. Such limitations may be imposed only by statute and must not violate the essence of freedoms and rights. In the Constitutional Tribunal's case law, "the 'only by statute' principle in respect of human rights does not rule out arrangements where certain cases linked to the exercise of constitutional rights and freedoms may be legislated by regulations (*rozporządzenia*)."[3] In the Constitutional Court's opinion, "the Constitution requires a full and exhaustive statutory coverage for all cases of high importance for the exercise of constitutionally guaranteed rights and freedoms of the individual and of the citizen. Only such cases which are not of high importance for the exercise of constitutionally guaranteed rights and freedoms of the individual and of the citizen may be legislated by regulations, with the proviso that the authorization to issue a regulation must conform to the requirements set out in Article 92 of the Constitution and that the regulation itself must comply with the terms laid down in said constitutional provision".[4]

By the Constitutional Court's reasoning, the law makers' intention has been to ensure that statutory-level legislation is provided to the fullest possible extent, and

[1] Cf. Taleb (2020), pp. 467ff.

[2] Cf. Piotrowski (2022a, b), pp. 11ff.

[3] See: e.g., the memorandum of explanation to Judgement in case P 10/02.

[4] See: the memorandum of explanation to Judgement in case U 3/01.

that the extent and contents of below-statutory-level legislation are constrained by the lawmakers' will.[5] This is because the regulation is an implementing instrument, issued on the basis of, and in order to implement, a statutory law.[6] For a regulation to be considered legal and constitutional, it must be issued on the basis of a statutory authorization that is clear, accurate and detailed (in terms of, both, *scope ratione personae* and *scope ratione materiae*). Should the issuer of a regulation transcend the material-scope bounds of the authorization, this would be equal to acting outside of their legislative competences, and would be comparable (effect-wise) to legislating generally binding norms without a proper statutory authorization. In this context, the Constitutional Tribunal has emphasized that each instance of improper implementation of statutory authorization represents a violation of procedural provisions contained in the Constitution.[7]

The case law of the Constitutional Tribunal reflects the conviction that the issuance of a regulation—as an implementing instrument to a statutory law—is contingent on "three conditions. These are: **1)** a regulation may only be issued on the basis of a statutory authorization that is clear—rather than a conjecture drawing on a teleological interpretation—and detailed; **2)** a regulation must be issued strictly within the bounds of the law makers' authorization to issue such an act (in terms of, both, *scope ratione personae* and *scope ratione materiae*) and also for the purpose of implementing the statutory law; and **3)** the content of the regulation must not contradict the norms of the Constitution, the statutory law on the basis of which it has been issued, or any other binding statutory law which directly or indirectly legislates the regulation's subject matter".[8]

These conditions represent a prohibition against issuing regulations which, respectively, **1)** are devoid of statutory authorization; **2)** do not constitute implementing instruments of the statutory law; and **3)** contradict the Constitution and binding statutory laws. Without a clear statutory authorization, a regulation must not deal with a subject matter already covered by other statutory laws; it must not transform, modify or even repeat the contents thereof. A failure to meet these conditions may give rise to accusations of the regulation being in breach of the law.[9]

In light of the consistency of the Constitutional Tribunal's case law, the regulation should be regarded as an implementing instrument issued on the basis of a statutory law and for the purpose of implementation thereof. Where the lawmakers' position on a given matter cannot be obtained due to inaccuracy of the authorization, this must be interpreted as failure to grant legislative authority in that respect. Authorization must not rest on the conjecture that its extent covers the subject-matter not specified therein. Nor is it susceptible to either teleological or extended interpretation.[10] Furthermore, where a regulation specifies the procedure to be

[5] See: the memorandum of explanation to Judgement in case U 3/06.

[6] See: the memorandum of explanation to Judgement in case U 16/02.

[7] See: the memorandum of explanation to Judgement in case U 1/01.

[8] See: the memorandum of explanation to Judgement in case U 3/06.

[9] Ibid.

[10] See: the memorandum of explanation to Judgement in case U 3/87.

followed, this should be in compliance with the provisions of the law.[11] The sphere of rights and freedoms is a constitutional subject-matter which does allow for constitutionally acceptable interference by statute—but not by lower-than-statutory acts.[12] The principle of statutory completeness must not be subject to any exceptions or exclusions.[13]

3 The COVID-19 Legislation as an Example of Constitutional Circumvention

The precepts presented above fully apply to such limitation of rights and freedoms of the individual that is necessary for combating a pandemic in ordinary constitutional circumstances. And it is in accordance with these precepts that one should assess the statutory arrangements designed to combat epidemic diseases in a situation where none of the three extraordinary states has been announced. These arrangements were provided in the Act on preventing and combatting infection and contagious diseases in humans,[14] which was subsequently amended—by an Act of 28 October 2020 for certain statutory amendments in connection with combatting crisis situations related to Covid-19—to receive such a legal shape that the provisions of said Act could be considered legally acceptable only under a state of natural disaster, one of the constitutionally permitted extraordinary states. In actual fact, though, no state of natural disaster was declared. Based on the just-amended statutory law, the government was combatting the pandemic via implementing regulations, while shunning arrangements that would be permitted under a constitutional state of natural disaster.

Thus, the Covid legislation so designed provides an example of constitutional circumvention: while no state of natural disaster was actually imposed, the legal arrangements were being introduced which could only be acceptable under such state. Thus, the boundary was removed between an ordinary state and an extraordinary state of public affairs.[15]

According to Article 228.1 of the Constitution of the Republic of Poland, in situations of particular danger, if ordinary constitutional measures are inadequate, there may be declared one of the extraordinary states: martial law, a state of emergency or a state of natural disaster. This is the prerogative of the Council of Ministers, seeking to prevent or remove the consequences of a natural catastrophe or a technological accident exhibiting characteristics of a natural disaster (Article 232 of the Constitution). This category, pursuant to Article 3 of the State of Natural Disaster

[11] See: the memorandum of explanation to Judgement in case U 7/98.

[12] See: the memorandum of explanation to Judgement in case U 6/93.

[13] See: the memorandum of explanation to Judgement in case U 5/97.

[14] Act of 5.12.2008, Journal of Laws, No. 234, item 1570.

[15] Cf. Albert and Roznai (2020), p. 18.

Act, is also understood as including an outbreak of contagious diseases in humans. And according to Article 233.3 of the Constitution, the statutory law defining the extent of limitations of rights and freedoms of the individual and the citizen under a state of natural disaster may limit the freedom of economic activity, personal freedom, inviolability of the home, freedom of movement and sojourn on Polish territory, the right to strike, the right of ownership, freedom to work, the right to safe and hygienic conditions of work, and the right to rest.

With no extraordinary state declared, the government evidently found as sufficient the ordinary constitutional arrangements specified in the Act on preventing and combatting contagious diseases in humans. And, as doctrine has it, in light of the Polish Constitution, the absence of an extraordinary state rules out any extraordinary limitation of rights and freedoms of the individual. This is because such limitations are subject to review in light of the precepts set out in Article 31.3 of the Constitution, which means that they must comply with the requirement of limitations being imposed statutorily, must respect the proportionality principle, and must not violate the essence of freedoms and rights.[16]

4 New Paradigm of Governance: A State of Emergency Without a State of Emergency

The pandemic has given a boost to the new paradigm of governance: a state of emergency without a state of emergency.[17] Its assumption is that the common instinct for survival and self preservation nudges people towards confidence in, and docile obedience to, those in power and away from disputing the legality of their actions. In this reasoning, the ruled are left with no other way of preserving their existence than passive acceptance of constitutional necessity and its consequences. A portion of the Constitution must be sacrificed in order to save the whole, something not quite uncommon in constitutional systems.[18] But this option is out of bounds in a situation where constitutionally required extraordinary measures have not been set in motion, which is precisely what happened—in contravention of the Constitution and despite the fact that such extraordinary measures were perfectly justifiable. A doctrinal argument has been presented to the effect that acceptance of limitations serving to protect health or prevent contagious diseases is "constitutionally undeniable", but if their "cumulativeness and universality" proves excessive, then we will witness a "circumvention of the constitutional caveat that the application of extraordinary measures in extraordinary circumstances, while acceptable, must be preceded by

[16] Cf. Florczak-Wątor (2020b), p. 20.

[17] Cf. Zizek (2020), pp. 79 ff.

[18] Cf. Wheare (1966).

the imposition of a proper state of emergency,"[19] something which was actually missing.

The government conviction that a declaration of the state of natural disaster was out of the question created a state of lawlessness where, against the constitutional standard, rights and freedoms were being limited by means of regulations.[20] Yet the statutory authorization for these regulations was designed faultily, rendering these regulations unconstitutional. And for some of the restrictive regulations, including those limiting the freedom of assembly (by banning certain types of assembly[21]), there was no statutory authorization at all, which, in view of the clear wording of the Constitution, leaves not a shred of doubt as to their illegitimacy.

A doctrinal argument has been propounded that the freedom of assembly must not be banned not only in a state of pandemic but also in a state of natural disaster, because that would violate the essence of freedoms and rights, which is prohibited under Article 31.3 of the Constitution. Such limitations are only permitted under a state of emergency or marshal law, where the freedom of assembly may indeed be prohibited.[22]

The statutory authorization to issue a regulation limiting the freedom of economic activity during an epidemic specifies the government agency which may issue such regulations and the extend of the subject matter that may be delegated thereto, but it provides no guidelines on the contents of the regulation. Even though the authorization does not refer to imposing a limitation of economic activity, such imposition is actually incorporated into the regulation, thus interfering with the essence of the freedom of economic activity. This kind of interference would indeed be acceptable if an extraordinary state were declared.[23]

In the jurisprudence of administrative courts, a point of view has been expressed to the effect that the Council of Ministers was only authorized to limit the extent to which the freedom of economic activity may be enjoyed, but that it was not authorized to ban this activity as such.[24] In this context, mention should be made of the line of juristic reasoning which points to Article 68.4 of the Constitution—requiring the public authorities to combat epidemic diseases—as a kind of intrinsic

---

[19] See Garlicki (2020), p. 461.

[20] Cf. Trociuk (2021), pp. 66 ff.

[21] Ibid. Art. 46.4.4 of the Act of 5.12.2008 on preventing and combatting infection and contagious diseases in humans (Journal of Laws of 2020, item 1845, as amended) provides for "prohibition of public shows and gatherings." But the authorization is about announcing "obligations, restrictions and injunctions" (Article 46b of the Act). A doctrinal point of view has been taken that the absence of the law makers' clear position must be interpreted that no legislative powers have been bestowed (see: Trociuk, p. 69). It was also pointed out that Article 233.3 of the Constitution "carries no authorisation to impose a limitation of the freedom of assembly, even under a formally declared state of natural disaster. This, therefore, provides an important interpretation hint for evaluating the proportionality of limitations of the freedom of assembly."—see: Bosek (2021), p. 818.

[22] Cf. Florczak-Wątor (2020a), pp. 644 ff.

[23] Cf. Trociuk (2021), p. 86.

[24] See: the memorandum of explanation to Judgement by Voivodship Administrative Court in Opole of 27.10. 2020, II S.A./Op 219/20, Legalis.

authorization to limit civil rights by regulation, given that "the state of epidemic is bound to provoke a verification and, often, a dissenting view of the established opinions about the interpretation of binding provisions of law.[25] But an epidemic does not invalidate the Constitution and its constraints on limitation of rights and freedoms of the individual.[26]

The pandemic has unleashed far-reaching, disproportionate restrictions of the individual's informational autonomy. The ad hoc law on presidential election contained provisions which posed the risk of voters' confidential data being exposed to unlimited access. Regrettably, such a possibility cannot be ruled out, given that under Article 15 of the Act of April 6 of 2020 on special procedure for a general presidential election announced in 2020[27]—it was subsequently repealed by the Act of May 12 2020 on special organizing rules for a general presidential election announced in 2020, with the option of mail voting,[28] according to which the presidential election was finally held—each municipality head, town mayor and city mayor was required to compile a list of voters in the given municipality and to "share it with the mail-voting operator as designated on the day of the present Act coming into force." The list specifies "the voter's name and surname, name of father, date of birth, PESEL resident identification number, and address." While it could be accepted that the designated mail-voting operator indeed needed the address data in order to properly deliver the voting papers, the other data (father's name, birthday, PESEL) were of no use whatever for that purpose. Neither the repealed law nor the binding law contained any guarantee that the data would not be intercepted by unauthorized parties interested in obtaining and processing these data without the knowledge or consent of the person concerned. Even though the Act of 6 April, which posed a threat to voters' safety, security and privacy, was repealed, the binding law contained no interim provisions that would deal with the threat resulting from the disclosure of PESEL-number data to an unauthorized party. This threat is of a totally disproportionate nature, given that it involves no interest protected by law—delivery of voting papers certainly cannot be regarded as such—while the sacrificed interests include citizens' security (Article 5 of the Constitution of the Republic of Poland), their right to privacy (Article 47) and the right not to be required to disclose information about oneself (Article 51).

Article 99 of the Act of 16 April 2020 on special support instruments in connection with the spread of SARS-CoV-2 virus[29] stipulated that "the designated operator, after submitting a request in electronic form, shall receive PESEL registry data … within two business days of receipt of the request." Citizens were offered no guarantee of protection of these data, nor was there any reasonable purpose for the postal

---

[25] Cf. Judgement by the Voivodship Administrative Court in Bydgoszcz of 17.11.2020, II S.A. Bd 834/20, Legalis.

[26] Cf. Piotrowski (2022a, b), p. 17.

[27] Journal of Laws, item 827.

[28] Journal of Laws, item 979.

[29] Journal of Laws, item 695.

service to acquire, to such an extent, confidential data of persons using, at that time or potentially, its services.

The informational autonomy of the individual was also compromised as a result of the disclosure—disproportionate to the actual needs—of data on persons crossing the state borders, which enabled many public entities, including commercial entities, to "track and document the behaviour of particular individuals."[30]

The pandemics has also provoked statutory amendments posing a threat to the right to a fair trial, in the extent to which this notion also means trial in open court. This is true of the proceedings before administrative courts,[31] and of civil proceedings.[32] Under the amended provisions, in-camera proceedings were allowed to be held during a state of epidemic threat or a state of epidemic, and also within a year of revocation of the last of such states.

5 The COVID-19 Pandemic and Its Coincidence with an Ongoing Constitutional Crisis

Rather than declaring an emergency state, the Polish authorities introduced a peculiar state of governance by the virus, which made its way to the official designation of statutory laws as well as serving as a vehicle to push for changes that otherwise would, probably, have not been adopted so easily and so effectively.

Against the doctrinal emphasis on durability of codified law, an inflation of laws has extended to areas covered by the Criminal Code and the Code of Criminal Procedure. Prior to the Covid-19 pandemic, the Criminal Code was extensively amended, changing the provisions of 18 statutory laws in line with the concept of a new penal policy, oriented towards harsher penalties for perpetrators of crimes against life, health, sexual freedom and property, with a view to strengthening the retributive and deterring functions of punishment.[33] The law introducing the amendment was referred to the Constitutional Tribunal by the president, using the powers granted him under Article 122.3 of the Constitution. The president did not question the constitutionality of harsher criminal punishment; rather, his referral[34] to the Constitutional Tribunal largely focused on the legislative procedure, and especially an infringement of the Sejm's rules of procedure. His objections were that the Criminal Code had been amended under ordinary legislative procedure and that the requirement of definiteness of criminal law provisions was not satisfied. The

[30] See: Trociuk (2021), p. 52.

[31] See: Article 4.1 of the Act of 28 May 2021 amending the Code of Civil Procedure Act and certain other statutory laws (Journal of Laws, item 1090).

[32] See: Article 4.3 of the Act of 28 May 2021 amending the Code of Civil Procedure Act and certain other statutory laws (Journal of Laws, item 1090).

[33] Act of 13 June 2019 amending the Criminal Code Act and certain other statutory laws.

[34] Presidential referral to the Constitutional Tribunal of 28.6.2019.

Constitutional Tribunal found the law questioned by the president to be unconstitutional in its entirety, thus sharing the referral's main lines of reasoning.[35]

But during the pandemic, the parliamentary majority felt encouraged to use it as a pretext to change criminal law exactly in a manner that had been described as unconstitutional by the president—in his referral to the Constitutional Tribunal, which was being considered right at the time of the said amendments. And when these amendments were incorporated into the body of laws serving to combat the pandemic, the Polish president was caught in a dilemma: either to underwrite statutory laws containing provisions that had been adopted in what he considered as unconstitutional manner, or to resort to various forms of obstructing the coming into force of these laws, something that the public would find hard to swallow during the pandemic. Thus the president, the guardian of the Constitution, found himself between the Scylla of constitutional infringement, which he had sought to avoid by referring to the Constitutional Tribunal a law previously passed in a similarly defective procedure, and the Charybdis of disobeying the constitutional requirement of diligence and efficiency in the work of public bodies, by placing roadblocks to a legislation designed to streamline the functioning of the state during the pandemic.[36] Having no authority to confine his objection to only a portion of the law, the president finally put his signature to statutes which contained provisions passed in a manner violating the Constitution of the Republic of Poland—as confirmed by the judgement which the Constitutional Tribunal eventually passed in response to the previously mentioned referral.[37] All that marked yet another instance—characteristic of the ongoing constitutional crisis—of constitutional lawlessness being assimilated and accustomed to. Eventually, a situation where constitutional infringement cannot be effectively called out or resisted leads to its veritable acceptance among the public.

The laws adopted to combat epidemics introduced wide-ranging changes in penal law—especially in the Criminal Code, the Code of Criminal Procedure and the Code of Petty Offences—which only in part dealt with countering plagues. For the legislators, an extraordinary occurrence of a public hazard provided an opportunity to hastily adopt such legal arrangements which they found useful. These were scattered among legislative packages covering diverse areas, which made it more difficult to properly evaluate them, and easier to "hide" these arrangements within binding laws.

The penal law changes were introduced by the Act of 31 March 2020 amending the Act on special measures to prevent, counter and combat Covid-19, other contagious diseases and the resulting crisis situations.[38] In particular, its Article 15t nullified criminal responsibility for the offence of mismanagement (Article 296.1-4 of the Criminal Code) by a person in managerial position who has neither recognized

---

[35] See: Judgement of 14.06.2020, case Kp 1/19.

[36] Cf. Piotrowski (2022a, b).

[37] In response to that referral, Judgement Kp 1/19 was passed.

[38] Journal of Laws of 2020, item 568.

nor demanded from a contractor amounts receivable due to the latter's Covid-19 related failure to perform or faulty performance under a public procurement order. The government's bill amending the Act on special measures to prevent, counter and combat Covid-19, other contagious diseases and the resulting crisis situations, and amending certain other statutory acts was sent to the Sejm on 26 March 2020. Its first, second and third reading (at the Sejm's plenary session) was squeezed into the next day, and the bill was made law due to the support of 343 Sejm deputies, including from opposition parties, with 73 deputies objecting and 19 abstaining. The Sejm discussed the Senate's position on the law, and accepted several of its amendments, on March 31, and on the same day the president added his signature to the document. Such was the manner in which changes were made in codified criminal law. The Criminal Code amendments introduced under the statutory law in question actually did not meet even the less rigorous requirements for passage of laws which do not provide for changes in legal codes. The president accepted this procedure, even though he previously questioned similar practices in respect of penal law amendments—in his referral to the Constitutional Tribunal of 28 June 2019 (case Kp 1/19), where he complained that "the Sejm took just two days for the three readings needed to pass the law." In that referral, the president questioned the practice of amending codified law "in ordinary legislative procedure, where the first reading of the relevant bill was completed on the next day after the bill's introduction, and the second reading a day after the release of the Legislative Committee's report." That, in the president's opinion, "warranted a referral to the Constitutional Tribunal for a constitutionality review of the law," to be found as wholly in breach of Article 7 of the Constitution and, as such, illegitimately passed. In 2020, though, the president refrained from referring the case to the Constitutional Tribunal despite a similarity in how the Sejm proceeded on both occasions. This inconsistency in presidential behaviour, and the consequent signing of a law passed in violation of the three-readings principle, must have probably been influenced by the argument that the other amendments provided in the law required to be passed.

Significant amendments to criminal responsibility law were passed in the Act of 19 June 2020 concerning subsidies to interest on bank loans granted to business entities affected by consequences of Covid-19 and also concerning a simplified procedure for arrangement-with-creditors approval in connection with Covid-19.[39] In particular, its Article 38 makes room for limitation of the right to defence, by modifying Article 250 of the Code of Penal Procedure in such a way that its Paragraph 3d now permits petitions for pre-trial detention to be examined at remote court hearings, where the detainee is held in an arrest cell and his or her defence counsel is at the seat of the court—which, in its consequence, limits the right to defence, guaranteed under Article 42.2 of the Constitution.

In the statutory law in question, the lawmakers also introduced other significant amendments to the Criminal Code and the Code of Penal Procedure, such as defining a new type of theft, introducing a new type of offence, changing the system of cumulative punishment, or enacting heavier penalties for some offences—all this in

[39] Journal of Laws of 2020, item 1086.

a statutory law designed to aid business during a pandemic, thus providing a salient example of legislative camouflage. Amendments of this kind should be preceded by public consultations and subjected to a procedure that is adequate for changes in codified law, but in actual fact they were inserted—during a session of the Sejm's Finance Committee—into an act of the legislature whose subject matter was unrelated to criminal law. It would likely be hard to find a rational connection between these changes in codified law and fight against the pandemic.

What was declared in Poland was none of the constitutionally defined extraordinary states but a peculiar state of combating an epidemic,[40] which served as a vehicle to proclaim changes which in other conditions could not be introduced so easily and so effectively. The outbreak of the pandemic coincided in Poland with an ongoing constitutional crisis, manifesting itself in the primacy of politics over law, and especially in a reduced role of the parliament and disrespect for law making formalities. Another feature of the constitutional crisis is the reduced role of the opposition in the legislative process.

The approach taken in the Act of 2 March 2020 on special measures to prevent, counter and combat Covid-19, other contagious diseases and the resulting crisis situations[41] was to amend the previous Act on preventing and combatting infection and contagious diseases in humans in such a way as to vest the Council of Ministers with the power to limit rights and freedoms of the individual—even though this empowerment, laid down in the amended law, did not rest on proper constitutional authorisation.[42] The reason why this path was chosen was not so much a desperate need to combat the pandemic, as rather the unconstitutional resistance to declaring a state of natural disaster—and that in a situation where ordinary constitutional measures proved insufficient. As a result, rights and freedoms of the individual were curtailed in a way that contradicted the constitution standards. Typical of the entire Covid-related legislation, this approach was dictated by neither constitutional nor medical considerations. Its underlying reason was political necessity resulting from the desire to avoid declaring a state of natural disaster.

6 Enterpreneurs and Deficit of Their Proper Legal Protection During Pandemic

The government's refusal to declare a state of natural disaster, dictated as it was by political considerations, played a considerable role in regulating the rights of the small and medium-size enterprises (SMEs) during the COVID-19 pandemic.

[40] It was introduced by the health minister's Regulation of 13.03.2020 announcing the imposition of a state of epidemic threat on territory of the Republic of Poland (Journal of Laws, item 433 as amended) and the health minister's Regulation of 20.03.2020 announcing a state of epidemic on territory of the Republic of Poland (Journal of Laws, item 491 as amended).

[41] Journal of Laws, item 1842 as amended.

[42] Trociuk (2021), p. 16.

According to the Polish Constitution, a state of natural disaster (one of three constitutionally defined emergency measures) may be imposed by the Council of Ministers "in order to prevent or remove the consequences of a natural catastrophe or a technological accident exhibiting characteristics of a natural disaster" (Article 232) where "ordinary constitutional measures are inadequate" (Article 228). The Act on preventing and combatting infection and contagious diseases in humans, in force at the time, allowed for the imposition—by regulation—of temporary restrictions[43] on the operation of certain institutions and workplaces, and also on certain lines of business activity. However, in the actual regulations that were issued, such activity was subject to either outright prohibition or certain conditions. That was in breach of the precept that the extent of competences must not be defined by conjecture, as deriving from Article 7 of the Polish Constitution, according to which public authorities act on the basis and within the limits of the law. Courts' reaction to this type of restriction on SME rights has varied. Some have ruled that there was no proper legal basis for prohibiting business activity. According to this line of jurisprudence, no provision of the Act "contained authorization to ban economic activity by regulation. The Council of Ministers was only empowered to impose regulatory restrictions on the exercise of the freedom of economic activity."[44] Other courts, however, stated that "in view of the widespread threat to the health and life of all persons on the territory of Poland, the applicable provisions must be interpreted in such a way as to offer citizens utmost protection from the behaviour of extremely irresponsible entities that fail to comply with regulations aimed at reducing the level of danger at the national level.[45]" This view has been described in doctrine as dangerous, because it allows SMEs to be punished without proper legal grounds, and only on the basis of the court's conviction,[46] which, in the practice of jurisprudence, contravenes the rule-of-law precept that public authorities may act only on the basis and within the limits of the law. The SMEs who conducted their activities in contravention of an unlawful prohibition were thus penalised for the government's failure to declare a state of natural disaster and, consequently, its failure to use the available legal instruments. And the reasons why such instruments were not applied were political. As it happened, the usual constitutional measures—which only allow for the freedom of economic activity to be restricted, not banned—were seen as inadequate by the government which believed that public health considerations called for outright prohibitions. And yet a state of natural disaster, permitting such prohibitions, was not declared because under the constitutional provisions governing extraordinary measures it would entail the postponement of presidential elections, something the ruling party wanted to avoid due to its own political calculations. As a result, there

---

[43] Cf. Articles 46a and 46b.2 of the Act on preventing and combatting infection and contagious diseases in humans of 5.12. 2008 r. (Journal of Laws of 2020, item 1845 as amended).

[44] See: e.g., the memorandum of explanation to Judgement by Voivodship Administrative Court in Opole of 27.10.2020, II S.A./Op 219/20, Legalis.

[45] See: the memorandum of explanation to Judgement by Voivodship Administrative Court Bydgoszcz of 17.11.2020, II S.A./Bd 834/20, Legalis.

[46] Cf. Trociuk (2021), p. 83.

was imposed a non-statutory ban on conducting business during an epidemic. It was promulgated in the implementing regulations issued on the strength of the Act on preventing and combatting infection and contagious diseases in humans. Violation of this ban was punishable by appropriate sanctions.

That had the effect of upending the principle of legal certainty, a key pillar of the freedom of economic activity. Businesses could not be certain that if they went on with their operations, in compliance with the Constitution and the relevant statutory law, they would not be penalised by court. As a matter of fact, the courts are subordinated only to the Constitution and statutory laws, and as such may judge government regulations in accordance with these regulations' conformity with constitutional and statutory provisions. In the practice of some courts, however, it happened that preventing the spread of the virus was found more important than respecting constitutional guarantees. Such judicial decisions may have been based on the belief in a certain state of necessity that requires sacrificing part of the Constitution in order to save the lives and health of those without whom the Constitution would become irrelevant.

The Covid-related legislation thus proved to be of limited use in regulating the legal environment for businesses under pandemic conditions. The fundamental problem requiring regulation—i.e. the imposition of a ban on economic activity, with all the consequences associated with non-compliance—was solved by promulgating such ban in a regulation, rather than a statutory law. That contravened the constitutional principles governing the sources of law, where the intention is to protect citizens and their activities, including business operations, from government arbitrariness.

According to contemporary scholarly literature that government should only act within the boundaries of the law "is an axiomatic precept of the rule of law. As a principle, legality requires that state action is carried out in accordance with transparent and democratically enacted laws, not mere – and unconstrained – discretion. It also requires that the process for enacting laws is transparent, democratic and subject to scrutiny. However, the exigencies of an emergency can place pressure on governments to act, and act rapidly. The need for a decisive response during a pandemic can favour swift executive action over inevitably slower legislative or consultative processes".[47]

However, the significant impact that the pandemic experience has made on the situation of SMEs and the legal framework for their activities is unlikely to be confined to undermining the certainty of the law governing these operations. During the pandemic, SMEs were also confronted with a blurring of the line between a constitutionally defined extraordinary measure, which the government did not wish to declare, and a situation where extraordinary measures were applied in practice without invoking the "extraordinary measure" description. With the line between an extraordinary measure and its opposite erased, a "new normal"[48] has developed.

---

[47] Cf. Grogan and Begiraj (2022), p. 201 ff.

[48] Cf. in particular Green (2020), p. 147.

One feature of this new normal is that it enforces disregard for constitutional values, being justified by a presumed temporary necessity. However, that which has been meant as ad hoc and short-lived may potentially turn into permanence, as a way of rationalising the enforced consent to lawlessness in government-business relations. This is an extremely risky threat, and not only for entrepreneurial freedom.

References

Albert R, Roznai Y (eds) (2020) Constitutionalism under extreme conditions. Cham

Bosek L (ed) (2021) Ustawa o zapobieganiu oraz zwalczaniu zakażeń i chorób zakaźnych u ludzi. Komentarz, Warszawa

Florczak-Wątor M (2020a) Granice ingerencji państwa w wolność zgromadzeń w czasach epidemii. In: Bodnar A, Płoszka A (eds) Wokół kryzysu demokracji, praworządności i praw człowieka. Księga jubileuszowa Profesora Mirosława Wyrzykowskiego, Warszawa

Florczak-Wątor F (2020b) Niekonstytucyjność ograniczeń praw i wolności jednostki wprowadzonych w związku z epidemią COVID-19 jako przesłanka odpowiedzialności odszkodowawczej państwa. Państwo i Prawo 12:20

Garlicki L (2020) Polskie prawo konstytucyjne. Warszawa

Green A (2020) Emergency powers in a time of pandemic. Bristol

Grogan J, Begiraj J (2022) The Rule of Law as the Perimeter of Legitimacy for COVID-19 Responses. In: Grogan J, Donald A (eds) Routledge Handbook of Law and the COVID-19 Pandemic. New York, p. 201

Grogan J, Donald A (eds) (2022) Routledge handbook of law and the COVID-19 pandemic. New York

Piotrowski R (2022a) Demokracja w stanie pandemii. Uwagi o doświadczeniach polskich. In: Grzebyk P, Uznańska P (eds) Prawo w czasie pandemii CIVID-19. Warszawa

Piotrowski R (2022b) Zakres zmian w polskim prawie karnym w dobie pandemii COVID-19 z perspektywy konstytucjonalisty. In: Kowalski S, Małolepszy M (eds) Prawo karne i postępowanie karne w dobie epidemii COVID-19. Doświadczenia polskie i wybranych państwa europejskich, Warszawa

Taleb NN (2020) Czarny łabędź. Jak nieprzewidywalne zdarzenia rządzą naszym życiem. Poznań

Trociuk S (2021) Prawa i wolności w stanie epidemii. Warszawa

Wheare KC (1966) Modern constitutions. Oxford

Zizek S (2020) Pandemia! Warszawa

Ryszard Piotrowski Professor of Constitutional Law at the Faculty of Law and Administration of the University of Warsaw, author of numerous academic publications on fundamental questions of constitutional law, comparative constitutional law, theory of law-making and human rights, member of the Committee of Legal Sciences of the Polish Academy of Sciences, author of numerous lectures and speeches delivered at conferences, symposia, and seminars, as well as numerous expert reports on constitutional law and human rights, commissioned by public institutions and private parties.

Liability for Damage Caused by Normative Restrictions in the State of Epidemic

Leszek Bosek

Abstract A State of Epidemic is a key anti-epidemic emergency regime under Polish law. It is defined as a legal situation introduced in a particular area in connection with an epidemic in order to undertake anti-epidemic and preventive measures specified in the Act to minimize the effects of the epidemic.

This article explores a problem of liability for damages caused by illegal or unconstitutional governmental regulations issued by Minister of Health and Council of Ministers as a reaction on COVID crisis and when the State of Epeidemic had been formaly announced.

The analysis demonstrates that certain restrictions introduced by the Goverment, in particularly those as intrusive as the ban on leaving the home, must be directly and comprehensively authorised by the Parliament. Governmental regulations must not, without comprehensive statutory authorisation, encroach upon spheres of personal and bussines interests.

However, claims for damages for normative restrictions—on the basis of the provisions of art. 417(1) § 1 of the c.c. and art. 77 of the Constitution– depends on a preliminary ruling of unconstitutionality or illegality of a particular restriction. If the Constitutional Tribunal is not finding the restriction unconstitutional or illegal, it is impossible to get compensation. However, there is only one first-instance judgment that has been issued in such cases so far. The court dismissed the entrepreneur's claim for payment of compensation by the State Treasury for profits lost by him in connection with the introduction of the ban on conducting business activity.

L. Bosek (✉)
Faculty of Law and Administration, University of Warsaw, Warsaw, Poland
e-mail: bosek@wpia.uw.edu.pl

E. Hadrowicz (ed.), *Polish Entrepreneurial Law in the Era of the COVID-19 Pandemic*, Ius Gentium: Comparative Perspectives on Law and Justice 114,
https://doi.org/10.1007/978-3-031-57480-1_3

1 Introduction

A State of Epidemic is a key anti-epidemic legal institution—emergency regime—in Poland. It is defined as a legal situation introduced in a particular area of the country in connection with an epidemic in order to undertake anti-epidemic and preventive measures specified in the Act to minimize the effects of the epidemic.[1] The State of Epidemic was announced on March 20, 2020[2] as a response to the SARS-CoV-2 crisis and revoked on May 16, 2022.[3]

This article explores a problem of liability for damages caused by illegal or unconstitutional normative restrictions issued by the Goverment under a vail of officially announced the State of Epidemic. Under this emergency regime dozens of governmental regulations were enacted by Minister of Health or Council of Ministers. Published articles and studies concern only selected issues.[4]

A binding model of liability for normative acts—enshrined in art. 77 § 1 of the Constitution and in art. 417-417[2] of the Civil Code—requires a formal declaration of illegality or unconstitutionality of a normative act. This means that legality of normative restriction is of crucial importance. For this reason, a legal structure of the State of Epidemic must be presented first and later other conditions of liability.

2 The State of Epidemic

The State of Epidemic was introduced into Polish Law for the first time by the Act of 6 September 2001 on infectious diseases and infections.[5] This regime was an instrument combined with a number of statutory authorisations for the executive to launch regulations ordering or banning activities in order to prevent and combat epidemic diseases. Restrictions could be introduced under Article 33 of the Act by

---

[1] Article 2 point 22 of the Act of December 5, 2008 on preventing and combating infections and infectious diseases [Ustawa o zapobieganiu oraz zwalczaniu zakażeń i chorob zakaźnych u ludzi] Journal of Laws 2020, position 1845. Later: "the Act".

[2] Decree of the Minister of Health of 20.3.2020 on the declaration of an epidemic state in the territory of the Republic of Poland [Rozporządzenie Ministra Zdrowia z 20.3.2020 r. w sprawie ogłoszenia na obszarze Rzeczypospolitej Polskiej stanu epidemii] Journal of Laws 2020, position 491.

[3] Decree of the Minister of Health of 12.05.2022 on the cancellation of an epidemic state in the territory of the Republic of Poland [Rozporządzeniem Ministra Zdrowia z 12.05.2022 r. w sprawie odwołania stanu epidemii na obszarze Rzeczypospolitej Polskiej] Journal of Laws 2022, position 1027.

[4] See: Bosek (2021a); Pecyna (2020), pp. 23–37; Pyziak-Szafnicka (2022), pp. 112–128; Strugała (2021), pp. 26–32; Zoll et al. (2021), pp. 6–27.

[5] Journal of Laws from 2001, item 1384.

executive regulations of the voivode,[6] for the territory of a region, or the Minister of Health for the entire country.

The binding Act of 2008 on preserved the model of anti-epidemic measures developed under the Act of 2001 and provided a legal basis for administrative and normative sanitary measures. This Act provides a balance between the need for efficient response to the rapidly changing epidemic reality and the need to protect lives and human rights. The Act neither suspends human rights nor—as a matter of principle—restricts them directly, but rather authorises the Minister of Health or the Council of Ministers in strictly defined areas to establish normative restrictions.[7]

The core of the Polish statutory anti-epidemic emergency powers is enshrined in Article 46 of the Act, opening Chapter 8 of the Act entitled "Principles of conduct in the state of epidemic threat and the state of epidemic". Article 46 provides a comprehensive regulation of the legal framework of both regimes. Article 46 (1) 1 authorizes the voivode, and Article 46 (2) the minister responsible for health, to declare (and also repeal) by regulation (decree) the State of Epidemic Threat or the State of Epidemic, respectively in a voivodship, several voivodships or the entire country.

The necessary precondition for the State of Epidemic Emergency to be declared is an epidemic. An epidemic is defined in Article 2 point 9 of the Act as the occurrence of infections or cases of infectious diseases in a particular area significantly larger than in the previous period, or the occurrence of such infections or infectious diseases that did not occur so far. The Act does not define the previous period nor a quantity or a quality of infections required to declare the State of Epidemic. Neither does the Act require an external declaration of pandemic by the WHO.

There are two formal requirements: a request by a regional state sanitary inspector (in case of a local epidemic announced by a voivode) or a request by the Chief Sanitary Inspector (in case of a nationwide epidemic announced by the Minister of Health) and infections covered within the categories recognised by the Act. The principle underpinning the 2008 Act is that enforcement of the Act is allowed only to 50 diseases enumerated in an annex Nr 1 to the Act.

Article 2 point 22 defines the State of Epidemic as a legal situation introduced in a particular area in connection with an epidemic in order to undertake anti-epidemic and preventive measures specified in the Act to minimize the effects of the epidemic.

While the Act defines this normative regime, its distinctive normative features and axiological consistency, related to the content of the introduced restrictions, orders and bans in the area designated in this regulation, can only be reconstructed from the provisions of Article 46. The provisions of Article 46 (3), (4) and (5) authorize the Ministry of Health or voivodes to fill the State of Epidemic with normative content, i.e. impose obligations by means of regulations (decrees) on institutions and private persons staying in the territory of the Republic of Poland. This is because

---

[6] Voivode is according to the Art. 152 Constitution a representative of the government in a voivodeship.

[7] Bosek (2022).

of the need to adjust emergency measures to rapid changes of epidemiological factors. Thus, a specific feature of the Polish model is that the anti-epidemic emergency regimes are mainly of a normative character and not administrative.

Regulations of the Minister of Health or voivode may lay down a temporary restriction of a specific method of movement, a temporary restriction or prohibition of the marketing and use of certain items or food products, a temporary restriction of the functioning of certain institutions or workplaces, a prohibition of organizing shows and other gatherings of people, an obligation to perform specific sanitary procedures, if their performance involves the functioning of certain production, service, commercial or other facilities, an order to supply real estate, premises, land and means of transport for anti-epidemic activities provided for by anti-epidemic plans, the obligation to carry out preventive vaccinations and the groups of persons subject to these vaccinations.

Under the amendment to the Act of 2 March 2020, extraordinary regulatory powers were given also to the Council of Ministers, in practice reducing the role of the Ministry of Health in managing the crisis.[8] According to Article 46a of the Act, the Council of Ministers is currently authorised in the event of the State of Epidemic or the State of Epidemic Emergency of the nature and dimensions exceeding the capacity of the competent governmental bodies and local governments, to determine, by regulation, on the basis of data provided by the minister responsible for health, the minister responsible for internal affairs, the minister responsible for public administration, Chief Sanitary Inspector and voivodes "the endangered area along with an indication of the type of zone in which the state of epidemic or the state of epidemic emergency occurred" and "the type of solutions used in the scope specified in Article 46b".

The scope of normative powers vested in the Council of Ministers is specified in Article 46b of the Act. The Council of Ministers may legislate in all areas, where the Minister of Health is empowered to legislate (as indicated in Article 46 of the Act) and above that to lay down temporary limitation of certain scopes of business activity, temporary regulation of supplies for a specific type of articles, medical examinations and the use of other preventive measures as well as treatments by sick and suspected persons, obligation to undergo quarantine, place of quarantine, temporary limitation of the use of sites or areas and the obligation to secure them, an evacuation order at specified times of specific places, areas and objects, an order or prohibition of staying in specific places and objects and in specific areas, prohibition to leave zero zone by sick and suspected, order to move in a specific manner.

The broad scope of this statutory delegation of powers to executives may be criticised. Although all emergency constitutions leave significant discretionary power to the executive during broadly defined states of emergency, delegation of legislative powers to executives in ordinary circumstances should be strictly defined in an act of parliament.[9] Nevertheless, the level of precision of the Polish anti-epidemic

[8] Journal of Laws from 2020, item 1842 with amendments.

[9] Art. 92 of the Constitution.

statutory delegations of powers is much higher than that in emergency constitutions and comparable to French, German and Italian statutory anti-epidemic models.

Moreover, the anti-epidemic statutory delegations of powers are backed by Article 5 of the Act. Article 5 of the Act obliges directly everyone in the territory of the Republic of Poland to meet the general obligations: undergo sanitary procedures, preventive vaccinations, sanitary and epidemiological examinations, epidemiological supervision, quarantine, treatment, hospitalization, isolation, isolation at home, post-exposure prophylactic use of drugs, providing information necessary for epidemiological supervision; it also imposes on the infected people with an infectious disease (carriers in the meaning of the Act) and ill persons the obligation to refrain from performing any work which may transmit an infection or an infectious disease to other people.

Although Article 5 establishes these obligations, each time requiring their reconstruction and application "on the principles set out in the Act", it aims at creating common and exhaustively listed statutory obligations of persons staying in the territory of the Republic of Poland. There is no doubt that it determines their statutory nature. Their source is the Act itself. Consequently, Article 5 ensures the internal axiological and constructive coherence of the Act and the Constitution. Failure to explicitly establish the obligations of private persons in this Article would raise a fundamental doubt whether interference in fundamental rights by executive regulations would be permissible.[10]

Article 46 (5) and (6) defines the formal condition for the entry into force of regulations announcing the State of Epidemic Emergency or the State of Epidemic: a promulgation in the relevant official journal (regulations of the Minister of Health and Council of Ministers must be published only in Journal of Laws, those issued by the voivode solely in the regional journals). They also require the voivode to inform about the obligations arising from the announcement of State of Epidemic Emergency or State of Epidemic in a manner customarily adopted in the voivodeship.

Specific feature of the Polish anti-epidemic emergency model is that it is based on two different regimes: the State of Epidemic and the State of Epidemic Emergency. However, as indicated above a quantity or a quality of infections in a particular area is not defined and therefore also "the risk of an epidemic" as a precondition of the state of epidemic emergency is not defined. Both definitions refer to a notion of an epidemic defined in Article 2 point 9 of the Act. It is also clear that the State of Epidemic Emergency cannot be announced because of a potential risk. The potential risk of an epidemic is neither a sufficient reason for far-reaching restrictions on fundamental rights nor a justification for exceptions to the principle of separation of powers.[11] The act must be interpreted in the light of the Constitution. Moreover, emergency powers in the state of Epidemic Emergency and the State of Epidemic attributed to the executives, the nature and legal effects of restrictions are

[10] Cf. Articles 2, 31 (3) of the Constitution.

[11] Bjørnskov, p. 108.

identical. Therefore, *de lege ferenda* one of the two emergency regimes should be removed. It seems that the State of Epidemic would be enough.

The parliament is not empowered to declare, approve, or repeal a nationwide state of epidemic—these powers are vested exclusively in the Minister of Health. The parliament (Sejm), empowered under the Constitution to political control of the government, to monitor the use of constitutional emergency powers, to investigate abuses, to extend these powers if necessary, and to suspend them if the emergency ends, may only force the Minister of Health and the whole Council of Minister to resign or be dismissed.

The power to monitor the legality of actions under statutory anti-epidemic emergency regimes is vested in the judiciary, and in particular in the Constitutional Tribunal. This is consistent with a global trend. However, there is only limited legal basis for a direct action for annulment against emergency measures in ordinary or administrative courts. Article 63 (1) of Governmental Administration in Voivodship Act (GAVA) allows to challenge only regulations of voivode before an administrative court. The purpose of Article 63 sec. 1 of the GAVA is to protect the rights of the complainant (subjective rights) and the mere objective illegality of an act does not constitute a basis for a complaint.[12] Regulations of the Ministry of Health or regulations of the Council of Ministers can be reviewed only by the Constitutional Tribunal or incidentally by courts in criminal or civil proceedings or by administrative courts (the jurisprudence emphasizes that if the court refuses to apply the provisions of a sub-statutory act, it "should independently conduct a detailed legal analysis").[13]

This restriction is of systemic character. Constitutional review of ministerial and governmental regulations is performed by the Constitutional Tribunal. Statutes and regulations may be challenged by constitutional complaint, but only if rights or freedoms of an individual have been violated by specific decision or ruling, which was based on an unconstitutional provision[14] and by court—by way of a legal question provided that the answer to such question will resolve an issue currently pending before that court.[15]

Moreover, according to the case law of the Constitutional Tribunal concerning martial law[16] it is unlikely that the announcement of the state of epidemic will be effectively controlled.[17] This is because of the very nature of a declaration which is not a norm, but an individual act focussed on a particular epidemic. However, other elements of the governmental regulations, in particular provisions imposing restrictions as "normative acts", can be constitutionally reviewed.

---

[12] Judgement of Supreme Administrative Court of 30.1.2020, No. II OSK 3574/18.

[13] Judgment of the Supreme Court 5.2.2008, No. II PK 150/07.

[14] Art. 79 of the Constitution.

[15] Art. 193 of the Constitution.

[16] Judgment of the Constitutional Tribunal of 16.3.2011, K 35/08.

[17] However, it is postulated in a legal literature: Bosek at 767–70 (*supra* note 112).

Judicial review concerns sanctions imposed by public authorities for non-compliance with sanitary restrictions. Ordinary courts have controlled the fines imposed by the police, and case-law confirmed that fines for disregarding obligation to wear masks or prohibition of leaving the house at the beginning of the epidemic are illegal, because they were established in a regulation that was issued in violation of statutory delegation, which did not authorise the Minister of Health to establish such an obligation.[18] Whereas the administrative courts dealt with complaints against decisions of sanitary inspection imposing fines for violating sanitary regulations.[19]

The model of anti-epidemic emergency powers under Polish law has evolved over the past century and currently is authorized directly by art. 68 paragraph 4 of the Constitution in Chapter 2 concerning basic rights. This model is sufficient to protect lives, mitigate natural hazards of infectious diseases and counteract epidemics. However, the Constitution established a complex regulation on 'extraordinary measures' in a separate chapter XI entitled 'extraordinary measures', including a principle of a closed catalogue of constitutional extraordinary regimes:[20] a state of martial law, a state of emergency and a state of natural disaster. Constitutional state of natural disaster may be introduced also in order to combat spread of infectious disease.[21] Article 3 (1) point 2 of the Act of 18 April 2002 on the state of natural disaster[22] classified an epidemic to the category of a natural catastrophe in the meaning of Article 232 of the Constitution.

This is the reason why a few influential authors contested legality of all anti-epidemic measures introduced in 2020 and 2021 under statutory regime of the State of Epidemic. According to their opinion, since the statutory regime is not envisaged in the Chapter XI of the Constitution, it means that it is not allowed.[23]

However, the statutory model of anti-epidemic emergency powers relies on a different constitutional basis. It is authorized by Article 68 (4) of the Constitution being an important element of a complex regulation of the basic right to health.[24] It states that public authorities shall combat epidemic illnesses and prevent the negative health consequences of degradation of the environment. Despite different views

[18] Decisions of: District Court in Kościan of 8.6.2020, Ref. No. II W 71/20; District Court in Siedlce of 29 September 2020, Ref. No. II W 924/20; District Court in Nysa from 9.11.2020, Ref. No. II W 981/20.

[19] Judgment of Regional Administrative Court in Gliwice from 20.9.2020, Ref. No. III SA/Gl 540/20; judgment of Regional Administrative Court in Gorzów Wielkopolski from 23.9.2020, Ref. No. II SA/Go 332/20; judgment of Regional Administrative Court in Białystok from 22 October 2020, Ref. No. II SA/Bk 528/20.

[20] Brzeziński (2007).

[21] Steinborn (2016), p. 1626.

[22] Journal of Laws 2017, item 1897.

[23] Florczak-Wątor (2020), pp. 5–22; Kardas (2020), pp. 5–28; Trociuk (2021); Tuleja (2020), pp. 5–21; Differently Roszkiewicz (2022), pp. 34–51.

[24] Cf. Bosek (2021b), pp. 113–141.

on a scope of application of this provision,[25] there is no doubt that it requires introduction of statutory scheme to combat infections and infectious diseases.[26]

3 Legal Basis of the Right to Be Compensated by Illegal Normative Restrictions

The heart of the Polish compensation system is the Art. 77 (1) of the Constitution. According to this provision "Everyone shall have the right to compensation for any harm done to him by any action of an organ of public authority contrary to law." This provision is located in the Chapter about basic rights in section "Means for the defence of freedoms and rights". This implies that the Constitution provides everyone with the basic right to be compensated for damage incurred by illegal act or omission of the public authorities, i.e. executive, legislative and judiciary branch of the government.

Art. 77 of the Constitution is implemented to the ordinary law by art. 417-417[2] of the c.c., as a result of amendment 2004 to the civil code, triggered by the judgement of the Constitutional Tribunal from December 4, 2001, SK 18/00. The Constitutional Tribunal in this and many other judgments questioned a number of code and non-code regulations on liability of the public bodies.[27]

Article 417 in new wording states: § 1. The State Treasury or a local government unit or another person exercising public authority by force of law is liable for any damage caused by an unlawful action or omission while exercising public authority.

§ 2. If performance of public authority tasks is contracted under an agreement to a local government unit or another legal person, joint and several liability for any damage caused is borne by the contractor and the local government unit contracting the tasks or the State Treasury

Article 417[1] § 1. If damage is caused by a legislative act, remedy thereof may be demanded once it has been declared incompliant with the Constitution, a ratified international treaty or the law in the course of appropriate proceedings.

§ 2. If damage is caused by a final and non-revisable court decision or other final decision, remedy thereof may be demanded once such decision has been declared incompliant with the law in the course of appropriate proceedings, unless separate

---

[25] It is argued that this regulation should be applicable to all epidemics (including f.eg. suicide) Miaskowska-Daszkiewicz (2017), pp. 69–71 or that it is applicable only to epidemics caused by infections [Bosek in Safjan (2016), pp. 1523–1565].

[26] Janik (2015), p. 105; Pałka (2018), pp. 601–624. See also Bosek and Roszkiewicz (2020), pp. 201–281.

[27] C.f. judgments of the CT: 4.12.2001, SK 18/00; 23.9.2003, K 20/02; 3.03.2004, K 29/03; 7.10.2003, K 4/02; 14.7.2004 r., SK 8/03; 20.1.2004, SK 26/03; 18.10.2005, SK 48/03; 7.2.2005, SK 49/03; 5.9.2005, P 18/04; 27.10.2015, SK 9/13; 27.09.2012, SK 4/11; 1.3.2011, P 21/09; 8.12.2009, SK 34/08; 24.2.2009, SK 34/07; 1.4.2008, SK 77/06; 1.9.2006, SK 14/05; judgment of the CT from 23.5.2006, SK 51/05.

regulations provide otherwise. This also applies to cases where a final and non-revisable court decision or other final decision has been issued based on a legislative act that is incompliant with the Constitution, a ratified international treaty or the law.

§ 3. If damage is caused through failure for a court decision or other decision to be issued and the obligation to issue the same is provided for by a legal regulation, remedy of damage may be demanded once the failure to issue the court decision or other decision is declared incompliant with the law in the course of appropriate proceedings unless separate regulations provide otherwise.

§ 4. If damage is caused by failure for a legislative act to be issued and the obligation to issue the same is provided for by a legal regulation, the failure to issue the act is declared incompliant with the law by the court hearing the case for remedy of damage.

According to Article 417^{2} if personal injury is caused through the lawful exercise of public authority, the aggrieved party may demand full or partial remedy of and monetary recompense for the harm caused if the circumstances, and especially the aggrieved party's inability to work or his difficult financial situation, indicate that the remedy is required under the equitable principle.

It is clear that the Constitution and the Civil Code grant the right to compensation for damage caused by normative omissions (art. 417^{1} § 4 of the c.c.) and for normative instruments incompatible with norms of higher rank (art. 417^{1} § 1 and § 2 of the c.c.).[28]

Liability for normative restrictions is based on art. 417^{1} § 1 and § 2 second sentence of the c.c. Both provisions indicate that first condition of liability depends on statement in "in the course of appropriate proceedings" inconformity of the act with the constitution, international law or the statue. Furthermore, the redress of damage may be demanded <<after>> the non-compliance of such instrument with the Constitution, ratified international agreement or act was stated.

There is no doubt that an "appropriate proceeding" is the proceeding before the Constitutional Tribunal. Language of the statue, historical background, and systemic context—a comparison of art. 417 of the C.C. with art. 190 (1) and art. 190 (3) as well as art. 190 (4) of the Constitution—convince that the legislator designated the Constitutional Tribunal as authorised to rule on the constitutionality of normative acts. This leads to the conclusion that a preliminary ruling in the form of a judgment of the Constitutional Tribunal stating the non-compliance of a normative act with the Constitution of the Republic of Poland is necessary to get compensation. The judgment of the Constitutional Tribunal should have retroactive effect (ex tunc effect). This means that if the Constitutional Tribunal postpones the date of expiry of the binding force of the regulation on the basis of art. 190 (3) of the Constitution, this excludes liability.

A preliminary ruling of the Constitutional Tribunal is thus of key importance for deciding on liability and is also required for governmental regulations.

---

[28] Resolution of the panel of 7 judges of the Supreme Court of 19.5.2009, III CZP 139/08.

More doubts are connected with the opinion that also European Court of Human Rights can deliver a required preliminary ruling. In the justification of the judgment of the Supreme Court of May 6, 2016, I CSK 364/15155, it was explained that even the so-called pilot judgment of the Grand Chamber of the ECtHR of June 19, 2006, 35014/97, Maria Hutten Czapska v. Poland, in which it was found that the Polish state violated Art. 1 of Protocol No. 1 to the ECHR, does not constitute a preliminary ruling in the meaning of art. 417[1] of the c.c. and does not trigger civil liability of the State Treasury. Similar opinion was presented by the Supereme Court in a judgment of the Supreme Court of June 14, 2012, I CSK 577/11158.

For these reasons it is even more controversial whether an ordinary court or an administrative court is impowered to declare for the purpose of art. 417^{1} of the c.c. unconstitutionality or illegality of the regulation without refering for a required preliminary ruling. However, there are doctrinal opinions presented by a group of scholars advocating that the court adjudicating in a case for compensation for normative unlawfulness may independently declare such an act unconstitutional.[29]

Furthermore, there is no doubt that liability for normative restrictions in the State of Epidemic depends on causal assessment (art. 361 of the c.c.). This means that everyone must indicate that a particular head of damage was caused exactly by uncessary illegal normative act. This could be difficult in practice as restrictions were issued for public health reasons and were necessary.

4 Conclusions

COVID-19 crisis damaged business and social life in Poland and in Europe. The announcement of the State of Epidemic in 2020 and not revocing it for over two years in Poland is prima facie considered justified and legal. It followed a declaration of the COVID-19 pandemic by the WHO and the fact that the SARS-CoV-2 crisis was not of sufficient magnitude to warrant the invocation of constitutional emergency powers. France, Germany, Italy, and Poland all chose to deal with the COVID-19 crisis by delegating powers to the executive by ordinary legislative means.[30]

The analysis of Polish case law demonstrates that certain restrictions introduced by the Government, in particularly those as intrusive as the ban on leaving one's house, must be directly and comprehensively authorised by the Parliament. Governmental regulations should not, without comprehensive statutory authorisation, infringe such important personal rights. Parliamentary supervision of the executive's use of its powers, exercised in principle by political control over the

[29] Florczak-Wątor, p. 19; Roszkiewicz, pp. 324–326, Zoll, Południak-Gierz, Bańczyk, pp. 10–12; see: also Pecyna, pp. 26–27; against Banaszczyk (2015), pp. 196–197; Bosek, p. 212; Strugała (2021), p. 30.

[30] Bosek, p. 141.

government and by virtue of new laws, is necessary and justified by the principle of separation of powers.

However, this analysis shows that pursuing claims for damages on the basis of the provisions of art. 417(1) § 1 of the Polish Civil Code is associated with substantial obstacles and limitations like duty to deliver a preliminary ruling of unconstitutionality or illegality of particular normative restriction. If the Constitutional Tribunal has not declared any anti-epidemic restriction unconstitutional or illegal, it is impossible to establish liability of the State Treasury.

Analysis of the case law indicates that so far there is only one first-instance judgment that has been issued in such cases.[31] The court dismissed the entrepreneur's claim for payment of compensation by the State Treasury for profits lost by him in connection with the introduction of the ban on conducting business activity, brought pursuant to Art. 417(1) § 1 of the Polish Civil Code. According to the Court, the plaintiff failed to demonstrate unlawfulness of the covid regulations. This requires obtaining a preliminary ruling in the form of a judgment of the Constitutional Tribunal, and not establishing this fact by the court examining the case for damages.

Furthermore, liability for damages always depends on a causal assessment. If there is no opinion according to which declaration of pandemic by WHO and declaration of the State of Epiemic by the Polish Minister of Health were not necessary, there is no causal nexus between anti-covid regulations and the damage of a particular person.

References

Banaszczyk Z (2015) Odpowiedzialność za szkody wyrządzone przy wykonywaniu władzy publicznej. Warszawa

Bosek L (2021a) Bezprawie legislacyjne. Warszawa

Bosek L (2021b) Anti-epidemic emergency regimes under Polish law in comparative, historical and jurisprudential perspective. Eur J Health Law 28:113–141

Bosek L (2022) Stan epidemii. Konstrukcja prawna, Warszawa

Bosek L, Roszkiewicz J (2020) Konstytucyjne uwarunkowania systemu udzielania świadczeń zdrowotnych [Constitutional conditions of the health care system]. In: Safjan M, Bosek L (eds) System Prawa Medycznego, vol 3 [System of Medical Law]. C.H. Beck, Warsaw

Brzeziński M (2007) Stany nadzwyczajne w polskich konstytucjach. Warszawa

Florczak-Wątor M (2020) Niekonstytucyjność ograniczeń praw i wolności jednostki wprowadzonych w związku z epidemią COVID-19 jako przesłanka odpowiedzialności odszkodowawczej państwa. Państwo i Prawo 12

Janik M (2015) Płaszczyzny działania organów policji sanitarnej w sferze nadzoru sanitarnego i epidemiologicznego. Studium administracyjnoprawne, Katowice

Kardas P (2020) Konstytucyjne podstawy rozstrzygania kolizji obowiązków i konfliktów dóbr w czasie epidemii. Palestra 6

Miaskowska-Daszkiewicz K (2017) Prawne instrumenty wspierające bezpieczeństwo epidemiczne biorców ludzkich komórek, tkanek i narządów. Studia Prawnicze KUL 3

[31] Judgement of the District Court for Warszawa-Śródmieście 31.3.2022 r., Ref. No. I C 1047/21.

Pałka K (2018) Świadczenia zdrowotne związane z chorobami zakaźnymi [Health services connected with infectious diseases]. In: Safjan M, Bosek L (eds) System Prawa Medycznego, vol 2 [System of Medical Law]. C.H. Beck, Warsaw

Pecyna M (2020) Odpowiedzialność odszkodowawcza Skarbu Państwa za ograniczenia praw i wolności w czasie epidemii COVID-19. Państwo i Prawo 12

Pyziak-Szafnicka M (2022) Naprawienie szkód spowodowanych ograniczeniami praw i wolności w czasie epidemii SARS-CoV-2 (głos w dyskusji). Państwo i Prawo 9

Roszkiewicz J (2022) Granice ograniczeń wolności gospodarczej wprowadzanych w celu przeciwdziałania epidemii (uwagi na tle orzecznictwa sądów administracyjnych). Zeszyty Naukowe Sądownictwa Administracyjnego 2

Safjan M, Bosek L (eds) (2016) Konstytucja Rzeczypospolitej Polskiej. Komentarz [Constitution of the Republic of Poland. Commentary], vol I. C.H.Beck, Warsaw

Steinborn S (2016) Id: Konstytucja RP. Tom II. Komentarz do art. 87–243, Safjan M, Bosek L, Warszawa

Strugała R (2021) Odpowiedzialność Skarbu Państwa za szkody wynikające z zakazów prowadzenia działalności gospodarczej w okresie epidemii COVID-19. Przegląd Prawa Handlowego 5

Trociuk S (2021) Prawa i wolności w stanie epidemii. Warszawa

Tuleja P (2020) Pandemia COVID-19 a konstytucyjne stany nadzwyczajne. Palestra 9

Zoll F, Południak-Gierz K, Bańczyk W (2021) Zakres odpowiedzialności odszkodowawczej Skarbu Państwa za szkody majątkowe spowodowane ograniczeniami wprowadzonymi w związku z COVID-19. Studia Prawa Prywatnego 3

Leszek Bosek Professor of Law at the Faculty of Law and Administration of the University of Warsaw, the Judge of the Supreme Court of the Republic of Poland; Head of the research project of National Science Center No. 2021/41/B/HS5/04277 (The role of codes of medical ethics and professional standards in biomedicine and their relevance for private law liability); this article is an element of the project.

The Liability of Public Authorities for "Legal Damages" During the Covid-19 Pandemic

Sandra Hadrowicz

Abstract The outbreak of the Covid-19 pandemic caused numerous changes in socio-economic life around the world. All countries around the world faced the challenge of dealing with the effects of the pandemic. However, the actions taken by the public authorities have not been without detriment to various spheres of human activity, in particular the sphere of economic activity. As a result, the affected entrepreneurs have suffered numerous losses, for which it is necessary to find an appropriate legal basis. For this reason, the chapter considers whether, and if so to what extent, a public authority may be held liable for Covid damages caused to entrepreneurs when the intrusive actions of the authority have been assessed as lawful. The analysis concerns the admissibility of holding public authorities liable for legal damages both in Poland and Germany.

1 The Covid-19 Pandemic and the Responsibility of Public Authorities

The outbreak of the Covid-19 pandemic has caused numerous changes in socioeconomic life around the world. The high level of danger associated with the spread of the still unexplored SARS-CoV-2 virus in 2020 has left national authorities with the challenge of combating the impact of the pandemic. However, the measures they have taken to limit the spread of the new virus and to protect the lives and health of

S. Hadrowicz (✉)
Faculty of Law and Administration, University of Warsaw, Warsaw, Poland
e-mail: s.hadrowicz@uw.edu.pl

E. Hadrowicz (ed.), *Polish Entrepreneurial Law in the Era of the COVID-19 Pandemic*, Ius Gentium: Comparative Perspectives on Law and Justice 114,
https://doi.org/10.1007/978-3-031-57480-1_4

billions of citizens,[1] have not been without detriment to various spheres of human activity. One of the areas that have been particularly badly affected was economic activity. By means of the so-called 'anti-covid' measures, a number of legal acts were issued that had the effect of limiting the freedom of economic activity. For example, cinemas, theatres, or gyms were ordered to close and restaurants were restricted to selling takeaway food only.[2] As a result, enterprises have suffered numerous losses for which an appropriate legal basis must be found. For this reason, the subject of damage caused by the actions of public authorities is of particular practical importance.

In the Polish legal order, the normative basis for liability for damage caused in connection with the exercise of public authority is Article 77(1) of the Polish Constitution. According to the wording of this provision, everyone shall have the right to compensation for any harm done to him by any action of an organ of public authority contrary to law. The liability of public authority is further regulated in ordinary legislation, namely in Articles 417-417^2 of the Polish Civil Code. However, the Civil Code regulations do not serve merely to replicate the content contained in the constitutional norm. They develop the prerequisites for asserting the right to compensation. In addition, the protection provided for in Article 77 of the Polish Constitution has been extended by the statutory regulations of liability for the exercise of public authority. This applies in particular to Article 417^2 of the Polish Civil Code. This provision regulates the liability of public authorities not only for the unlawful exercise of power but also for lawful damage.

Article 417^2 of the Polish Civil Code may thus acquire particular significance in the era of post-pandemic reality.[3] This is due to the fact that the constitutionality of the adopted covid acts is still unsettled, while the actualization of the liability of public authority for the unlawful exercise of powers (Article 417-417^1 of the Polish Civil Code) is conditional on the unlawfulness of the failure to adopt a judicial or other decision which is to be established in the course of the relevant proceedings.[4] However, this issue remains open for the time being.[5] There are also no legal regulations providing a legal basis for compensation claims to compensate for the damage suffered by entrepreneurs as a result of restrictions introduced to combat pandemic.[6]

---

[1] Judgment of the LG w Hannover from 9.7.2020, 8 O 2/20, NJW 2020, 3469; judgment of the LG w Hannover from 11.12.2020, 8 O 4/20, https://dejure.org/dienste/vernetzung/rechtsprechung?Text=8%20O%204/20; judgment of the BGH from 17.3.2022, III ZR 79/21, openJur 2022, 7945.

[2] See for example § 32 Infektionsschutzgesetzes (IfSG) i.V.m. § 2 Infektionszuständigkeitsverordnung durch die Ministerin für Soziales, Gesundheit, Integration und Verbraucherschutz die "Verordnung über Maßnahmen zur Eindämmung des neuartigen Coronavirus SARS-CoV-2 und COVID-19 in Brandenburg" (GVBl. II Nr. 11).

[3] Bosek (2022), p. 27. See also: Pyziak-Szafnicka (2022), p. 117.

[4] Strugała (2021), p. 31.

[5] See more extensively: in the German legal order: Hofstätter (2021); in the Polish legal order: Bosek (2022), who discusses the issue of the constitutionality of covid ordinances in detail.

[6] Pyziak-Szafnicka (2022), p. 118.

At the same time, the provision of Article 417^2 of the Polish Civil Code is an unusual legislative solution even on a European scale. For example, the German Civil Code has no similar legal regulation. Nevertheless, German jurisprudence attempts to find an appropriate legal basis for the compensation of legal damages by invoking the concept of the so-called self-sacrifice remedy (German: *Aufopferungsentschädigung*).

2 Damage to Entrepreneurs

The damage suffered by entrepreneurs resulted mainly from the imposition of numerous bans and restrictions on business activities. For example, hotels, gyms, or hairdressing salons were closed for more than a few months.[7] Additional negative impacts arose indirectly from restrictions on people's mobility. These include, for example, the closure of national borders, which had a negative impact on tourist traffic, or the temporary restriction of mobility.[8] This has consequently led to a reduction in income for many entrepreneurs, especially in places that can be described as 'recreational'. However, it is not only entrepreneurs' income that has been reduced, because they also had to incur certain expenses. Such damages include, for example, costs related to the provision of hygiene measures (e.g. purchase of disinfectants, disposable gloves), which were supposed to ensure the safety of both the people using the services and the entire staff of the enterprises.

The damage suffered by entrepreneurs was therefore primarily damage to property. This is because the damage of this kind consists of negative consequences of infringement of property and other property rights of the injured party.[9] Thus the above-mentioned types of damage fall within the scope of damage to property. However, this does not mean that it is not possible to indicate damages of other types among all the damages suffered by entrepreneurs. In this respect, personal injury can also be mentioned. For example, traders may have suffered a health disorder (e.g. depression) as a result of the deterioration of their professional situation due to the imposed restrictions.[10] Such damage will include both the pecuniary effects of this disorder (e.g. psychiatric treatment costs) and the non-pecuniary effects (e.g. mental pain and suffering).[11]

However, when classifying a particular injury suffered by entrepreneurs as a legally relevant damage, the principles of compensation law must be borne in mind. Not every damage in the natural sense is subject to compensation.[12] It is only cov-

---

[7] Zoll et al. (2021), p. 14.

[8] Zoll et al. (2021), p. 14.

[9] Brzozowski et al. (2016), p. 235.

[10] Juranek (2021), p. 103.

[11] See: Kaliński (2021a), p. 19.

[12] Wandt (2017), p. 27.

ered by the obligation to compensate if the law expressly provides for it.[13] Thus, a specific legal meaning is only acquired when the damage is qualified as the result of a breach of a legal situation.[14] Different rules determine which damage is compensable and to what extent.[15] As a consequence, damage to entrepreneurs can only be compensated if an appropriate legal basis for compensation is indicated.

3 Liability of Public Authorities for Legal Damage in Poland

3.1 General Observations

Article 417^2 of the Polish Civil Code falls within the scope of the regulation of State Treasury liability.[16] It stipulates the liability of public authority for legal damage. The introduction of this regulation was based on the assumption that there are cases where public authority is exercised in such a way that the illegality of a sovereign act or omission cannot be alleged, but at the same time, it would be unjust for the negative consequences of this behavior to be borne solely by the injured party.[17] Article 417^2 of the Polish Civil Code has a subsidiary function to the other provisions on the liability of public authorities.[18] This means that it is applicable only in those cases where there are no grounds for assuming that the event causing the damage was unlawful.[19] In this respect, the case law indicates that courts should consider its application in cases involving personal injury caused in connection with the exercise of public authority only after excluding the possibility that the perpetrator's act or omission was unlawful.[20]

Liability for damage caused by the lawful exercise of public authority is expressed in a provision of a special nature, which justifies the prohibition of its extensive interpretation (*exceptiones non sunt extendendae*).[21] The provision of Article 417^2

[13] Sinkiewicz (1998), p. 61.

[14] Castronovo (1997), p. 11.

[15] Larenz and Canaris (1994), p. 351; Fikentscher and Heinemann (2017), p. 365.

[16] Judgment of the SA (Polish Court of Appeal) in Szczecin from 22.8.2018, I ACa 173/18, Legalis.

[17] Radwański (2004), p. 22.

[18] Dzienis (2008), p. 37. This was also the position presented: w judgment of the SA in Warszawa from 17.1.2014, VI ACa 868/13, Legalis; judgment of the SA in Gdańsku from 23.2.2017, V ACa 370/16, Legalis; judgment of the SA in Katowice from 11.9.2018, V ACa 560/17, Legalis.

[19] Also compare to: judgment of the SN (Supreme Court of Poland) from 14.1.1970, II CR 609/69, Legalis; judgment of the SA in Kraków from 19.12.2019, I ACa 691/18, Legalis.

[20] See: judgment of the SN (Supreme Court of Poland) from 13.4.2012, I CSK 398/11, Legalis; judgment of the SN from 247.2009, II CSK 39/09, Legalis; judgment of the SN from 4.3.2008, I CSK 453/07, Legalis.

[21] See: judgment of the SN (Supreme Court of Poland) from 22.3.2012, V CSK 135/11, Legalis; judgment of the SA in Warszawa from 27.5.2014, I ACa 1411/13, Legalis; judgment of the SA in Gdańsk from 23.2.2017, V ACa 370/16, Legalis.

of the Polish Civil Code should therefore be interpreted strictly. For this reason, it is necessary to analyze the individual prerequisites for the application of Article 417^2 of the Polish Civil Code in order to determine whether this provision can be invoked as a legal basis for compensating entrepreneurs for covid damages. The prerequisites for the application of this provision are: the equitable principle, the lawful action of the public authority, personal damage, and the existence of causal link.

3.2 *The "Equitable Principle" Rationale*

Article 417^2 of the Polish Civil Code makes the emergence and extent of the obligation to pay damages dependent on the criterion of equitable principle. The courts are consequently obliged to apply this general clause when deciding whether to accept or dismiss a claim for damages under this provision.[22] In applying the equity clause, these authorities should therefore consider the specific circumstances of the case and resolve it on the basis of appropriate equitable, ethical as well as moral justification.[23] It is neither possible nor advisable to give a comprehensive identification of the criteria to be taken into account in assessing the existence of equitable principle.[24] However, it should be stated that the court's decision based on equity must be objectively and factually justified. The court should therefore make a comprehensive assessment of all the circumstances of the case which may justify the assumption of liability of the state, a local or regional authority, or another legal person exercising public authority or which may be of significance for the determination of the extent of the damage to be compensated.[25] Such circumstances include, in particular, the financial situation of the parties, the aggrieved party's inability to work or his difficult financial situation,[26] and the existence of a general interest underlying a specific action of the public authority.[27]

The literature and case law unanimously indicate that the court should also take into account the circumstances of the causative event, i.e. the severity of the harm suffered or its permanence,[28] the conduct of the injured party[29] (for example,

[22] See: judgment of the SN (Supreme Court of Poland) from 22.3.2012, V CSK 135/11, Legalis.

[23] Kuźmicka-Sulikowska (2019), art. 417^2, Rn 6. Compare to: judgment of the SA in Katowice from 7.2.2018, I ACa 838/17, Legalis.

[24] Safjan (2004), p. 83.

[25] Więzowska-Czepiel (2009), p. 53; judgment of the SN (Supreme Court of Poland) from 22.3.2012, V CSK 135/11, Legalis.

[26] See: judgment of the SN (Supreme Court of Poland) from 21.3.2014, IV CSK 380/13, Legalis; judgment of the SN from 22.3.2012 r., V CSK 135/11, Legalis.

[27] Więzowska (2009), p. 202.

[28] Safjan (2004), p. 8; Dzienis (2006), p. 234. See also: judgment of the SN (Supreme Court of Poland) from 14.6.2018, V CSK 371/17, Legalis.

[29] See: judgment of the SN (Supreme Court of Poland) from 22.5.2003, II CKN 96/01, Legalis. See also: judgment of the SA in Warszawa from 22.9.2020 r., I ACa 340/20, Legalis; judgment of the

altruistic conduct in terms of providing assistance to state or local government bodies would be in favor of awarding compensation[30]) or the personal situation of the injured party.[31] Importantly, the case law of the Supreme Court points out that it would be inaccurate to assume that the circumstances constituting the ground for awarding compensation based on equitable principle, in particular the injured party's inability to work or his or her material hardship, must be consequential to the causal event.[32] From the wording of Article 417^2 of the Polish Civil Code the Supreme Court infers the possibility to claim damages also if the circumstances of the case concerning the injured party existed beforehand, but only their scope has changed—as a result of the damage caused by the public authority.

In the case of entrepreneurs, the most relevant factors to be considered by the court when assessing whether the condition of equitable principle is met will be their difficult economic situation involving, in particular, the negative financial impact of the pandemic. Numerous restrictions have often led to a significant deterioration of the financial situation of many entrepreneurs. Moreover, the current difficult socio-economic situation and rising inflation may constitute an additional circumstance justifying the redress of entrepreneurs' damages.

3.3 *Lawful Action of Public Authority*

Compensation based on 417^2 of the Polish Civil Code is subject only to damage caused by "acts of public authority", which should be understood as both acts and omissions falling within the sphere of imperium.[33] This sphere encompasses legal relations in which the state in the narrow sense of the term (the State Treasury) or a local government unit (commune, district, voivodeship) is in a superior position, i.e. may unilaterally, within the framework of the imperium, shape the rights or obligations of another entity and use coercive means to ensure the realization of those rights or obligations.[34] As a result, damage caused by public authorities that act outside the sphere of imperium is not covered by 417^2 of the Polish Civil Code.[35]

SA in Kraków from 20.6.2013, I ACa 498/13, Legalis.

[30] See: judgment of the SN (Supreme Court of Poland) from 6.1.1975, II CR 779/74, Legalis.

[31] See: judgment of the SN (Supreme Court of Poland) from 22.3.2012, V CSK 135/11, Legalis; judgment of the SA in Warszawa from 19.9.2018,V ACa 424/17, Legalis.

[32] See: judgment of the SN (Supreme Court of Poland) from 22.3.2012, V CSK 135/1, Legalis. See also: judgment of the SN (Supreme Court of Poland) from 21.3.2014 r., IV CSK 380/13, Legalis; judgment of the TK (Polish Constitutional Tribunal) from 4.12.2001, SK 18/00, OTK 2001, No. 8, item 256.

[33] Kuźmicka-Sulikowska (2019), art. 417, Rn 3.

[34] Sobolewski (2020), art. 417, Rn 27.

[35] See: Banaszczyk (2020), art. *417,* Rn 46.

The relevant tort provisions governing the tortious liability of legal persons (i.e. Articles 416, 427, 429, and 430 of the Polish Civil Code) shall then apply.[36] At the same time, the act of the public authority must be lawful and, therefore, in order to claim compensation under Article 417^2 of the Polish Civil Code, the aggrieved party does not have to prove the unlawfulness of the act or omission of the public authority. Legitimate action, on the other hand, is to be understood as fully corresponding to the legal norms regulating the scope of activity of the public administration.[37]

Thus, the issuance by the government of a series of legal acts (in particular regulations) that imposed new restrictions on entrepreneurs can be qualified as a lawful act of the public authority. However, this matter has not yet been fully resolved and there is still plenty of opinions in the legal doctrine that the aforementioned acts were unlawful.[38] If this position will be shared by the relevant authority, it should be considered that the application of Article 417^2 of the Polish Civil Code will be excluded. In such a case, however, it will be possible to compensate the damage suffered by the injured parties on the basis of other provisions, i.e. 417-417^1 of the Polish Civil Code.

3.4 *Causality*

Another prerequisite is the existence of a causal link between the action of the public authority and the damage suffered by the aggrieved party. In the legal doctrine, it is disputed whether, in the case of the regulation of liability based on equitable principle, the concept of an adequate causal link (Article 361 § 1 of the Polish Civil Code) is applicable, or whether only a conditio sine qua non link is required.[39] According to the position prevailing both in literature[40] and case law,[41] the application of Article 417^2 of the Polish Civil Code as a basis for liability for the lawful exercise of public authority requires, as a rule, the existence of an adequate (normal)

---

[36] Radwański (2004), p. 12.

[37] Parchomiuk (2010), p. 99.

[38] See for example: Pecyna (2021), p. 29; Florczak-Wątor (2020), p. 18.

[39] Banaszczyk (2020), art. 417^2, Rn 2.

[40] Compare to: Safjan (2004), p. 27; Banaszczyk (2020), art. $417^{2.}$, Rn 2.

[41] See: judgment of the SN (Supreme Court of Poland) from 7.12.2012, II CSK 239/12, Legalis; judgment of the SN from 14.6.2018, V CSK 371/17, Legalis; judgment of the SN (Supreme Court of Poland) from 1.1.2004, II CK 134/03, Legalis; judgment of the SN (Supreme Court of Poland) from 21.3.2014, IV CSK 380/13, Legalis; judgment of the SA in Warsaw from 203.2019, I ACa 1788/17, Legalis; judgment of the SA in Warszawa from 19.9.2018, V ACa 424/17, Legalis; judgment of the SA in Kraków from 24.4.2014, I ACa 233/14, Legalis; judgment of the SA in Kraków from 18.1.2013, I ACa 262/13, Legalis; judgment of the SA in Kraków from 11.4.2013, I ACa 225/13, Legalis.

causal link between the damage caused and the exercise of public authority. However, it is pointed out that, if justified by considerations of equity, it is possible—by way of exception—to depart from adequate causation towards conditio sine qua non causation.[42] However, it has also been noted that the negative side of the adequate theory is the elimination of responsibility for "abnormal" results,[43] which *a casu ad casum* may lead to wrongful decisions. On the other hand, the provisions governing liability for damages based on equitable principles have a protective function and their purpose is to correct wrongful solutions. Nevertheless, this view is incorrect. Because of the vagueness of the concept of "normality" in borderline situations, it is still possible for the court to balance assessments according to reasons of equity.[44] In the case of liability based on equitable principle, this is particularly relevant as this principle itself refers *expressis verbis* to equity. This means that when doubts arise as to whether there was a normal consequence of the harmful event or whether it was abnormal in its nature, the court should be inclined to interpret in favor of recognising the existence of an adequate causality.

Thus, the view that the requirement of an adequate causal link can be omitted in exceptional situations must be rejected. Such a view would lead to an unacceptable, from the point of view of the axiology of tort liability, differentiation of the situation of victims. The criticized view is further based on the assumption that, in the case of an exceptional situation, the court will be free to choose between the application of an adequate causal link or a *conditio sine qua non* causal link. The point is, however, that this concept does not find its legal basis in the wording of the Civil Code. Therefore, it should be thought that the general norm expressed in Article 361 § 1 of the Polish Civil Code is applicable to the regulation of liability based on equitable principle. Since Article 417^2 of the Polish Civil Code does not provide for any modification of the causal link, the liability in this case, too, will only become effective if the condition of normal consequences is met. It has been correctly pointed out that the equitable principle abandons the requirement of fault or illegality, but not the general regulation of causation.[45]

Therefore the requirement of the existence of causality as defined in of Article 361 § 1 of the Polish Civil Code should not represent a premise disqualifying the entrepreneurs' claims for damages. As a result, if the damage to their legally protected interests is the normal consequence of the harmful event, there will be no obstacle to concluding that there is an adequate causal link. However, this issue is to be assessed only after considering the specific injury.

---

[42] Olejniczak (2010), p. 381. Compare to: Śmieja (1990), p. 331.

[43] Lewaszkiewicz-Petrykowska (1978), p. 67.

[44] Dybowski (1961), p. 29.

[45] Kaliński (2018), p. 53.

3.5 Personal Damage

The last prerequisite analysed is the requirement of personal damage. The scope of application of Article 417² of the Polish Civil Code is limited, as the injured party may not claim compensation for every damage suffered as a result of the action of the public authority, but only for damage of a specific type—personal damage.[46] Therefore, the scope of compensation does not include the negative consequences of the violation of property and other property rights of the injured party (so-called property damage)[47] or pure economic loss. The provision of Article 417² of the Polish Civil Code does not specify which personal injuries are subject to compensation. Thus, it should be thought that there is no statutory narrowing, and the concept should be understood as damage resulting from the violation of the personal rights and interests of the injured party[48] (life, health, as well as other personal goods such as freedom and autonomy of will).[49]

However, there is a dispute in the legal doctrine as to whether "personal damage" should be understood exclusively as the consequences of the violation of the personal rights and interests of the injured party of a material nature or also of a non-material nature. Some of academics indicate that this concept may encompass not only material damage but also non-material damage.[50] However, based on Article 417² of the Polish Civil Code, an apt thesis has been put forward that personal injury can only be of a material nature, which results from the fact that the legislator distinguishes in this provision between the notion of 'personal damage' and 'non-material damage'.[51] This interpretation is therefore supported by the linguistic interpretation of Article 417² of the Polish Civil Code.

Based on the analyzed provision, it is also possible to award compensation for the harm (non-material damage) suffered. Awarding it may be justified only by causing health disorder, bodily injury (Article 417² of the Polish Civil Code in connection with Article 445 of the Polish Civil Code) or death of the injured party (Article 417² of the Polish Civil Code in connection with Article 446 §4 of the Polish Civil Code) which arose in conjunction with the exercise of public authority.[52] Thus, in the case of violation of other personal rights, it is not possible to award compensation based on Article 448 of the Polish Civil Code, even if they were a

[46] Radwański (2004), p. 22. See: judgment of the SA in Katowicach from 2.8.2018, I ACa 86/18, Legalis; judgment of the SA in Gdańsk from 28.2.2018,V ACa 7/17, Legalis; judgment of the SA in Łodź from 28.2.2017, I ACa 1127/16, Legalis; judgment of the SA in Katowice from 25.4.2013, I ACa 137/13, Legalis.

[47] Kaliński (2021b), p. 233.

[48] Brzozowski et al. (2016), p. 82; Kaliński (2021b), p. 236; Szpunar (1999), p. 44; Fellman and Kottmann (2012), p. 54; Czachórski (2009), p. 88.

[49] Bagińska and Bączyk-Rozwadowska (2021), p. 681.

[50] Radwański and Olejniczak (2016), p. 93; Szpunar (1999), p. 54.

[51] Brzozowski et al. (2016), p. 233.

[52] Radwański (2004), p. 23; Banaszczyk (2015), p. 363.

negative consequence of lawful action of public authority. This follows from the linguistic interpretation of Article 417^2 of the Polish Civil Code, which makes not only the award of damages, but also of pecuniary reparation, conditional on personal injury.[53] Moreover, from the wording of this provision, it must be concluded that the claim for compensation is only possible if the non-material damage coexists with the material damage. Therefore, if the victim suffers non-material damage alone, no compensation can be awarded. Furthermore, according to the prevailing position in the legal doctrine, Article 448 of the Polish Civil Code makes the possibility of awarding compensation conditional on the premise of the unlawfulness of the infringement of personal rights,[54] which is not present in the case of liability for legal damage.

The limitation of damage compensation in Article 417^2 of the Polish Civil Code to personal injury and related non-property (non-physical) damage is the biggest obstacle to effective redress by entrepreneurs based on equity. Meanwhile, as has already been pointed out, most of the entrepreneurs' damages took the form of damage to property. These damages will therefore not be compensable under Article 417^2 of the Polish Civil Code. Its scope, however, includes such damages as, for example, the costs of psychiatric treatment of depression.

4 Liability of Public Authorities for Legal Damages in Germany

Sections 56(1) and 65(1) of the German Infection Protection Act (German: Infektionsschutzgesetz) do not grant a claim for damages to entrepreneurs who have suffered losses because of the actions of state authorities counteracting the effects of the Covid pandemic-19.[55] Furthermore, compensation claims under police and regulatory law (e.g. § 39 Abs. 1 Buchstabe b OBG NRW) are also excluded. This is due to the fact that the compensation provisions contained in the twelfth chapter of the Infection Protection Act—at least with regard to lawful infection control measures—constitute a lex specialis in relation to the provisions of police and regulatory law, which excludes their applicability.[56] For this reason, it is necessary to consider whether the legal basis for the claims of entrepreneurs can be found in the general regulations governing the liability of public authorities.

In German law, the issue of public authority liability is regulated in Article 34 GG and Section 839 BGB.[57] Thus, as in Poland, the relevant legal regulation is found in both the Constitution and the Civil Code. However, the German system of

[53] Compare to: judgment of the SA in Warsaw from 5.2.2014, I ACa 1618/13, Legalis.

[54] Brzozowski et al. (2016), pp. 254–255.

[55] Judgment of the BGH from 17.3.2022, III ZR 79/21, NJW 2022, 2252.

[56] Judgment of the BGH from 17.3.2022, III ZR 79/21, NJW 2022, 2252.

[57] Fuchs and Pauker (2012), p. 203.

public authority liability is much more complicated than the Polish one. The claim for damages based solely on § 839 BGB is directed only against public officials.[58] This provision regulates the liability for damages of a public (civil) servant for an intentional or negligent breach of his or her official duty towards a third party. However, it is only by linking the claim under Section 839 BGB with Article 34 GG that the liability of the state can be extended to situations where the damage was caused by any state functionary taking action of a sovereign nature.[59] According to Article 34 GG, if, in the exercise of the public office entrusted to him or her, someone violates a duty owed to a third party, the State or the authority in whose service he or she is employed shall in principle be liable. Thus the difference between the code regulation and the constitutional regulation amounts to the fact that § 839 BGB is the substantive legal basis for the liability of public servants, while Article 34 GG is the basis for shifting liability to the state.[60] Only the combined application of § 839 BGB in conjunction with Article 34 GG, therefore, provides a uniform basis for the attribution of liability to public authorities.

The decisive factor for the attribution of liability is whether the public official acted in the exercise of a public function, i.e. in a position of authority.[61] However, Article 34 GG contains the expression "someone" (German: *jemand*). This means that liability for the unlawful exercise of public authority is to be understood in a broad sense.[62] As a result, it has to be assumed that not only the conduct of a public official but also of other persons acting in the sphere of imperium will give rise to liability.[63] The scope of the regulation of Article 34 GG will therefore include also the actions of private persons which the state "uses" (e.g. on a contractual basis) to exercise public authority.[64]

Official duties referred to in section 34 GG and section 839 BGB may in turn arise from all sources of law (e.g. laws, regulations), including administrative regulations and other internal regulations of public authorities.[65] The essential requirement, however, is that the official duty that has been breached, leading to the damage, must exist vis-à-vis a third party.[66] Outside the scope of the norms of § 839 BGB are therefore such duties that exist only towards the public. This requirement has the function of limiting the liability of the public authority. Nevertheless, it is considered sufficient if the official duty—in addition to the general interest—also serves to safeguard the interests of the individual, even if no claim for the

[58] Fuchs and Pauker (2012), p. 204.

[59] Fuchs and Pauker (2012), p. 204.

[60] Fuchs and Pauker (2012), p. 204.

[61] Fikentscher and Heinemann (2017), p. 975.

[62] Fikentscher and Heinemann (2017), p. 975.

[63] Fikentscher and Heinemann (2017), p. 975.

[64] Compare to: judgment of the BGH from 21.1.1993, III ZR 189/91, BGHZ 121, 161 and BGH JZ 2006, 920 m. Anm. Ossenbühl.

[65] Fuchs and Pauker (2012), p. 204.

[66] Fuchs and Pauker (2012), p. 205.

performance of an official act is provided for.[67] Therefore, in this respect, doubts arise as to whether the actions of the public authority in preventing the spread of the pandemic would meet the criterion of , "duty to a third party", or whether it should rather be thought that it was a general duty to the public.

However, the greatest limitation to the possibility of compensating for covid damages is that, under German law, the public authority will only be liable for culpable and unlawful conduct.[68] Therefore, as in the Polish legal system, this means that holding a public authority liable under Article 34 GG in conjunction with § 839 BGB for covid damages of entrepreneurs can be excluded. This is because it requires a prior determination that the measures taken by the public authority were not only disproportionate but also unlawful, resulting in damage to entrepreneurs. The issue is hence complex and still unresolved. Meanwhile, there is no provision in the German legal order similar in content to Polish Article 417^2 of the Polish Civil Code, that would regulate the issue of public authority liability for legal damages. Thus, in German law, in principle, only unlawful interference by a public authority with the legally protected interests of others gives rise to liability for damages of that authority.

However, German jurisprudence attempts to derive from the provisions of the German Constitution the admissibility of compensation for damage also caused by the lawful exercise of public authority (the concept of the so-called self-sacrifice remedy, German: *Aufopferungsentschädigung*). Article 20(3) GG, which states that justice is exercised based on the statute and the law (German: *Gesetz und Recht*), is indicated as the legal basis for such liability of public authority. As a result, this provision serves as a justification for the judiciary to correct and develop law.[69] Thus, by way of exception, a lawful interference with another's rights, if it has led to damages, gives rise to a claim for compensation.[70]

All of the exceptions to the compensation of legal damages identified in German case law are based on special emergency or conflict situations. They make the state interference necessary and lawful. At the same time, this means that the special self-sacrifice associated with it—taking into account the criterion of equity—requires compensation. The decisive factor in this respect is whether the self-sacrifice was imposed on the individual in the general interest and was not expected from others.[71] Claims for compensation may therefore be considered if the sovereign measures are lawful but lead to unusual and unforeseen inconvenience for the injured party that exceeds the threshold of what is reasonable under the law.[72] An example

[67] Judgment of the BGH from 3.3.1977, III ZR 10/74, BGHZ 68, 142, 145.

[68] Fikentscher and Heinemann (2017), p. 977; Fuchs and Pauker (2012), pp. 207–208.

[69] Hoyningen-Huene (1978), p. 34.

[70] Fikentscher and Heinemann (2017), p. 1006.

[71] BGHZ 48, 101; BGHZ 65.

[72] Judgment of the BGH from 14.3.2013, III ZR 253/12, BGHZ 197, 43; judgment of the BGH from 15.12.2016, III ZR 387/14, BGHZ 213, 200; judgment of the BGH from 29.3.1984, III ZR 11/83, BGHZ 91, 20, 26 f; judgment of the BGH from 17.3.2022, III ZR 79/21, NJW 2022, 2252.

of such cases in which claims based on self-sacrifice are accepted by the German jurisprudence are cases for compensation for damage caused by compulsory vaccination.[73] In this respect, however, the legislator has safeguarded the claims of the vaccinated against Covid-19 in § 60 IfSG.[74]

Nevertheless, it should be borne in mind that the concept of self-sacrifice is used as an exception. The principle is that lawful acts of public authority do not give rise to liability for damages. This is primarily due to the concept of a general risk of life that everyone must bear, and which cannot be passed on to the public.[75] It is therefore not a foregone conclusion that the concept of self-sacrifice can be applied to the covid damages suffered by entrepreneurs. In particular, the fact that governmental restrictions to combat the Covid-19 pandemic has affected most entrepreneurs across the country and not just within one industry (e.g. catering) may be an obstacle in this respect. Therefore, the nature of the measures taken in order to stop the Covid-19 pandemic speaks against considering that there was an individual, specific sacrifice,[76] which is the basic premise of the concept of self-sacrifice developed by the case law.

Recent German jurisprudence further notes that the application of the legal institution of self-sacrifice is not possible when it comes to compensation for damage caused by comprehensive infection control measures during a pandemic.[77] This is due to the fact that liability for legal damages under the concept of self-sacrifice is not an appropriate basis for compensation for damages of a mass nature (German: *massenhaft auftretende Schäden*).[78] This concept was not designed to compensate for damage caused by such a global phenomenon as the Covid-19 pandemic.[79] Furthermore, in the previous jurisprudence of the German courts, the liability of the public authority on the basis of self-sacrifice has only been accepted in the case of individual property damage caused by acts of an administrative-legal nature.[80]

Granting mass compensation claims to entrepreneurs solely on the basis of the criterion of equity could also be considered incompatible with the principle of separation of powers and the principle of democracy (German: *Grundsatz der Gewaltenteilung und dem demokratischen Prinzip*).[81] The granting of mass compensation claims should be reserved exclusively for the competence of the legislature. This is also reflected in recent judgments of the BGH. They expressed the view

---

[73] Fikentscher, Heinemann (2017), p. 958.

[74] Act on the Prevention and Control of Infectious Diseases in Humans of 20.7.2000, Federal Law Gazette I, p. 1045.

[75] BGHZ 46, 327; Fikentscher and Heinemann (2017), p. 1007.

[76] Judgment of the BGH from17.3.2022, III ZR 79/21, NJW 2022, 2252.

[77] Judgment of the BGH from17.3.2022, III ZR 79/21, NJW 2022, 2252.

[78] Judgment of the BGH from 10.12.1987, III ZR 220/86, NJW 1988, 478.

[79] Judgment of the BGH from 17.3.2022, III ZR 79/21, NJW 2022, 2252.

[80] See: judgment of the BGH from 29.1.1998, III ZR 110/97, NJW 1998, 1398, 1399. See also: judgment of the BGH from 17.3.2022, III ZR 79/21, NJW 2022, 2252.

[81] Judgment of the BGH from 17.3.2022, III ZR 79/21, NJW 2022, 2252.

that the allowance of claims for property damage caused by nationwide infection protection measures during the Covid-19 pandemic (i.e. closure of businesses or restriction of business activities) based on judicial law alone would amount to an impermissible addition to the Infection Protection Act.[82]

5 Conclusion

The analysis leads to the conclusion that the current legal regulations, both in Poland and Germany, do not provide effective juridical tools to pursue claims by entrepreneurs for damages suffered as a consequence of the pandemic. Especially if it is determined that the actions of the public authorities to counteract the effects of the Covid-19 pandemic were lawful. In the Polish legal order, in such a case the relevant legal regulation will be applicable, i.e. Article 417^2 of the Polish Civil Code. However, the normative scope of Article 417^2 of the Polish Civil Code is rather narrow. In particular, the limitation of the public authority's liability only to compensation for personal injury is a significant restriction on entrepreneurs' compensation claims. This is due to the fact that most of the damage they suffered was of a property damage nature, which the Polish legislator excluded from the scope of liability of the public authority for the lawful exercise of this authority. However, in the case of personal injury suffered by entrepreneurs, which was caused by the imposition of numerous restrictions and limitations by the public authority, it will be possible to apply Article 417^2 of the Polish Civil Code.

The issue of public liability for legal damages in connection with measures to combat the effects of the Covid-19 pandemic is even more complex under German law. In this legal order there is no regulation like Article 417^2 of the Polish Civil Code, regulating in a general way the liability of public authorities for lawful damage. Liability for the lawful exercise of public authority is mainly a creation of case law functioning under the name of the concept of self-sacrifice remedy (German: *Aufopferungsentschädigung*). The attribution of public authority liability for covid damages in the event of the lawful exercise of that authority may therefore be questionable in the absence of a relevant legal provision. Particularly as the damage suffered by the entrepreneurs was massive and a global phenomenon. Thus, it should be considered insufficient to adopt a legal basis for redressing such damages solely on the basis of judicial law.

References

Bagińska E, Bączyk-Rozwadowska K (2021) In: Bagińska E (ed) System Prawa Medycznego. Odpowiedzialność prywatnoprawna, vol 5. Warszawa

[82] Judgment of the BGH from 17.3.2022, III ZR 79/21, NJW 2022, 2252.

Banaszczyk Z (2015) Odpowiedzialność za szkody wyrządzone przy wykonywaniu władzy publicznej. Warszawa
Banaszczyk Z (2020) In: Pietrzykowski K (ed) Kodeks cywilny. Komentarz. Art. 1–449[10], vol I. Legalis
Bosek L (2022) Stan epidemii. Konstrukcja prawna, Warszawa
Brzozowski A, Jastrzębski J, Kaliński M, Skowrońska-Bocian E (2016) Zobowiązania – część ogólna. Warszawa
Castronovo C (1997) La nuova responsabilita civile. Milano
Czachórski W (2009) Zobowiązania. Zarys wykładu, Warszawa
Dybowski T (1961) Adekwatny czy konieczny związek przyczynowy - cz. 1. Palestra 42(6):76–83
Dzienis P (2006) Odpowiedzialność cywilna władzy publicznej. Warszawa
Dzienis P (2008) Znaczenie zasad słuszności w odpowiedzialności odszkodowawczej władzy publicznej. Białostockie Studia Prawnicze 3:33–45
Fellman W, Kottmann A (2012) Schweizerisches Haftpflichtrecht. Bern
Fikentscher W, Heinemann A (2017) Schuldrecht Allgemeiner und Besonderer Teil. Berlin
Florczak-Wątor M (2020) Niekonstytucyjność ograniczeń praw i wolności jednostki wprowadzonych w związku z epidemią COVID-19 jako przesłanka odpowiedzialności odszkodowawczej państwa. Państwo i Prawo 12:5–22
Fuchs M, Pauker W (2012) Delikts- und Schadenserstazrecht. Heidelberg-Dordrecht-London-New York
Hofstätter C (2021) Amtshaftung bei rechtswidriger COVID-19-Verordnungserlassung. ZfV 57:4
Hoyningen-Huene GF (1978) Die Billigkeit im Arbeitsrecht. Munich
Juranek A (2021) O zwyczajnej odpowiedzialności w niezwyczajnych czasach, czyli analiza odpowiedzialności deliktowej Skarbu Państwa w związku z wykonywaniem władzy publicznej w stanach zagrożenia epidemicznego, epidemii i innych, równie niezwyczajnych. Transformacje Prawa Prywatnego 4:89–109
Kaliński M (2018) In: Olejniczak A (ed) System Prawa Prywatnego. Prawo zobowiązań – część ogólna, vol 6. Warszawa
Kaliński M (2021a) Szkoda na mieniu i jej naprawienie. Warszawa
Kaliński M (2021b) Szkoda na osobie i jej naprawienie. Warszawa
Kuźmicka-Sulikowska (2019) In: Gniewek E, Machnikowski P (eds) Kodeks cywilny. Komentarz, Legalis
Larenz K, Canaris C (1994) Lehrbuch des Schuldrecht. Band II: Besonderer Teil, 2. Halbband, München
Lewaszkiewicz-Petrykowska B (1978) Wyrządzenie szkody przez kilka osób. Warszawa
Olejniczak A (2010) In: Kidyba A (ed) Kodeks cywilny. Komentarz. Zobowiązania. *Część* ogólna, vol III, part 1. Warszawa
Parchomiuk J (2010) Odpowiedzialność odszkodowawcza władzy publicznej na zasadzie słuszności w prawie polskim. Roczniki Wydziału Nauk Prawnych i Ekonomicznych 6(1):93–103
Pecyna M (2021) Odpowiedzialność odszkodowawcza Skarbu Państwa za ograniczenia praw i wolności w czasie epidemii COVID-19. Państwo i Prawo 12:23–37
Pyziak-Szafnicka M (2022) Naprawienie szkód spowodowanych ograniczeniami praw i wolności w czasach epidemii SARS-CoV-2 (głos w dyskusji). Państwo i Prawo 9:112–128
Radwański Z (2004) Odpowiedzialność odszkodowawcza za szkody wyrządzone przy wykonywaniu władzy publicznej w świetle projektowanej nowelizacji kodeksu cywilnego, Ruch Prawniczy. Ekonomiczny i Socjologiczny 66(2):7–24
Radwański Z, Olejniczak A (2016) Zobowiązania część ogólna. Warszawa
Safjan M (2004) Odpowiedzialność odszkodowawcza władzy publicznej (po 1 września 2004 roku). Warszawa
Sinkiewicz A (1998) Pojęcie i rodzaj szkody w polskim prawie cywilnym. Rejent 2:59–74
Śmieja A (1990) Związek przyczynowy i zasady współżycia społecznego w świetle art. 419 KC. Acta Universitatis Wratislaviensis 186:331–349
Sobolewski P (2020) In: Osajda K (ed) Kodeks cywilny. Komentarz, Legalis

Strugała R (2021) Odpowiedzialność Skarbu Państwa za szkody wynikające z zakazów prowadzenia działalności gospodarczej w okresie pandemii Covid-19. Przegląd Prawa Handlowego 5:26–32
Szpunar A (1999) Odszkodowanie za szkodę majątkową. Szkoda na mieniu i na osobie, Bydgoszcz
Wandt M (2017) Gesetzliche Schuldverhaltnisse. Frankfut am Main
Więzowska B (2009) Odpowiedzialność cywilna na zasadzie słuszności. Warszawa
Więzowska-Czepiel B (2009) Odpowiedzialność za zgodne z prawem wykonywanie władzy publicznej na zasadzie słuszności. Studia Prawnicze: Rozprawy i Materiały 7:39–56
Zoll F, Południak-Gierz K, Bańczyk W (2021) Zakres odpowiedzialności odszkodowawczej Skarbu Państwa za szkody majątkowe spowodowane ograniczeniami wprowadzonymi w związku z COVID-19. Studia Prawa Prywatnego 3–4:3–29

Sandra Hadrowicz Ph.D. student at Warsaw University, the author of many publications concerning tort law, speaker at numerous scientific conferences of national importance.

Legislation During the COVID-19 Pandemic: Revolution, Patholegislation or Continuation?

Krzysztof Koźmiński

Abstract The article presents some observations on the reality of law-making during the COVID-19 pandemic and the state of epidemic legislation. On the one hand, it confronts the contemporary experience of the changing legal system with the Enlightenment ideals of good law (such as, among others, rationality, hierarchy, consistency, predictability, clarity of regulations), and on the other hand, it justifies the thesis that these ideals have long been only an imagination not reflected in the legislative practice of continental European countries and Anglo-Saxon countries. Contrary to the belief that the challenges of COVID-19 led to the 'state of emergency', an 'exception' to the rule of law and good law-making—it is argued that for at least several decades, phenomena such as inflation of law, juridization of socio-economic life, and even postmodernization of the legal system or after the crisis of the law was a reality well known by lawyers, entrepreneurs, citizens and commentators. As a result, epidemic legislation is rather the culmination, continuation or intensification of previously observed negative trends, rather than a breakthrough or a new quality. According to the author, this state of affairs leads to the need to search for new instruments of description and understanding of the law in force—including innovative methods of interpreting provisions, legal reasoning and methods of argumentation.

1 Introduction

A great deal has already been said about the legislation of the COVID-19 era—both in foreign and Polish literature. It would even appear that in the last two years such a myriad of publications have been put out, including scientific studies, devoted to mistakes of the legislator, retroactive regulations, dysfunctional provisions,

K. Koźmiński (✉)
Faculty of Law and Administration, University of Warsaw, Warsaw, Poland
e-mail: k.kozminski@wpia.uw.edu.pl

E. Hadrowicz (ed.), *Polish Entrepreneurial Law in the Era of the COVID-19 Pandemic*, Ius Gentium: Comparative Perspectives on Law and Justice 114,
https://doi.org/10.1007/978-3-031-57480-1_5

violations of the constitution and other examples of the so-called 'epidemic patholegislation', that it is now difficult to formulate innovative and groundbreaking conclusions. One can get the impression that commentators are in principle unanimous in their critical assessments of legislators and their activity during the pandemic, especially in 2020, when most of the new regulations were adopted in a state of uncertainty, a dearth of medical knowledge about the coronavirus, in connection with the subsequent alarming statistics of new infections and deaths.

Particular victims of the epidemic legislative crisis were primarily entrepreneurs who—due to the unpredictability of the legislator's actions, legislators' mistakes, haste in the decision-making process, as well as disproportionate limitations and restrictions imposed by regulations coming into force without the necessary vacatio legis—incurred costs and were forced to change the way running a business or even went bankrupt.

This paper shall proffer and defend a hypothesis according to which legislative experiences in the pandemic era do not set up a 'new quality', but are, at best, an amplification of well-known lawmaking-related shortcomings discernible in Poland, in other countries of continental Europe, and in contemporary Anglo-Saxon countries alike. In other words, I will venture to show that the negative aspects of legislative activity in liberal-democratic states, including the disruption of the hierarchy of sources of law, the dubious rationality of the draft regulations, repeated violations of constitutional principles (especially such as proportionality, separation of powers and human rights), degradation of legal language, a fiction of legislative planning and apparent regulatory impact assessments—are phenomena that have manifested themselves for at least several decades. For this reason, the often expressed surprise, sharp criticism, or even more so—conclusions and corollaries about the 'uniqueness' of the state of legislation between 2020–2022 are unfounded.

Moreover, an attempt will be made to demonstrate that the legal order has indeed undergone a 'postmodernization' process for a long time, and as a consequence, the traditional model of educating lawyers and legislators is outdated and was so long before the outbreak of the COVID-19 epidemic. This happened in defiance of academic professors, law practitioners, and commentators—who would like, in accordance with the Enlightenment paradigm, to perceive the law as coherent, consistent, rationally designed and having autotelic value. As a consequence, paradoxically, 'epidemic patholegislation' can serve as a starting point for a general and broader reflection on the usefulness of such categories as rationality, hierarchy, coherence, unambiguity and reasonableness for law-making. It cannot be ruled out that it was the COVID-19 epidemic that finally discredited modern legal myths about legislation, especially related to legal positivism and the imagination of liberal political thinkers. Myths, the illusions of which few observers were aware of, and which have now become universally recognized.

Surprisingly, therefore, it may transpire that the problem does not lie in the state of emergency or the extraordinary nature of the epidemic period, but in the power of modernist illusions, which for many decades have made it difficult to realize the actual state of legislation in Western European countries, Anglo-Saxon countries, as well as at the supranational level (especially within the European Union).

2 Enlightenment Myths About Legislation in a Modern Liberal State

Although the issue of good law has received many studies in the scientific literature and numerous statements in judicial decisions (both national and supranational courts), there is no single universal definition of good regulation or a universally respected set of criteria.[1] On the other hand, regardless of the multiplicity of views of individual thinkers, differences in legal traditions, political systems and different experiences and legacies in the field of legislation of different countries—several fundamental and universal directives in the field of lawmaking can be identified. Most of them are assumptions and principles based on Enlightenment ideas, inspired by individualism, the concept of separation of powers, legalism and the desire to guarantee the rights and freedoms of the individual.

However, despite the passage of several centuries, in the light of the currently available literature on lawmaking, especially the practical education of legislators, the said directives appear to be still alive and presented as unquestionable dogma.[2] Worth mentioning here are, in particular, the following:

- humanitarianism and proportionality of regulation (including the prohibition of excessive interference with the situation of the individual, the mandate to respect their rights and freedoms);
- respect for the freedoms and rights of the individual, as well as freedom of the market and freedom of economic activity (including respecting the limits of the law, i.e. lack of regulations in spheres treated as a space of free choice, one's private or intimate sphere, or simply those in which actual and effective enforcement of legal obligations is impossible or burdened with excessive costs);
- hierarchy of law respecting the primacy of the constitution and laws as acts of parliament (stemming from the English principle of parliamentary sovereignty or the French principle of popular sovereignty);
- rationality of the legislator (understood not only as secularism, but also the ability to choose the most effective instrument, analytically balancing profits and losses) and rationalization of the law-making process as a decision-making process (legislative planning, evidence-based, costs-benefits analysis, openness to the opinions of experts and the voices of external stakeholders);
- prospectiveness of law-making (avoidance of retroactivity, respect for acquired rights and respect for existing social relations, predictability of legislative actions and trust in the legislator, public promulgation of new regulations, respecting the relevant *vacatio legis*);
- coherence of legal regulations and the special role of codes as acts integrating individual areas of law (including, *inter alia*, terminological consistency, no gaps or contradictions in the system);

---

[1] Kosielińska-Grabowska (2013), p. 160. See also: Baldwin et al. (2012), p. 26.

[2] For example: Martin and Saalfeld (2014). See also: Malinowski (2009), p. 22.

- stability of regulations, legal certainty and security of legal transactions;
- correctness, clarity and intelligibility of the legal text.

The works of leading thinkers from the past confirm their potentially universal and timeless character. It is no accident that these ideas were reflected in treatises by thinkers representing various European nationalities and epochs. Regardless of the origin of philosophers and the legal culture in which they operated, similar directives to the ones laid out above can be found in publications by ideologists active during the English revolution of the seventeenth century, Montesquieu (French), Cesare Beccaria (Italian), or later authors such as Jeremy Bentham or Robert von Mohl (German).

The French author of "*The Spirit of Laws*" emphasized that laws should be concise, devoid of vague terms, and that the general principles of legislation are clarity, brevity, simplicity.[3] Meanwhile, the Italian writer stigmatized not only the inhumane shape of the solutions of the criminal law at the time, along with drastic penalties and irrational methods of inference and evidence, but also the form of legislation as he saw it: the use of ambiguous concepts, which inevitably leads to subjectivity and discretion in the process of applying the law.[4] At the same time, he demanded that regulations be precise and clear, which would conduce to legal certainty and comprehensibility for the average citizen, the common man.[5] Even Thomas Hobbes, regarded as a pro-absolutist thinker, was aware that the actual meaning of the law is ultimately determined by its form. Public promulgation and clarity of the message are essential for the implementation of the sovereign's will.[6]

Bentham's achievements in the field of political philosophy notwithstanding, his remarks on legislation were of a rather 'technical' nature, which prompts some commentators to view his publications as a starting point for contemporary standards of legislative technique.[7] A perusal of the works of Jeremy Bentham, called the 'legislator of the world' or 'Newton of legislation', leads to the conclusion that this nineteenth-century liberal, an Anglo-Saxon promoter of legal positivism, stigmatized such defects of legal texts as ambiguity and obscurity whist promoting the consistency and consequentiality of the legislator, the directive to use one concept to express one meaning, conciseness of the legal text (brevity), the use of short sentences, avoidance of the use of technical terms, to the extent practicable.[8] All this so that legal texts are universally understandable, do not leave excessive room for interpretation or give rise to difficulties on the part of authorities purporting to apply the same. At the same time, they shall be convenient for their addressees and serve their safety, and any code penned in line with these directives is to stand out from other books owing to its great simplicity, unambiguity, publicity and completeness,

[3] Canale et al. (2009), p. 83.

[4] Beccaria (1959), p. 63.

[5] Sójka-Zielińska (1995), p. 39.

[6] Poole (2012), p. 83.

[7] Ilbert (1914), p. 94.

[8] Alfange (1969), pp. 58–77.

thus allowing the father of the family to take it in his hand and teach his children without any outside help.[9] Since earlier 'judge-made' English law was, according to the author of the 'calculus of happiness', full of contradictions, unpredictable, subject to arbitrary and inconsistent decisions of judges, expressed in various forms—written law should be free from these weaknesses, and instead be associated with stability, security and predictability of the decision.[10] Bentham addressed his suggestions not only to a specific group of politicians and lawyers in order to reform some local legal system (e.g. the English one, which he criticized very harshly), but to a universal audience; his guidelines were to be universally applicable. And so, one of the most important and unfinished works of the Constitutional Code, although formally dedicated to the Spaniards and Portuguese, was actually addressed not only to the two countries of the Iberian Peninsula, but to all nations of the Earth.[11] Bentham believed that—regardless of climatic conditions, geography, accepted religions and established customs—his action plan for codification would be appropriate for every country in the world. Thus, he can be classified as a representative of legal cosmopolitanism.[12]

Robert von Mohl—a nineteenth-century German lawyer and politician, known more widely for juxtaposing the idea of the rule of law (*Rechtsstaat*) with the absolute police state (*Polizeistaat*)—emphasized that the former is characterized by, *inter alia*, that the rules in force are intended not only for officials, but also, or rather above all, for the people, so it is a duty and a good thing that their meaning be understood by all subjects.

Despite the passage of several hundred years and major political, social and technological changes (including the increase in the importance of supranational law coinciding with globalization, the evolution of the legal language, the emergence of new branches of law and the expansion of the legal system, as well as progress in legal theoretical research)—handbooks for legislators as well as academic papers devoted to legisprudence as 'the new theory of legislation or 'rational theory of legislation' still emphasize the importance of such principles as the stability of regulations, the hierarchy of the legal system, the rationality of legislation, plain language or the prospective nature of law-making, along with the general prohibition of retroactivity.

It is worth emphasizing that the paradigm of rational law-making is particularly strongly reflected in the Polish theory of law. Views of such authors from the past as Leon Petrażycki, Bronisław and Jerzy Wróblewscy, Kazimierz Opałek, as well as Zygmunt Ziembiński, Adama Podgórecki, Stanisław Ehrlich oraz Aleksander Peczenik,[13] lead one to surmise as much as that the rationality of the legislator, as

[9] Bentham (1983), p. 209.

[10] Hezel (1972), pp. 253–267.

[11] Fuller (2000), pp. 1–14.

[12] Loring (2014), pp. 1–12.

[13] Alexy (2006), pp. 245–248.

well as the logic and analytical method related thereto, are the hallmark of the Polish tradition of legal thinking.[14]

On the other hand, despite completely different foundations embedded in the common law legal culture, analogous standards and values of good legislation are emphasized also in the Anglo-Saxon tradition.[15] It is even suggested that the origins of this way of thinking are reflected in some Roman maxims such as: '*simplicitas legibus amica*' (simplicity is the friend of laws), '*leges ab omnibus intellegi debent*' (laws should be understandable to everyone), or '*in legibus magis simplicitas quam difficultas placet*' (law is more pleasing to simplicity than complexity), '*legem brevem esse oportet, quo facilus ab imperitis teneatur*' (the law should be concise so that the inexperienced can more easily follow it), '*de minimis non curat lex*' (the law does not care about trifles).[16]

These directives and values are necessary, but not sufficient, in order to implement the principle of good legislation. For example, the OECD has differentiated the following standards of good legislation: clarity, simplicity, and accessibility for private citizens and businesses; design standards such as flexibility and consistency with other rules and international standards; structure, orderliness, clear drafting, terminology along with economic and analytical standards such as benefit-cost and cost-effectiveness tests.[17] What is particularly interesting: Enlightenment, liberal and positivist ideas of the legal system determine specific methods of interpreting provisions of applicable law. This, in turn, compels one to focus on the legal text, attach great importance to the terminology used by the legislator, and treat law as a disciplined system, a hierarchical structure in which each element (legal norm, normative act, regulation, etc.) has its proper place, and even if there is a conflict between these elements, their relationship can be explained by legal reasoning or conflict rules of interpretation (such as, for example, *lex specialis derogat legi generali*). One could even risk a hypothesis that in the perspective presented above, a rational legislator cannot ever be wrong, and an interpreter using reliable methods of text analysis will become Montesquieu's '*la bouche de la loi*'.[18]

The problem is, however, that already long before the COVID-19 pandemic, constitutional law-making directives, modernist assumptions about regulations and optimistic ideas about the standards of good legislation had only been little more than wishful thinking, deviating markedly from the actual practice of liberal-democratic states. The contemporary law-making practice, as evinced in the passage of at least several dozen recent laws, has not had much in common with the idealized ideas of thinkers, theorists and ideologists.

---

[14] Ziembiński (1987), p. 40.

[15] Dickerson (1955), pp. 14–27. See also: Dickerson (1954), pp. 635–637; Dickerson (1965).

[16] Zabłocka (2004), pp. 72–77.

[17] OECD (1994), p. 12.

[18] Schönfeld (2008), pp. 274–301.

3 Pre-pandemic Reality: Legislative Inflation, Juridization of Socio-economic Life, Post-modernization of the Legal Order and the Crisis of Law

Although this proposition may seem surprising at first glance, pessimistic assessments of the crisis of law were formulated by lawyers of the European continent and Anglo-Saxon jurists already a hundred years ago. Criticism of then-current regulations and the actual course of the legislative process—taking into account exactly the same allegations and arguments that are formulated contemporarily during the COVID-19 pandemic—has a very long tradition.

As an example, the Polish author of an article with the eloquent title 'Inflation of Regulations' wrote as far back as in 1929: "The incredible amount of regulations in force in our country and their mass production, exceeding both the capacity of civil servants' brains and the endurance of the citizen, is, as we mentioned before, primarily the result of the conditions in which the Polish State was established. The fast pace of legislative work is not conducive to their perfection (...) The effects of this inflation are disastrous from the point of view of offices and administration, and dangerous from the point of view of a state ruled by law. The law is becoming more and more secret knowledge. For a citizen it has been for a long time something strange and completely incomprehensible, like a labyrinth in which the citizen does not even try to wander. The law, however, is secret knowledge even for officials".[19]

Another author explained in the 1930s: "The issue of legislative technique is not an end in itself but is part of the broader problem of raising the level of existing regulation, and to this end one of the means, but not the only one, is better legislative technique; and this broader problem of "improvement of legislation" is only a part of the great issue that has been occupying minds for a long time under the name of 'crisis of law' (...) we still (and not only us) have huge amounts of regulations. In the face of this mass of norms, even the bravest lose their courage, and the citizen becomes helpless. Inflation of regulations can be counteracted in two ways: to reduce the number of regulations and to make them smaller in volume".[20]

For example, the following phenomena are not new at all:

- hypertrophy of statutory (positive, written) law and creeping legal intervention (the omnipresence of regulations and the dynamically growing purview of regulatory activity of public authorities affecting the social, economic and private spheres of individuals relying upon provisions of positive law);
- legislative inflation (writers who avail themselves of this term intuitively understand under this umbrella at least several different, not necessarily identical, phenomena: juridization of socio-economic life, a tendency to meticulously regulate every manifestation of human activity,[21] excessive detail and casuistry of legal

[19] Hausner (1929), pp. 1–2.

[20] Aker et al. (1934), p. 4.

[21] Dziedzic (2012), p. 251.

provisions,[22] inconsistency within the legal system as a result of inconsistency and inconsequentiality of the legislator and ill-considered legislative changes,[23] dynamic changes in the legal status as a result of amendments,[24] prolixity and fastidiousness of the legislator by including provisions in the texts of normative acts that are in fact *superfluum*[25]);

- juridization of socio-economic life (a situation in which "an increasing range of social matters is being regulated by law. The attention of lawyers is focused on both theoretical aspects of law-making activity as well as very technical and detailed problems of editing legal texts"[26]);
- 'colonization of life' by law facilitating the development of the welfare state, bureaucratism and statism, interventionism related to disproportionate power interference with private relationships, spheres of autonomy of the individual, their individual rights and freedoms;[27]
- coexistence and rivalry of numerous centers of public authority that make and interpret the law,[28] not necessarily in a coherent manner, located at different levels of public authority and having different legitimacy (concepts known as 'multicentricity', 'polycentrism' or 'multicentrism' of legal order/legal systems. These theories, inspired by postmodern theory of law and the so-called legal realism, reject the 'classical' vision of the legal system as a rational, hierarchical system);[29]
- decodification and disintegration of the legal system, including in particular the loss of real significance by codes in favor of so-called specialacts;[30]
- degradation of legal language (manifested, for example, by the legislator using many different definitions in various acts for one term—e.g. divergent definitions of "entrepreneur" in private and administrative law in the Polish legal system);
- so-called special acts, counted in dozens to date, introducing, as *leges speciales*, exceptional, usually 'simplified' modes of government interference with the sphere of rights and freedoms of private entities[31] (which inevitably involves restricting the rights of agents and parties to proceedings; although such special acts were originally supposed to be exceptional and incidental in nature, they have now become a rather undesirable 'standard' of legislative intervention in

---

[22] Mastalski (2016), p. 27.

[23] Chochowski (2012), p. 301.

[24] Teszner (2017), p. 78.

[25] Hofmański and Stefański (2016), p. 549.

[26] Sarkowicz and Stelmach (1996), p. 107.

[27] Deflem (2013), p. 81.

[28] MacCormick (2001), p. 94.

[29] Lang (2005), pp. 95–99.

[30] Genner (2006); Murillo (2001), pp. 163–183; Longchamps de Bérier (2017); Rudnicki (2017), pp. 15–25.

[31] Bródka (2022), pp. 22–43. See also: Gdesz (2022), pp. 36–48.

areas where a public authority acts ineffectively), conferring broad discretionary power on the executive;[32]
- criticism of bodies, institutions, experts and external stakeholders involved in the legislative procedure and the practices of the legislative process[33] (directed, *inter alia*, at the lack of consultation, insufficient consideration of the voices of experts and stakeholders, the lack of a reliable assessment of the effects of regulations, lthe ack of or defective lobbying procedures).

It is worth expanding on selected observations.

In general, attention is drawn to two aspects of legal inflation: quantitative and qualitative, i.e. a situation in which the saturation of legal regulation is accompanied by a gradual decrease in its value. This is perceived similarly in foreign literature where the notion of legal inflation (legislative inflation, inflation of law, *l'inflation législative*), albeit rarely defined, is associated rather with specific causes and exposed consequences. At the forefront are: the need to implement EU law, state interventionism, the national legislator's desire to guarantee the fullest possible implementation of human rights (the principle of the rule of law requiring the legal basis for the activity of a public authority to be sought in statutory law), progressive technological development, changes in social and economic life, issues requiring regulation (e.g. in the field of biotechnology, environmental protection), errors in the legislative process and insufficient assessment of the effects of regulations, the activity of interest groups.[34]

It follows that the state of law understood in this way is such that statutory law (the effect of legislation) is ubiquitous, and the socio-economic reality, including the individual sphere (private, home) is subject to legal regulation unknown hitherto. The problem of juridization of life or colonization by law of subsequent spheres of existence is noticed not only by philosophers and sociologists, but also by lawyers. As an example, the former president of the Polish Constitutional Tribunal and a current judge of the Court of Justice of the European Union explains that "there is a gradual and unprecedented juridization of public, social and economic life. The scale of what is happening in front of our eyes in this field is unprecedented and incomparable to anything previously (which is, after all, a logical effect of the rule of law model) (…). The dispute about the law, about what is due to whom, penetrates more and more strongly all spheres of life, where before no one thought of asking questions about the law. It is no longer shocking to decide on law in the area of education (school grades, criteria and rules of examinations are subject to control), medicine (the law is supposed to answer questions that until recently belonged only to philosophy, ethics and theology, such as the question of permissibility of having a ventilator turned off or sex changes)".[35]

---

[32] Greene (2020), p. 96. See also: Powell and Durojaye (2022), p. 29.

[33] Koźmiński (2018), pp. 212–231; Koźmiński (2022), pp. 6–34.

[34] Eng (2002), p. 65; Ost and van den Kerchove (1999), p. 147; Duprat and Xanthaki (2017), p. 112.

[35] Safjan (2003).

The juridization of social life entails the gradual interference of public authority with the life/activity of subordinated individuals by way of legally issued normative acts which regulate in more and more detail—hitherto unregulated—areas of life. Along with the expansion of the scope of matters regulated by the norms of statutory law, other normative systems—religious, moral and moral—are displaced. The legislator assumes that norms inherent to the legal system should provide answers to questions that until recently belonged to philosophy, ethics or theology (examples are the admissibility of sex reassignment surgery and disconnection of a patient from a ventilator). Statutory norms interfere to a greater degree with family life, limit parental authority, set a top-down model of raising children, shape relations between spouses, regulate the conduct of business activity or the way of spending free time (e.g. detailed bans on playing on the beach, permissible demeanour in the forest or museums). The progress of juridization is favored by trends such as legal paternalism, state interventionism, globalization and the expansion of the functions of the democratic-liberal welfare state. This process could be said to have culminated in 2020, when—under the guise of a rush to stop the coronavirus—public authorities introduced bans on movement (e.g. in Poland a ban on entering forests), restrictions on religious practices and gatherings, standards for spending free time in one's own private home (e.g. limiting the number of guests during Easter) or interfering with the secrecy of correspondence and communication (e.g. tracking the activity of telephone line users in Israel).

However, the legislator's ambition for further regulation does not go hand in hand with the quality of legislation. The volume of provisions skyrockets, but they are of lower quality: the new laws are less well thought out, incoherent in the systemic context, often prompted by a current socio-economic problem and motivated by a pressing political need. A good example of such legislative pathology (not only in the period 2019–2023) is the phenomenon of so-called 'special acts', which have become a negative standard of a parliamentary source of law not only in Poland.

Another contemporary problem is the so-called special act. Although the concept of a "specific statute" does not have its strict statutory definition, such an act is generally considered to be an incidental regulation, adopted due to immediate needs and to achieve effects impossible to attain under pertinent "ordinary" general provisions. In doing so, specific acts purport to cover legal norms from various fields of law, amend numerous applicable normative acts, whilst mixing institutions in the field of private and public law in the process. A classic example is the so-called COVID-19 special laws—which, by way of a single act, modified in one stroke the law of contracts, labour, tax, administrative and criminal law. They were justified by the need for a temporary (exceptional, extraordinary) change to the existing rules, including standards resulting from the codes (Civil Code, Penal Code, Code of Administrative Procedure). Immediately afterwards, a special act was adopted addressing the problems caused by the war in Ukraine and the energy crisis. Coincidentally, numerous special acts had been adopted in Poland many years ago—for example, the special act on organization of the European football championship, the special act governing the investment in the Central Communication Port, or the special act on road investments. One must share the view that the increasing number of 'special laws' in force in Poland has a negative impact on the actual weight of the constitutional guarantee of rights and freedoms (especially property rights) due to the fact that they introduce, as *leges speciales*, exceptional, usually simplified modes of expropriation of real estate whilst broadening the scope of administrative interference with the sphere of rights and freedoms of private entities. The idea behind the 'special acts' is the pursuit of accelerating and streamlining investment processes (administrative proceedings), which, however, necessitates impinging upon the rights of the other subjects. The normative acts discussed are, at their root, an undesirable phenomenon as they operate to supersede ordinary statutes and at the same time attain the objectives of the legislator, albeit by a 'shortcut', perhaps beneficial for public authorities to carry out the entrusted tasks or objectives, but limiting the rights of citizens specified in 'ordinary' laws.

Moreover, the preponderance of acts of dubious status is also worth highlighting. This is a grouping of administrative acts, court rulings, other acts of official application or interpretation of law as well as sources atypical for the positivist image of 'hard law' such as soft law and behavioral interventions such as nudges. Admittedly, we realized their importance and potential, especially during and in connection with the COVID-19 pandemic (when some bans and orders turned out to be ineffective, e.g. the obligation to wear masks or respect social distance),[36] although they were also used earlier[37] (e.g. in Poland, the National Receipt Lottery under the auspices of the Ministry of Finance).

The Polish legislator of the times of the "first waves of COVID" was, above all, very inconsistent and acted excessively quickly. There can be no justification for situations in which the actions of the legislator—especially those resulting in restrictions on rights and freedoms as well as freedom of economic activity—are characterized by internal contradiction and lack of any reflection. A good example were the restrictions on trade, in particular the functioning of shopping malls. Without entering into a discussion about their effectiveness in stopping the spread of the virus, let's remind of a few facts from autumn 2020, when the second lockdown was introduced:

- contrary to earlier declarations of politicians, as well as the draft regulation, the mandatory closure eventually also covered furniture stores (which these entities and their customers found out at the time when the regulation was published);
- at the same time, those whose predominant activity consists in the sale of construction or renovation products (i.e. entities competing with furniture stores, as most of them also offer furniture in their assortment) were excluded from the general trade ban;
- the sales ban also covered electronics, household appliances and IT stores;

[36] By way of example: Sibony (2020), pp. 350–357; Hume et al. (2021); Soofi et al. (2020), pp. 345–350.

[37] Sunstein (2014), pp. 583–588; Hertwig and Grüne-Yanoff (2017), pp. 973–986; Alemanno and Sibony (2015).

– at the same time, representatives of the authorities announced "the transition of society to remote mode", i.e. extension of remote work to professional groups other than teachers, e.g. public administration officials, declaring support in the form of subsidies for the purchase of necessary electronic equipment for teachers, with the government's appeal to simultaneously cover private sector employees with remote work and with the currently widespread remote learning of all students and students of all school categories.

In sum, the understanding of the contemporary legal system is aided by the perspective inspired by the postmodern theory of law and so-called legal realism, which rejects the 'classical' vision of the legal system (as an orderly, hierarchical, consistent, coherent system, based on fully recognized assumptions, established by a rational, conscious and fully informed legislator, knowing the only one truth).[38] In this context, it is worth asking a few questions: what data or arguments prompted the decision-makers to allow gardening and DIY stores to operate (especially in late autumn, when the interest in their offer is lower than in the spring-summer period), obliging at the same time to stop operating showrooms with furniture and showrooms with household appliances, electronics and IT? Does such a solution meet the constitutional standards of equality before the law, proportionality and competition related to the freedom of economic activity and the social market economy? Is the actual recognition by the authorities of electronic devices for remote communication as one of the goods of "first need" during the epidemic (the purchase of which should be supported with state vouchers in the amount of PLN 500) with the simultaneous closure of stationary electronics, household appliances and IT stores, an example of a consistent legislative policy?

On the other hand, the Polish authorities legislated "in real time", i.e. new regulations were drafted and implemented so quickly that there was no real opportunity to learn about (and adapt to) the new obligations. It has become a norm for the rulers to report on the latest changes in the legal status at a press conference or in the form of a general announcement on the government's website. It happened that the announcement was reflected in the regulations entering into force a few hours or days later. At other times, the action of the authorities was "based" only on a project (e.g. activity related to the preparation of voting by correspondence), and sometimes it was clearly contrary to the law in force (e.g. fines for violating a legally dubious ban on movement). It was hard to resist the impression that the regulations became an addition to the spontaneous ideas of politicians, and the laws and regulations published in the Journal of Laws are a clumsy attempt to repeat the contents of the power point slides displayed a moment earlier. In addition, there were shortcomings in the legislative technique—internal contradictions, gaps and the non-transparent arrangement of the "COVID-19 Laws".

In addition, the legislator, with ad hoc, day-to-day actions, interferes and disrupts the economic ties built over the years. As a consequence, it seemed that working under enormous time pressure, without knowledge of economic realities, led to the

[38] For example: Feldman (2000); Farber and Sherry (1997). See also: Balkin (1992), pp. 1966–1990.

drafting of normative acts, which in fact constituted an experiment on a living organism. An expression of this was the state in which amendments to recently passed laws were so frequent that the decision-makers themselves were confused in their answers to the question about the current legal status.

It should be noted that in the context of the "epidemic legislation", the situation of entrepreneurs was special because, on the one hand, legislative interventions allowed business entities to obtain new rights, benefits (financial support, loans, deferral of payment deadlines) and exemptions (including tax), but on the other hand, exposing them to the risk of a sudden change in the legal status, uncertainty as to future regulations, and even a definitive ban on conducting business activity. Even though entrepreneurs were already facing permanent legal risks already in 2019, the time of the coronavirus epidemic brought such significant changes in the legal framework for conducting business activities that rational planning of profits and costs, thoughtful company management or long-term HR policy became impossible.

4 Legislation in the COVID-19 Era: Revolution, Patholegislation or (Just) Continuation?

The legislation of the COVID-19 era has been commented upon as follows: "The introduction of the state of epidemic in Poland in connection with the prevention, counteracting and combating of COVID-19 brought about restrictions of basic human rights in this state";[39] "The period of the COVID-19 epidemic increased the Council of Ministers' legislative activity (…) regulations issued by the Council of Ministers contained several prohibitions, orders and other types of restrictions touching upon a broad spectrum of citizens' functioning, not only political, social and economic life but above all everyday and personal life";[40] "COVID-19 legislation fulfils the characteristics of statutory legal nihilism".[41] These assessments are hard to underestimate, and critical reviews such as 'patholegislation', 'irrational regulation', 'dysfunctionality', 'law inflation' seem justified.

However, are alarmist voices about some radical qualitative change, a revolution in law or a breakthrough in legislation warranted?

In papers published jointly with *Jan Rudnicki*[42] we argued that—contrary to the dominant comments evaluating legislative actions taken by governments in connection with the epidemic as non-standard phenomena, deviating from both the standard generally accepted in the prevailing theory of democratic-liberal law in the West, and from the practice of the times before the pandemic—the practices of

[39] Trociuk (2021), p. 11.

[40] Prokop (2022), p. 39.

[41] Izdebski (2020), p. 37.

[42] Koźmiński and Rudnicki (2022), pp. 28–39; Koźmiński and Rudnicki (2020), pp. 105–121.

creation and application of the COVID-19 pandemic laws are indeed not particularly compatible with the theoretical, often idealized, standards of the rule of law, yet they do not fundamentally differ from regular existing practices. In other words, although over the last three years allegations of unconstitutionality of various legal solutions entering into force have been raised particularly often, and the attitude of the legislator has provided exceptionally glaring examples that has given grounds to undermine its rationality—phenomena such as inflation of the law, excessive juridization of socio-economic life, decodification of or even actual post-modernization of the legal order (understood as disruption of its hierarchy, cohesion, meaning, stability) had been discernible long before the coronavirus epidemic, and a subject of extensive scientific literature, which had critically perceived them as symptoms of a general crisis of law.[43]

According to our assessment: "a superficial view of lawmakers' reaction to the current pandemic crisis is that we are witnessing an aberration and a concentration of bad practices. This paper presents a partially opposite thesis that the response of legal systems to this situation is not surprising and an accumulation of several phenomena very characteristic of the contemporary evolution of law. The restriction of personal freedoms, often imposed by means far from the theoretical scope of sources of law described by demo-liberal constitutions, combined with the broad scope and curious details of the extraordinary regulations complete the general trend towards the juridisation of almost every aspect of human activities. Today, the law serves as the dominant tool of creating social and economic order, taking the fields once occupied by other (and now almost extinct) normative systems and at the same time, displacing them. Thus, the more law exists in the everyday circulation, the more demand it creates for further and even more casuistic legal regulation. In this reality, this is the only tool that can be applied in extraordinary circumstances. In addition, the applied legislative techniques are not new. The Polish act known commonly and semi-officially as the 'anti-crisis shield' is atypical 'complex act' aimed at dealing with a particular matter thoroughly through the use of all traditional methods of regulation: civilian, administrative, and penal mixed together in a single text of law. Thus, this regulation also constitutes a perfect (and perhaps the most striking) example of the phenomenon of decodification, especially in the field of private law, since it deals with particular contractual and tort issues as if there were no relevant regulations in the Civil Code, which should (at least theoretically) constitute the core of the private law system".[44]

Ultimately, therefore, it is entirely possible that the time of crisis brought about by the COVID-19 pandemic serves only as a kind of "magnifying glass", a lens highlighting certain undesirable phenomena, which, however, have a much more complex nature and a longer tradition. Although these phenomena have intensified (and will probably intensify further as the epidemic and economic situation worsen) in connection with the COVID-19 epidemic, they are part of a series of events and

---

[43] Koźmiński (2019), p. 277.

[44] Koźmiński and Rudnicki (2020), p. 105.

trends that have been occurring for a long time. All this is liable to give rise to a radical discrepancy between constitutional principles (including the rule of law, good governance, legal certainty and legal security), recommendations of international organizations, political declarations on good legislation and experts' postulates, on the one hand, and practice on the other.

Freedom of economic activity and related legal guarantees for entrepreneurs have been significantly eroded during the epidemic, although they had already been weakened earlier. Negative processes had already started earlier, the pandemic intensified them. The same happened with other spheres of life—e.g. the public sphere: "democracy was in global retreat even before COVID-19, and the pandemic shrunk and fractured the global map of democracies still further".[45]

Will it be possible to overcome the deficiencies of the legislative process as expounded upon in this paper and what will be their possible consequences for the legal system, lawyers and the addressees of legal norms? These are questions that legal theorists will be compelled to face up to for years to come.

References

Aker J, Berezowski C et al (1934) Zasady techniki ustawodawczej. 4 referaty. Warszawa

Alemanno A, Sibony A (2015) Nudge and the law: a European perspective. Oxford

Alexy R (2006) Aleksander Peczenik: In Memoriam. Ratio Juris 19(2):245–248

Alfange D Jr (1969) Jeremy Bentham and the codification of law. Cornell Law Rev 55:58–77

Baldwin R, Cave M, Lodge M (2012) Understanding regulation. Theory, strategy and practice

Balkin JM (1992) What is a postmodern constitutionalism? Mich Law Rev 90(7):1966–1990

Beccaria C (1959) O przestępstwach i karach. Warszawa

Bentham J (1983) Constitutional code. Oxford

Bródka A (2022) Zarys ewolucji prawa wywłaszczeniowego w Polsce. In: Martysz C (ed) Skuteczność w prawie administracyjnym. Warszawa

Canale D, Grossi P, Hofmann H (2009) A treatise of legal philosophy and general jurisprudence. In: Pattaro E (ed) A history of the philosophy of law in the civil law world, 1600–1900. Dordrecht–Heidelberg–New York–London

Chochowski K (2012) Kryzys prawa administracyjnego w administracji publicznej – rzeczywistość czy fikcja? In: Doliwa A, Kijowski D et al (eds) Kryzys prawa administracyjnego? Tom III: Wypieranie prawa administracyjnego przez prawo cywilne. Warszawa

Deflem M (2013) The legal theory of Jürgen Habermas. In: Banakar R, Travers M (eds) Law and social theory. Oxford

Dickerson R (1954) Legislative drafting: a challenge to the legal profession. Am Bar Assoc J 40:635–637

Dickerson R (1955) How to write a law. Notre Dame Law Rev 1(31):14–27

Dickerson R (1965) The fundamentals of legal drafting. Boston

Duprat J-P, Xanthaki H (2017) Legislative drafting techniques. In: Karpen U, Xanthaki H (eds) Legislation in Europe: a comprehensive guide for scholars and practitioners. Oxford 2017

Dziedzic J (2012) Sądowa kontrola administracji a wykładnia twórcza. In: Kijowski D, Radwanowicz-Wanczewska J et al (eds) Kryzys prawa administracyjnego? Wykładnia i stosowanie prawa administracyjnego. Warszawa

[45] Grogan and Donald (2022), p. 18.

Eng S (2002) Legislative inflation and the quality of law. In: Wintgens L (ed) Legisprudence: a new theoretical approach to legislation. Oxford
Farber DA, Sherry S (1997) Beyond all reason: the radical assault on truth in American law. Oxford
Feldman SM (2000) American legal thought from premodernism to postmodernism: an intellectual. New York-Oxford
Fuller C (2000) 'Primeiro e mais antigo Constitucional da Europa': Bentham's contact with Portuguese liberals 1820–23. J Bentham Stud 3:1–13
Gdesz M (2022) Zasada korzyści w prawie wywłaszczeniowym. Zeszyty Naukowe Sądownictwa Administracyjnego 1(100):36–48
Genner S (2006) Dekodifikation. Zur Auflösung der kodifikatorischen Einheit im schweizerischen Zivilrecht. Basel–Genf–München
Greene A (2020) Emergency powers in a time of pandemic. Bristol
Grogan J, Donald A (2022) Routledge handbook of law and the COVID-19 pandemic. London-New York
Hausner R (1929) Inflacja przepisów. Gazeta Administracji i Policji Państwowej 2:10–19
Hertwig R, Grüne-Yanoff T (2017) Nudging and boosting: steering or empowering good decisions. Perspect Psychol Sci 12(6):721–726
Hezel G (1972) The influence of Bentham's philosophy of law on the early nineteenth century codification movement in the United States. Buffalo Law Rev 22:253–268
Hofmański P, Stefański R (2016) System Prawa Karnego Procesowego. Tom X: Postępowanie przygotowawcze, Warszawa
Hume S, John P et al (2021) Nudge in the time of coronavirus: the compliance to behavioural messages during crisis. https://doi.org/10.2139/ssrn.3644165
Ilbert C (1914) Mechanics of law-making. New York
Izdebski H (2020) Legislacja dotycząca COVID-19 i ustawowy nihilizm prawny. In: Gardocka T, Jagiełło D (eds) Pandemia Covid-19 a prawa i wolności obywatela. Warszawa
Kosielińska-Grabowska U (2013) Dobre prawo jako element Strategii Bezpieczeństwa Narodowego. In: Żebrowski A, Jaeschke A, Kłaczyński R (eds) Bezpieczeństwo RP: historia, ekonomia, polityka: studia z zakresu bezpieczeństwa państwa: 160–174
Koźmiński K (2018) Ograniczenie handlu w niedziele: przewidywanie skutków regulacji czy wróżenie z fusów? Studia Iuridica 78:212–231
Koźmiński K (2019) Technika prawodawcza II Rzeczypospolitej. Warszawa
Koźmiński K (2022) Ekonomiczna analiza prawa w procesie stanowienia i stosowania prawa: doświadczenia polskie i zagraniczne. Opinie i Analizy Instytutu De Republica 3:5–36
Koźmiński K, Rudnicki J (2020) The COVID crisis as a sample tube with contemporary legal phenomena. Central Eur J Comp Law 2:105–121
Koźmiński K, Rudnicki J (2022) Doświadczenia doby COVID-19 a tendencje rozwojowe współczesnego prawa. In: Grzebyk P, Uznańska P (eds) Prawo w czasie pandemii COVID-19. Warszawa
Lang W (2005) Wokół problemu "multicentryczności systemu prawa". Państwo i Prawo 7:95–110
Longchamps de Bérier F (2017) Dekodyfikacja prawa prywatnego. Warszawa
Loring R (2014) The role of universal jurisprudence in Bentham's legal cosmopolitanism. Revue d'études benthamiennes 13:1–68
MacCormick N (2001) Questioning sovereignty. Law, state, and nation in the European commonwealth. New York
Malinowski A (2009) Zarys metodyki pracy legislatora. Ustawy - akty wykonawcze - prawo miejscowe, Warszawa
Martin S, Saalfeld T (2014) The Oxford handbook of legislative studies. Oxford
Mastalski R (2016) Tworzenie prawa podatkowego a jego stosowanie. Warszawa
Murillo M (2001) The evolution of codification in the civil law legal systems: towards decodification and recodification. J Transnatl Law Policy 1:1–20
OECD (1994) Improving the quality of laws and regulations: economic, legal and managerial techniques. Paris

Ost F, van den Kerchove M (1999) Constructing the complexity of the law: towards a dialectic theory. In: Wintgens L (ed) The law in philosophical perspectives: my philosophy of law. Brussels
Poole T (2012) Hobbes on law and prerogative. In: Dyzenhaus D, Poole T (eds) Hobbes and the law. New York
Powell D, Durojaye E (2022) Constitutional resilience and the Covid-19 pandemic. Cham
Prokop K (2022) Political system of the Republic of Poland during the COVID-19 pandemic: continuity and change. Siedlce
Rudnicki J (2017) Kształtowanie się prawa pracy a specyfika procesów kodyfikacji i dekodyfikacji prawa w Polsce. Forum Prawnicze 3:15–25
Safjan M (2003) Wystąpienie Prezesa Trybunału Konstytucyjnego Prof. Marka Safjana wygłoszone 3 marca 2003 roku podczas uroczystości zorganizowanej prze redakcję "Rzeczpospolitej" z okazji ogłoszenia rankingu kancelarii prawniczych http://www.trybunal.gov.pl/Wiadom/Prezes/003.htm
Sarkowicz R, Stelmach J (1996) Teoria prawa. Kraków
Schönfeld K (2008) Rex, Lex et Judex: Montesquieu and la bouche de la loi revisited. Eur Const Law Rev 4:274–301
Sibony A-L (2020) The UK Covid-19 response: a behavioural irony? Eur J Risk Regul 11(2):350–357
Sójka-Zielińska K (1995) Cesare Beccaria a ochrona praw człowieka w procesie karnym. Analecta 4(8)
Soofi M, Najafi F et al (2020) Using insights from behavioral economics to mitigate the spread of Covid-19. Appl Health Econ Health Policy 18(3):345–350
Sunstein CR (2014) Nudging: a very short guide. J Consum Policy 37(4):583–588
Teszner K (2017) Stosowanie prawa przez administrację podatkową a wartości aksjologiczne. In: Zimmermann J (ed) Aksjologia prawa administracyjnego. Warszawa
Trociuk S (2021) Prawa i wolności w stanie epidemii. Warszawa
Zabłocka M (2004) U źródeł współczesnego prawodawstwa. In: Wąsowicz M (ed) Z dziejów kultury prawnej. Studia ofiarowane Profesorowi Juliuszowi Bardachowi w dziewięćdziesięciolecie urodzin. Warszawa
Ziembiński Z (1987) The methodological problems of theory and philosophy of law: a survey. In: Ziembiński Z (ed) Polish contributions to the theory and philosophy of law. Amsterdam

Krzysztof Koźmiński Head of the Law and Economics Department, Chair of the Centre for Regulations Impact Assessment at the University of Warsaw, researcher and lecturer at the Faculty of Law and Administration of the University of Warsaw, member of the Polish Prime Minister's Covid-19 Council. Author of numerous legal opinions and drafts of normative acts commissioned by Polish and foreign public authorities, speaker at numerous international scientific conferences in China, India, South Africa, England, Portugal, Croatia, and Ukraine.

The Impact of Legislative Changes Caused by the Outbreak of the COVID-19 Pandemic on the Functioning of Contracts in Economic Turnover

Angelika Kozyra

Abstract The COVID-19 pandemic not only significantly reduced the activity of entrepreneurs, but also largely crowded out their functioning in business. The existing condition magnified by legislative changes has become a determinant of changes also at the level of contracts entered into by entrepreneurs. The purpose of the following paper is to present the changes in the rules of contract formation. The first part of the article deals with modifications in contracts concluded within the framework of public procurement in connection with the impact of circumstances defined by COVID-19 on the proper execution of a contract. This is followed by amendments to financing and M&A (Mergers and Acquisitions) contracts with regard to the introduction of clauses in them: material adverse effect, material adverse change and hardship. These clauses significantly emphasise the negotiating role of business-to-business contracts at the level of breach of a contract, evasion of performance of the transaction as well as define the limits of the event contained in the contract in terms of the executing party's liability.

1 Introduction

The outbreak of the Covid-19 pandemic has created a new reality and from its very beginning, countries have faced challenges such as dealing with the virus effectively and compliance with the democratic constitutional framework, including respect for the regulations of law.[1] The Covid-19 pandemic has questioned the ability of political and legal systems to respond to emergency situations. This situation has

[1] Grogan and Donald (2022a, b), p. 6.

A. Kozyra (✉)
Trigon Orthopedia Clinic and Softmed-Laser Clinic, Warsaw, Poland

E. Hadrowicz (ed.), *Polish Entrepreneurial Law in the Era of the COVID-19 Pandemic*, Ius Gentium: Comparative Perspectives on Law and Justice 114,
https://doi.org/10.1007/978-3-031-57480-1_6

fundamentally changed assumptions about the functions of national institutions, crisis management and the role of law.[2]

The international response to the pandemic was governed by international legal frameworks, in particular public health, human rights and constitutional law, which, depending on the circumstances, may complement each other. Most governments have resorted to emergency executive powers in response to the pandemic. This could be a necessary measure to take decisive action in the field of, for instance, public health. However, it should be borne in mind that the use of emergency powers has suspended or weakened constitutional control mechanisms that in normal times apply to executive actions. The balance between the legislature, executive and judiciary has shifted significantly towards governments.[3]

In the field of countries emergency powers, trends emerge in the choices countries have made regarding the structure and use of emergency powers. One of the choices concerned the framework governing emergency powers, namely whether to introduce a state of emergency in the constitution, in legislation, or in the constitution and legislation. The model of emergency powers a given state chooses is a basic normative decision shaped by the combination of political, economic and social stimuli, in particular whether the basis of the legal order of a given state is parliamentary or constitutional supremacy. The next choice concerned the legal regime to be applied in response to the pandemic, whether to declare a state of emergency in accordance with the norms of international law or to apply targeted disaster management or public health legal measures.[4]

It should also be remembered that states of emergency constitute a premise for increased legislative activity by states and departures from basic norms. In turn, what ultimately justifies the departure from basic norms is that it is a temporary situation and should not constitute a permanent and irrevocable change. Therefore, emergencies are a temporary response to a temporary threat.[5]

Undoubtedly, one of the consequences of the pandemic was legislative activity aimed at improving the functioning of the state in emergency conditions. This activity in particular led to the implementation of new normative solutions into existing legal acts and the suspension of existing legal solutions that could not function in the circumstances of the pandemic. What is also worth emphasizing is the fact that the existing legal standards did not necessarily constitute reliable guidelines regarding the actions that countries should take after the outbreak of the Covid-19 pandemic, which is why the actions taken had a diverse scope. To give an example, Colombia and Thailand used existing statutory or constitutional emergency frameworks, while India and Turkey did not invoke such frameworks and Germany quickly changed them. Some countries, such as France and Great Britain, quickly

[2] Grogan and Donald (2022a, b), p. xvi.

[3] Durojaye and Powell (2022), p. 5.

[4] Durojaye and Powell (2022), p. 25.

[5] Greene (2020), p. 12.

introduced regulations to respond to Covid-19, while Iran and Pakistan created centralized bodies for this purpose, sometimes without appropriately delegated powers. Sweden, on the other hand, was the only country to abandon legal measures and instead relied on non-binding recommendations and decentralized administration. Post-pandemic responses also differed in whether countries that declared a formal state of emergency reported derogations or restrictions to relevant international institutions (like Colombia) or did not do so (like Hungary).[6]

When assessing the functioning of individual countries during the pandemic in the context of their preparation for future crisis situations, it is undoubtedly necessary to draw conclusions from the diversity of experiences documented in this volume. In this regard, it is of crucial importance to bear in mind that even in countries that generally performed poorly in terms of public health or the rule of law, there was also a noticeable application of good practices: in the usage of technology to enable people to have access to justice, education and etc. Exploring the review and reform of the legal framework for emergencies is undoubtedly urgent. It also should not be forgotten that: „In legislation drafted during emergencies, we see a microcosm of the challenges to adherence to rule of law standards where ostensibly 'higher' demands for immediate action to save lives can lead to the sacrifice of procedural and substantive requirements of legal process, leading to legal uncertainty, lack of accountability, and unrestricted discretion beyond the proper boundaries of legality".[7]

It cannot be ignored that the speed in which emergency regulations were introduced during the Covid-19 pandemic, granting unquestionable decision-making freedom, which sometimes remained in statutes for a long time, often revealed a clear disregard for the rules of law and democratic norms. The political rhetoric of justifying the uniqueness of given circumstances on the basis of which certain provisions were introduced may ultimately influence the legal culture and law-making processes. Therefore, in the case "where such provisions are extended until they become permanent fixtures of the law, countries risk the "permanence of the temporary[8]" and the 'emergency creep' of exceptional powers into ordinary modes of governance".[9]

2 Legislative Changes of Public Procurement Contracts

The outbreak of the Sara-coV-2 coronavirus pandemic in the world and the declaration of an pandemic state in the Republic of Poland, in accordance with the Decree of the Minister of Health of March 20, 2020 (Regulation of the Minister of Health

[6] Grogan and Donald (2022a, b), p. 3.

[7] Grogan and Donald (2022a, b), p. 5.

[8] Grogan and Donald (2022a, b), p. 5.

[9] Grogan and Donald (2022a, b), p. 5. Quotation from: Dyzenhaus (2001).

of March 20, 2020 on declaring a state of pandemic in the territory of the Republic of Poland, OJ 2020 pos. 491), has had an enormous impact and far-reaching effects in the sphere of economic relations through the introduced restrictions resulting in numerous bans and limitations, which have led to a significant diminution in the activities of entrepreneurs. The situation has forced the entrepreneurs to adapt to the new conditions in the implementation of contracts. With regard to the state of the pandemic and the real problems that have arisen as a result of it, special consideration should be given to the Act of March 2, 2020 on special solutions related to the prevention, counteracting and combating COVID-19, other infectious diseases and crisis situations caused by them (OJ 2020 pos. 374 as amended)—hereinafter referred to as the Covid Act.

The regulations incorporated in the aforementioned act were a manifestation of legislative intervention, the primary purpose of which was to mitigate the economic impact created by the COVID-19 pandemic on businesses, in particular by enabling the implementation of contractual amendment mechanisms in the public procurement space. The above Act introduced regulations allowing the Procuring Entity and the Contractor to amend the contract in matters of public procurement due to the impact of circumstances related to the occurrence of COVID-19 on appropriate execution of the contract. The regulation in question was amended by the Act of 16 April 2020 on special support instruments in connection with the spread of the SARS-CoV-2 virus (OJ 2020 pos. 695 as amended) and by the Act of 14 May 2020 amending certain acts in the field of protective measures in connection with the spread of the SARS-CoV-2 virus (OJ 2020 pos. 288 as amended).

The Covid Act in Article 15r confirms the possibility of implementing changes to the concluded contracts, the effectiveness of making such changes, however, involves an obligation to inform. The parties to the contract are obliged, under the above provision, to inform each other of the impact of the circumstances related to the occurrence of COVID-19 on appropriate execution of the contract in a situation where such an impact has occurred or may occur. Additionally, the failure to promptly inform the contracting authority of the possible negative impact of the restrictions resulting from the pandemic will preclude the possibility of negotiating an amendment to the contract. More importantly, the mere notification in this legal rigor will not be sufficient since the regulation also requires to submit the proof of the impact of the above circumstances by means of documents or statements, which may include a wide range of circumstances, including, but are not limited to, absence of employees or persons providing work on a basis other than employment, decisions issued by the Chief Sanitary Inspector or the state provincial sanitary inspector imposing an obligation on a party to the contract to take certain actions, withholding the supply of products or components of those products or materials, as well as other circumstances that prevent or significantly limit a party's ability to perform the contract. Documents and statements may also present circumstances concerning a subcontractor as well as a further subcontractor of the contract. The above obligations also apply to contractors with a registered office or performing activities related to the execution of the contract outside the territory of the Republic of Poland, but they will be required to submit documents issued by the relevant institutions of the country, and in a situation when in a given country such documents are not issued or their procurement is obstructed due to pandemics, the contractors' own statement.

It is of considerable importance that it is in the contractor's interest to correctly and reliably prove the impact of the occurrence of COVID-19 on the inability to properly execute the contract. It should be emphasised that the cited catalog of documents is not complete, thus, either party to the contract may demand that the other party submit additional statements or documents to confirm the impact of the circumstances associated with COVID-19 on the appropriate execution of the contract. Simultaneously, the contracting party, on the basis of the received statements and documents, shall, within 14 days from the date of their receipt, communicate to the other party its position with reasons. As Article 15r (3) of the Covid Act indicates, if a party to the contract has received further statements or documents, the 14-day period is calculated from the date of their receipt. In view of the above, the contract may be amended only after the contracting authority determines, based on its analysis of the statements and documents presented by the contractor, that the circumstances related to the occurrence of covid-19 affect or may affect the appropriate execution of the contract.

The legislator's introduction of a 14-day deadline for communicating the position to the other party is intended to counteract the protraction of actions taken by the contracting parties. Furthermore, it is noteworthy that the information obligation in question is not directly linked to the term of the contract, so regardless of the fact that a particular party to the contract (the ordering party or the contractor) takes the initiative to amend it, each time the parties to the contract are obliged to inform each other about the occurrence of circumstances related to COVID-19 affecting the appropriate execution of the contract. What is important, with regard to the obligation to inform each other regarding the occurrence of circumstances related to COVID-19, the legislator did not define what is to be understood by this term, therefore an analysis based on purposive and systemic interpretation indicates that the above issue should be interpreted as any possible circumstances related to the occurrence of COVID-19 such as production limitation, quarantine of employees, restriction in the conduct of a given activity, lack of availability of products.

What is more, the obligation of a party to a public procurement contract that the circumstances related to the occurrence of COVID-19 have arisen does not generate the obligation of the contracting parties to inform each other. This obligation arises only when the given circumstances related to the occurrence of COVID-19 affect or may affect the appropriate execution of the contract, e.g. when a limitation in the availability of materials affects the schedule of deliveries, or when the restriction of movement and the observance of sanitary restrictions may affect the performance of the given activities included in the contract on time. Not every circumstance related to the occurrence of COVID-19 will affect the performance of the contract and generate information obligations, and thus there will be no grounds for amending the contract, by way of example, we can use public procurement related to the sale of electricity carried out regardless of the occurrence of COVID-19, the regulation in question in Article 15r of the Covid Act does not cover events of a general, universal nature, admittedly related to the occurrence of COVID-19 but not adversely affecting the process of performance of the contract in question.

Concluding, the mutual obligation of the parties to inform each other in case of a public procurement are dependent on the circumstances connected with COVID-19 as well as either the influence or the possibility of the influence of those circumstances on the appropriate execution of the contract. Nevertheless, the key factor in referring to the aforementioned circumstances is the indication of the specific situations or, alternatively, the indication of the limitations including the citing the legal basis of the imposed restrictions on the execution of the contract, however not on the general impact on the situation of either party of the contract. Every time the circumstances mentioned above are supposed to be analysed in accordance to the contract in question since the legislator strongly emphasised that the influence concerns the appropriate execution of the contract not the general situation of the contractor.

The impact of the indicated circumstances on the appropriate execution of the contract cannot be based on common knowledge, and the indication of the circumstances and their impact on the appropriate execution of the contract should be clearly indicated by the party.

Examples of circumstances affecting the appropriate execution of the contract include:

1. reduction in the supply of products or materials by the manufacturer restrictions in the production of finished products or components, as well as the breaking of supply chains, which consequently lead to a significant reduction in the availability of the final product, affect the punctuality of deliveries, as well as an increase in the previously offered price.
2. plant closures due to quarantine of employees which may lead to inability to carry out partial or final works despite notification of readiness for acceptance by the contractor.

In pursuance of Article 15 r (4) of the Covid Act, the contracting authority, upon determining that circumstances related to the occurrence of COVID-19; affect appropriate execution of the contract, in consultation with the contractor, is supposed to amend the contract, in particular by:

1. changing the deadline for performance of the contract or part thereof, or temporarily suspending performance of the contract or part thereof
2. changing the manner of the delivery of supplies, services or building works
3. changing the scope of the contractor's performance and a corresponding change in the contractor's remuneration

Provided that the increase in remuneration caused by each subsequent change does not exceed 50% of the value of the original contract.

The above-mentioned catalog indicating permissible changes in the contract is not complete, which is identical to the possibility of further introduction of other modifications to the contract, obviously, only if the need to change the contract is due to the circumstances caused by the COVID-19 pandemic, which consequently indicates that the legislator allows the possibility of changing any contractual provision that is related to the impossibility of appropriate execution of the contract,, while the decision on the scope of changes to the contract is determined by mutual agreements of the parties, cited circumstances affecting its appropriate execution. Accordingly, the parties to the contract may make changes to it, for instance the date of the execution of the subject of the contract or the given stages of the execution of the contract due to the presence of employees in quarantine, delivery dates, the price of goods, etc. It should also be emphasised that the parties to the contract may shape the contract in such a way that the circumstances related to the occurrence of COVID-19 affect the appropriate execution of the contract as little as possible. The parties may, for example, suspend the execution of the contract as well as execute the contract taking into account the limitations resulting from the introduced state of the covid-19 pandemic while extending the deadline for the execution of the contract.

Another prerequisite for amending a contract is the requirement that the changes made do not exceed 50% of the value of the original contract. What is significant, the legislator has not introduced restrictions on the number of changes made to a given contract as long as there are prerequisites for them, nevertheless any changes made must not cause the total increase in remuneration to exceed the threshold of 50% of the original value of the contract. If, by virtue of the changes made to the contract, 50% of the original value of the contract were exceeded, it would not be permissible for the parties to conclude such changes, and in the situation of a violation of the above restriction, it would be necessary to assess whether there is a violation of public finance discipline, i.e. the Act of 17 December 2004 on liability for violation of public finance discipline (Journal Laws of 2021, item 289 as amended). If the public procurement contract contains regulations that shape the situation of a contracting party more favourably than it is apparent from Article 15r (4) of the Covid Act, those regulations apply to amend the contract, with the proviso that circumstances related to the occurrence of COVID-19 may not constitute an independent basis for exercising the contractual right to withdraw from the contract. Despite the occurrence of circumstances related to COVID-19 affecting the proper execution of the contract, a party is not obliged to amend the contract, there is merely the possibility of amending it. Despite this, the unreasonable refusal to amend the contract may be a premise for liability for damages or a premise for the reduction of contractual penalties by the court.

The regulations of the Covid Act, insofar as they apply to public procurement contracts, are also applicable to the contracting authority's assertion of contractual penalties or damages in the event of non-performance or improper performance of the contract. Article 15 r (6) of the Covid Act indicates that if a public procurement contract contains in its wording provisions for contractual penalties or damages for liability for non-performance or improper performance due to designated circumstances, a party to the contract shall present the impact of the circumstances related to the occurrence of COVID-19 on the proper execution of the contract and the impact of the circumstances related to the occurrence on the legitimacy of determining and claiming such penalties or damages or their amount. In addition, Article 15r1 of the Covid Act prevents the contracting authority from deducting the accrued contractual penalty reserved for non-performance or improper performance of the contract from the contractor's remuneration or from its other receivables, as well as from claiming gratification from the security for proper execution of this contract, provided that the event in connection with which the penalty was reserved occurred during the period of the pandemic.

3 Material Adverse Effect Clause (MAE) in Contracts

The subsequent section of this article constitutes the amendments to financing agreements and M&A (Merger and Acquisitions) with regard to the introduction of material adverse effect clauses into them (hereinafter as MAE or material adverse effect). The effects of the COVID-19 pandemic and the regulations introduced in this regard, primarily with regard to strictures and prohibitions and new obligations, have had an adverse effect on entrepreneurs and financial markets, and above all have affected the poor financial condition of companies. In such a reality, parties to agreements on financing, mergers and acquisitions of companies are forced to apply non-standard solutions forced by an exceptional situation in the form of, for example, material adverse effect clauses—the presence of a material adverse effect, which can be applied in these extraordinary circumstances. The MAE as a contractual clause applicable in financing, merger or acquisition agreements, depending on the will of the parties to the contract and their desire to shape the legal relationship between them, can appear in various forms, which is why the MAE is almost always subject to negotiations. Depending on the type of contract being entered into, these clauses have different functions:

1. In financing agreements, they often provide a trigger/premise for the procedures applicable in the event of a breach. The occurrence of a material adverse effect on, for example, a loan may entitle the lender to suspend the financing or put the outstanding loan into immediate default. In credit agreements, lenders use a similar provision in the event of the realisation of a disruption event, which allows the lender to suspend financing when there is a material disruption in the financial markets that affects the making of payments and is beyond the control of a party to the agreement.
2. In merger and corporate transactions, material adverse effect clauses are typically used to allow the buyer to evade the transaction if the acquired company has been materially adversely affected by certain factors. A material adverse effect clause written into a contract usually specifies events that, in a reasonable assessment, have or may have a material adverse effect on the company, the financial condition of the enterprise, realistic development prospects, ability to perform obligations under the contract, as well as the validity of the effectiveness, enforceability or degree of priority of the collateral established by the party. Each application of the material adverse effect clause is individual in nature therefore in each case of its application in a contract it is essential to consider the precise wording of the clause in question and the circumstances in which the party is. Such analysis may also be influenced by government responses and regulatory

considerations such as declarations to take special measures or enact emergency laws. In the case of material adverse effect clauses, the parties do not specify an amount threshold or other objective criteria for considering a particular impact as relevant. Ultimately, the court decides whether a material adverse effect has occurred.[10]

MAE clauses have been transferred to contracts concluded in the Polish legal system from the models used in the legal systems of the United States and the United Kingdom, where the manner of their interpretation and assessment is to some extent established, although not as significant as it might seem, which is why in the Polish reality leaving the assessment to the court may be one of the drawbacks of this type of solution. The MEA clause begins with a base definition, followed by the placement of exceptions transferring risk categories called MEA exceptions, some of which are further in such a way as to shift back the disproportionate materialization of the of the relevant risks, relying on the disproportionality exception.[11]

Typical Definition of Material Adverse Effect in Business Combination Agreements

Material Adverse Effect shall mean

Base Definition

Underlying *any event, fact, occurrence,*

Predicate *circumstance, development of change*

Event *that, either singly or in the aggregate*

Expectation *has, or would (alternatively could)*

Metric *reasonably be expected to have,*

Undefined Term *a material adverse effect on*

MAE Objects *the company and its subsidiaries taken as a whole, or its (a) business, (b) financial condition, (c) results of operations, (d) assets, (e) properties, (f) liabilities, (g) condition, other than financial condition, (h) capitalization, or (i) prospects,*

MAE Exceptions

except that none of the following, nor any event, fact, occurrence, circumstance, development or change, arising from any of the following shall constitute a Material Adverse Effect:

Systematic Risks: (a) general changes in the economy or economic or business conditions, (b) general changes in conditions in financial, credit, debt, capital, or securities markets, (c) general changes in the industries or lines of business in which the company operates, (d) general changes in law or legal

[10] Janiszewski and Hovarth III (2020), pp. 1–4.

[11] Miller (2021), p. 684.

or regulatory conditions, (e) general changes in GAAP, (f) general changes in political or social conditions, (g) general changes in weather or climatic conditions, (h) acts of war, terrorism, or sabotage, (i) hurricanes, tornadoes, earthquakes, tsunamis, floods, or pandemics, (j) calamities or natural disasters,

Indicator Risks: (k) failures to meet financial projections prepared by the company, industry or securities analysts, or other parties (but not the underlying cause of any such failure), (l) downgrades or similar adverse actions by rating agencies relating to the company or its debt or equity securities (but not the underlying causes of any such downgrades or actions), (m) changes in the prices or trading volumes of the company's shares or other securities (but not the underlying causes of any such changes),

Agreement Risks: (n) the agreement between the parties, (o) the public announcement or disclosure of the agreement between the parties, (p) any action (or omission) taken (or omitted) by the company as required or permitted by the agreement, or (q) any action (or omission) taken (or omitted) by the company with the prior written consent of the acquirer,

Disproportionality Exclusion except, with respect to (a) through (j) above, to extent that such events, facts, circumstances, developments or changes disproportionately affect the company as compared to other companies or persons operating in the same industries and geographical regions.[12]

Material adverse effect clause, similarly to material adverse change, was borrowed from Anglo-Saxon law and credit agreements and is similar in nature to force majeure. Important from the point of view of this work is the analysis of the relationship of the force majeure clause in commercial contracts and the definition of the MEA. At this point it should be stated that: *"force majeure exceptions refer to extraordinary events arising without human agency that tend to disrupt commercial transactions, and both become valid when a party seeks relief from the performance of a contractual promise. At this point, however, the similarity ends. In all other respects, the two are almost exact opposites."*[13] In view of the above: *"the MEA exception for force majeure events is just that - an exception - and its purpose and effect is to remove from the definition of MEA force majeure events that, were it not for the exception, could be considered a material adverse effect. This makes the legal effect of the MEA exception for force majeure events essentially the exact opposite of the force majeure clause. This means that under the force majeure clause, the occurrence of a force majeure event relieves the seller of an obligation. Under the MAE clause with the MAE exception for force majeure events, the occurrence of a force majeure event does not relieve the buyer of an obligation. The effect*

---

[12] Miller (2021), pp. 685–687.

[13] Miller (2021), p. 688.

of the MAE exception is to take an event that, but for the exception, would have had a Material Adverse Effect, and therefore relieves the buyer from closing the transaction and reversing that result: even if the company has suffered a Material Adverse Effect, if the effect is due to a force majeure event, the buyer must still close the transaction".[14]

4 Material Adverse Change Clause (MAC) in Contracts

Besides the implementation of the material adverse effect clause there is also the possibility to apply the material adverse change (hereinafter as MAC ort material adverse change). Its wording may be different in each contract, however, this clause, as in the case of material adverse effect, relates to the occurrence of any circumstances that may have a material adverse effect on the business, property or financial condition of the debtor (borrower or bond issuer). Such circumstance may also be the incident unrelated to the debtor's actions. Material adverse effect clauses cover events that are a major threat to a party's overall revenue-generating potential for a significant period of time, as temporary or transitory circumstances will not qualify as material adverse effect, so the rationale for considering an event as material adverse effect is very narrow.[15] The purpose of the MAC clause is to create options by which the buyer can refuse to close the merger or acquisition under the circumstances.[16] The MAC clause can be understood in terms of the sharing of risk between the buyer and seller during the period between the signing of the agreement and the closing of the transaction (the transition period).[17] It is also important to bear in mind about the possibility of risk that the value of the seller's company may change during the time between signing and closing. The aforementioned interim period can last several months, and can extend up to a year for some transactions.

With the above in mind, it should be concluded that the overriding purpose of the MAC clause is to allow the buyer to walk away from the transaction when the seller's value changes in a sufficiently significant and adverse way.[18]

It also cannot be ruled out that the effects of the COVID-19 pandemic will determine the application of the material adverse effect or material adverse change clause if they cause an adverse effect on the business, property and financial situation of the debtor. In this situation, the existence of aforementioned effect must be demonstrated by the creditor. It should also be pointed out that the action of a creditor in the form of terminating a credit, a loan agreement or demanding early redemption of bonds may be considered an abuse of subjective right by that creditor (Art. 5 of

[14] Miller (2021), p. 695.

[15] Clifford Chance (2020), p. 2.

[16] Alexander Jr (2005), p. 51; Elken (2009), p. 295.

[17] Rod (2000), pp. 217 and 221; Elken (2009), p. 295.

[18] Elken (2009), p. 295.

Civil Code). The abuse of a subjective right will occur when the creditor uses it in a manner contrary to the social and economic purpose of that right or to the principles of social interaction. Therefore, in the circumstances of an pandemic or threat of an pandemic, taking action by the creditor(s) resulting in termination of the contract based on the material adverse effect and material adverse change clauses requires caution due to the risk of allegations of abuse of subjective right by the creditor.

Another point of determination that needs attention is that the MAC in the contract can be equated with a force majeure clause. The biggest difference between MAC and the force majeure clause is that MAC is vague and does not specify the event triggering its possible enforcement, while the force majeure clause specifies circumstances that justify the execution performance of the contract.[19]

5 Hardship Clause in Contracts

In addition to the above, there is also a hardship clause. This clause refers to a situation in which the performance of the contract is still possible but becomes extremely burdensome, so the essence of the hardship clauses is to maintain the contract in force despite the changed circumstances. The main consequence of the occurrence of a hardship event under the regulations of the relevant clause is to trigger a procedure that will lead to adapt the contract to the changed circumstances (as a rule, through renegotiation between the parties). The stipulation of a hardship clause in the contract, also known as a renegotiation clause, imposes an obligation on the parties to the contract to negotiate in the event of a change in the circumstances indicated in the clause and to work together to adapt the content of the contractual relationship to the changed circumstances.[20] For many long-term projects where performance of contractual obligations is spread over years, parties to the contract may include an addendum to the contract to specify when and how to change the terms of the contract e.g. in the event of loss of economic stability by one of the parties to the contract. A hardship clause may oblige the parties to negotiate alternative contract terms therefore the purpose of the hardship clause is to provide a higher level of flexibility and to balance risks between the parties.

6 Conclusions

At this point, it is difficult to assess the long-term impact of COVID-19, although extreme and unprecedented actions such as border closures and business shutdowns may have long-term effects causing a material adverse effect on the execution of

[19] Andrew and Schwartz (2010), p. 57; Dep, p. 45.

[20] ICCWBO (2020), pp. 5–6.

business contracts. Time and practice will tell whether, e.g., banks will consider deterioration resulting from COVID-19 as a reason to place a loan in default, and whether governments will take steps to preclude such a possibility and buyers will invoke these clauses to avoid executing corporate takeovers.

In Poland, there has not yet been a court dispute over the application of the material adverse effect clause in the context of financing or M&A transactions specifically due to the pandemic, therefore it is difficult to claim conclusively what the final outcome of such a dispute would be. However, it is certain that the contracting parties applying these clauses in Poland want to give it a similar meaning to the one in the legal system from which it originates (i.e., as the ultimate trigger for taking corrective measures). Polish courts lacking knowledge of foreign doctrine may create their own interpretations that do not necessarily coincide with the goals the contracting parties aimed to achieve when agreeing on the material adverse effect clause.

MAEs, MACs and hardship clauses are not the only remedy, there are also two institutions in the Polish legal system which may be applicable in today's circumstances namely *rebus sic stantibus* and force majeure. However, it should be borne in mind that the COVID-19 pandemic that has been going on since the beginning of 2020, as well as its effects, has changed the situation in the M&A market and for that reason it requires a new approach from both a business and legal perspective

References

Alexander JB Jr (2005) The material adverse change clause. Prac Law 51:11

Andrew A, Schwartz A (2010) Standard clause analysis of the frustration doctrine and the material adverse change clause. UCLA Law Rev 789

Clifford Chance (2020) Impact of the Covid-19 pandemic on debt financing transactions on the polish market. https://www.cliffordchance.com/content/dam/cliffordchance/briefings/2020/03/covid-19-effect-on-debt-financing-transactions%20.pdf

Durojaye E, Powell DM (2022) Constitutional resilience and the COVID-19 pandemic: perspectives from sub-Saharan Africa. Palgrave Macmillan

Dyzenhaus D (2001) The permanence of the temporary: can emergency powers be normalized? In: Daniels RJ et al (eds) The security of freedom. University of Toronto Press

Elken AC (2009) Notes rethinking the material adverse change clause in merger and acquisition agreements: should the United States consider the British model? South Calif Law Rev

Greene A (2020) Emergency powers in a time of pandemic. Bristol University Press

Grogan J, Donald A (eds) (2022a) Routledge handbook of law and the COVID-19 pandemic, 1st edn. Routledge

Grogan J, Donald A (2022b) 38. Lessons for a 'Post-Pandemic' future. In: Grogan J, Donald A (eds) Routledge handbook of law and the COVID-19 pandemic. Routledge. (forthcoming)

ICCWBO (2020) ICC force majeure and hardship clauses

Janiszewski A, Hovarth SJ III (2020) Coronavirus disease (COVID-19) – financing and M&A agreements in Poland. Greenberg Traurig LLP

Miller RT (2021) Pandemic risk and the interpretation of exceptions in MAE clauses. J Corp Law

Rod JH (2000) Deal risk, announcement risk and interim changes—allocating risks in recent technology M&A agreements. Drafting Corporate Agreements 2000–2001, pp 217, 221 (PLI Corporate Law & Practice)

Angelika Kozyra PhD of Law (Faculty of Law and Administration, Jagiellonian University), Doctor of Juristic Science, a corporate and medical law practitioner at Trigon Orthopedia Clinic and Softmed-Laser Clinic, runs sole proprietorship in terms of legal advice and legal services for business and medical entities.

The Amount of Rent Under the CoVid-19 Pandemic. Between Poland and Germany

Piotr Ratusznik

Abstract The outbreak of the CoVid-19 pandemic has led to unprecedented changes in the practice of law. Significant transformations have taken place in the field of contract law. The sustainability of rental agreements is a good example. Before the outbreak of the pandemic, it might have been thought that civil law in Europe was without exception based on the principle *pacta sunt servanda*. However, the extraordinary times of the pandemic led the judicature to apply exceptional solutions. Both in Poland and Germany, the courts as well as legal doctrine began to invoke special regulations to break the *pacta sunt servanda* principle. Despite the differences separating these two legal orders, both rejected any automatic solutions. The key role was played by the individual assessment of specific facts of the case.

1 Starting Point: The Principle of *Pacta Sunt Servanda* in the Polish Civil Code and the German BGB

The rapid outbreak of the CoVid-19 pandemic brought social life and the world's economy to a standstill for more than a year. Although it was not the first epidemic caused by the Sars-CoV virus, CoVid-19 reminded humanity of the spectre of epidemics that once tragically—and cyclically—visited the continents, such as the so-called 'Spanish flu' pandemic, which spread the death toll just after the end of the First World War. The governments, aware of the possible consequences of the CoVid-19 pandemic, tried to prevent the spread of this virus as quickly and effectively as possible. Despite the differences in the individual models adopted to combat CoVid-19, it can be said that in the European region it was more than often decided to introduce a so-called lockdown.

P. Ratusznik (✉)
Faculty of Law and Administration, University of Warsaw, Warsaw, Poland
e-mail: p.ratusznik@student.uw.edu.pl

E. Hadrowicz (ed.), *Polish Entrepreneurial Law in the Era of the COVID-19 Pandemic*, Ius Gentium: Comparative Perspectives on Law and Justice 114,
https://doi.org/10.1007/978-3-031-57480-1_7

As a result—and for the sake of the population—social mobility and the freedom to carry out economic activities were significantly restricted. This was not without an impact on the mood of the population, already sufficiently aggravated by the mere possibility of being infected. One of the major legal problems that arose was the question of the sustainability of the contractual obligations of the parties to the rental agreement in those situations where, as a result of the introduction of lock-down, the operation of shopping malls, shops, restaurants, etc., lost its sense for the tenants, while the landlords were still, in principle, ready to perform their obligation.

A typical example from the practice of law in the era of the pandemic was characterized by the following features: **(1)** the entrepreneur rented the premises on the basis of a rental agreement concluded before the outbreak of the CoVid-19 pandemic; **(2)** the rapid spread of the virus led to the closure of various commercial locations and office spaces; **(3)** under such conditions, the entrepreneurs' profits were significantly reduced; **(4)** and they themselves saw no point in paying rent to their landlords at the previous—pre-pandemic—amount.

(5) Landlords, on the other hand, generally turned a deaf ear to tenants' requests, emphasizing that the rented property they provided was still fit for use. In this way, they highlighted the permanence of their obligations, which was supposed to justify the impossibility of changing the rent payable under the rental agreement. At the same time, the landlords noted that their counterparties generally received state aid from the government under various social programmes, the so-called "anti-crisis shield", which was said to be an additional circumstance demonstrating that any rent reduction was unjustified.

This difference of opinions between the two parties to the rental agreement created the need for tenants to resort to the courts to protect their rights. At the same time, a fundamental question arose—how solid was the root of the *pacta sunt servanda* principle during the CoVid-19 pandemic?

This paper refers to the solutions proposed in two countries—Poland and Germany. For several reasons. Firstly, the *pacta sunt servanda* principle is valid in both Polish and German civil laws. In this context, one wonders whether this principle is breached in situations such as the rapid spread of the CoVid-19 pandemic.

Secondly, it is believed that Polish law provides for a specific institution that allows for the judicial apportionment of contractual risk and the modification of the contract primarily due to economic difficulties (Article 357[1] of the Polish Civil Code). In Germany, on the other hand, it is argued that a solution has been adopted that also makes such effects possible, however this occurs by taking into account more circumstances than just economic difficulties (§ 313 BGB).[1] This approach needs to be verified and it should be determined whether, in practice, both legal norms—regardless of their differences—are not applied in the same manner.

Thirdly, so far in Poland, the issue of rent reduction under a rental agreement is—especially as a consequence of the overloading of the civil departments of courts with so-called cases of loans denominated in foreign currency—still in the early

[1] Kadner-Graziano (2019), p. 438.

stages. As a consequence there is no established line of the most important judicial authorities, such as Courts of Appeal or the Polish Supreme Court. What we are dealing with here is an issue that is primarily keenly debated in the doctrine. In Germany, on the other hand, despite the fact that the issue of a possible rent reduction is a new one, it is already possible to identify a considerable number of rulings concerning this matter. In particular, the rulings of the German Federal Supreme Court (BGH) should be mentioned. This raises the question—what conclusions does Polish doctrine reach and what lessons can be drawn from German case law? Are they different in comparison to each other? Does the doctrinal perspective (Poland) on the CoVid-19 pandemic outbreak differ from the approach developed by case law (Germany)?

At the same time, it must be borne in mind that in both countries approaches to the permanence of rental agreement obligations are still in the process of formation. Therefore, it requires continuous and in-depth reflection. Particularly since the negative socio-economic effects originating in the spread of the Covid-19 virus place lawyers and, above all, the courts in a special position—that of an arbiter.

At the most generalized level, this study is about determining the method and how to distribute contractual risk between the parties to an existing rental agreement affected by the CoVid-19 pandemic.

2 Possibility to Reduce Rent Under a Rental Agreement Under Polish Law

2.1 The Essence of the Rebus Sic Stantibus Clause

When a fortuitous event occurs that regularly appears in business relations, the provisions of the Polish Civil Code generally provide for imposing its negative consequences on only one party to the legal relationship.[2] The provision of Article 353 § 1 of the Polish Civil Code is relevant here. It indicates that the essence of an obligation is that the creditor may demand performance from the debtor and the debtor should fulfil this performance. However, in times of crisis, which include the spread of the CoVid-19 pandemic and its consequences, the possibility of applying a special regulation—Article 357[1] of the Polish Civil Code—arises (the so-called *rebus sic stantibus* clause).

This provision states that if, due to an extraordinary change of relations, the fulfilment of the obligation would be connected with excessive difficulties or would threaten one of the parties with a gross loss, which the parties did not foresee when concluding the agreement, the court may, after considering the interests of the parties, in accordance with the principles of social co-existence, determine the manner

[2] Cf. Article 663 of the Polish Civil Code, which makes it clear that the rule is that necessary repairs are to be borne by the landlord.

of fulfilment of the obligation, the amount of the obligation or even decide to terminate the agreement. When terminating the contract, the court may, where necessary, rule on the parties' settlements, following the principles set out in the previous sentence.

The substantive legal prerequisites for the application of Article 357^1 of the Polish Civil Code are: **(1)** the contract as the source of the obligation;[3] **(2)** an extraordinary change in relations characterised by the fact that the parties did not take into account its effect on the obligation when concluding the contract; **(3)** it can be proven that the continuation of the contractual obligation in its unchanged form and the performance of the contractual obligations lead to an unreasonable hardship in fulfilling the obligation or a threat of a gross loss for one of the parties; **(4)** a causal connection between both (2 and 3) of the above prerequisites.[4]

The provision of Article 357^1 of the Polish Civil Code[5] serves to distribute the contractual risk between the parties in a special way in order to take into account the difficult financial situation of the party that has to fulfil an obligation. The *rebus sic stantibus* clause allows the court to intervene in the legal relationship between the parties.[6] This interference of the court consists, firstly, in the authority to alter the value of the mutual obligations of the parties to the contract. What is at stake here is a reduction or an increase in one of the benefits of either party. Only as a last resort—bearing in mind the directive to keep the contract in force (favor contractus)—is the court entitled to issue a judgment terminating the contract.

Although at first glance it appears that Article 357^1 of the Polish Civil Code leads to a breach of the principle of *pacta sunt servanda*, in the Polish legal doctrine the opposite position has also been expressed, according to which Article 357^1 of the Polish Civil Code does not constitute an exception to the principle of *pacta sunt servanda* at all, but actually complements or reinforces this principle.[7] The matter cannot be determined with complete conviction. On the one hand, it can be argued that the *pacta sunt servanda* principle applies only in as much as it does not become a justification for the existence of contracts which grossly violate the interests of one of the parties. In this view, the rebus sic stantibus clause reinforces this principle by acting as a "safety bar" designed to be applied in exceptional situations. It is a situation where ignoring the negative impact of changed circumstances on the

---

[3] It has been established in case law that Article 357^1 of the Polish Civil Code is applicable to every contract—judgment of the SA (Polish Court of Appeal) in Warsaw from 6.6.2018, I ACa 190/17, Legalis; judgment of the SA (Polish Court of Appeal) in Katowice from 25.6.2013, I ACa 226/13, Legalis.

[4] Brzozowski (2014), p. 15.

[5] The rebus sic stantibus clause from Article 357^1 of the Polish Civil Code is described in the legal doctrine as the "large clause", which allows it to be contrasted with the so-called 'small clause' from Article 358^1 (3) and (4) of the Polish Civil Code, which relates only to cases of a significant change in the purchasing power of money after the obligation has arisen.

[6] Kowalów-Ziułkowska and Stasiewicz (2022), p. 1.

[7] Kowalów-Ziułkowska and Stasiewicz (2022), p. 1; judgment of the SA (Polish Court of Appeal) in Szczecin from 21.4.2016, I ACa 9/16, Legalis. Otherwise: Nowak-Górski et al. (2020), p. 3.

parties' interests would lead to an unfair disturbance of the contractual balance.[8] On the other hand however, the view that the *rebus sic stantibus* clause is an exception to the *pacta sunt servanda* principle is also defensible. Such a position has the advantage of justifying, in a systemic way, the need for cautious use of this institution.[9]

2.2 The Application of the Rebus Sic Stantibus Clause to Rental Agreements in Poland Under the Conditions of the CoVid-19 Pandemic

The question arises as to whether, under the conditions of the CoVid-19 pandemic, Polish tenants could make use of the right provided in Article 357[1] of the Polish Civil Code in order to demand that the court shape the legal relationship arising from the rental agreement, including a demand for its termination. Hitherto, the issue has not been resolved by the highest Polish judicial authorities. So far, it has primarily been dealt with by courts of first instance.[10] At this point, the trend that can be observed tends to favour the application of the rebus sic stantibus clause to rental agreements in Poland in the case of the CoVid-19 pandemic.

Nevertheless, these issues are primarily of interest to legal scholars. This does not mean, however, that the considerations in this article have the value of legal abstraction. The views expressed by the Polish legal doctrine concerning the possible application of Article 357[1] of the Polish Civil Code to modifications of rental agreements in the conditions of the CoVid-19 pandemic are built upon the statements of the jurisprudence developed on the basis of the long-standing practice of application of Article 357[1] of the Polish Civil Code. Over the years, this provision was often used to deal with the sudden drop in the value of money, which was associated with Poland's transition to a capitalist economy, that took place in the 1990s. It is enough to say that the legal doctrine refers to the established view of the Supreme Court regarding whether an epidemic can be an event justifying a party's invocation of Article 357[1]of the Civil Code.

This is not surprising. After all, it is case law that is of key importance when it comes to the interpretation of Article 357[1] of the Polish Civil Code, as it is accepted that it is a provision of so-called judicial law.[11] This is an important fact, because Article 357[1] of the Polish Civil Code is the most relevant provision allowing such

---

[8] Nowak-Górski et al. (2020), p. 3.

[9] Kaliński (2022), p. 168.

[10] According to article 321 § 1 of the Polish Code of Civil Procedure: The court cannot rule on a matter not included in the claim or award beyond what was requested.

Judgment of the SR (Polish District Court) for Łodź-Śródmieście in Łodź from 21.5.2021, XIII GC 1439/20, LEX No. 3278505; judgment of the SR (Polish District Court) for Poznań-Stare Miasto in Poznań from 20.1.2021, I C 957/20, LEX No. 3175155.

[11] Judgment of the SN (Supreme Court of Poland) from 14.1.2009, IV CSK 385/08, Legalis.

losses, which were not covered by the usual contractual risk, to be shared between the parties to the contract. In applying the rebus sic stantibus clause, the court exercises considerable degree of discretion. It is even entitled to shape the legal relationship in a manner different from that indicated in the wording of the lawsuit, which constitutes an exception to Article 321 § 1 of the Polish Code of Civil Procedure.[12]

Furthermore, it has been noted in the legal doctrine that the legislator has not determined whether a judgment shaping a legal relationship between the parties to the contract has effects from the date it becomes binding, i.e. ex nunc, or whether it acquires retroactive effect, i.e. ex tunc. Therefore, it has been assumed that it is the court that ultimately chooses the moment when the legal effects of its decision shaping a legal relationship occur.[13] However judicial discretion has its limits. Not all rental agreements can be regarded in terms of the possible application of Article 357[1] of the Polish Civil Code. In the judgment of the Polish Supreme Court from 18.5.2006, the view was expressed that if the parties concluded the agreement in abnormal conditions, counting on the stabilization of them during the execution of the agreement, and this did not occur, then the premise of an extraordinary change of relations does not exist.[14] This means that the possibility to invoke rebus sic stantibus clauses suffers from some major preliminary limitations.

When considering the applicability of Article 357[1] of the Polish Civil Code to rental agreements in Poland under the conditions of the CoVid-19 pandemic, one should start from the fact that the jurisprudence of the Polish Supreme Court accepts that an epidemic can be the cause of an extraordinary change in relations.[15] Especially as this is not a regularly occurring event that would fit within a typical contractual risk. Furthermore, it must be assumed that the extraordinary impact of the CoVid-19 pandemic on the contractual situation of the parties could not have been foreseen. As a rule, the agreements that tenants of office or retail space entered into were from a time when no pandemic could be expected to break out.

At the same time, it must be borne in mind that the extraordinary nature of the situation from Article 357[1] of the Polish Civil Code refers not to the event itself which brought about the change in relations, but to the change in relations.[16] In other words—for the application of Article 357[1] of the Polish Civil Code to rental agreements during the CoVid-19 pandemic, it is not sufficient that the parties simply did not expect, for example, a pandemic (whose outbreaks are recurrent), but that its outbreak would lead to massive lockdowns resulting in the pointlessness of renting premises on the original contractual terms.

Regardless of the way in which this issue can be distinguished, it should be noted that in cases of CoVid-19 pandemic we are dealing with both an event bearing the characteristics of an extraordinary event (pandemic) and its effect, i.e. an

---

[12] See judgment of the SN (Supreme Court of Poland) from 14 1.2009, IV CSK 385/08, Legalis.

[13] Brzozowski (2014), p. 49.

[14] Nowak-Górski et al. (2020), p. 9.

[15] Judgment of the SN (Supreme Court of Poland) from 8.3.2018, II CSK 303/17, Legalis.

[16] Judgment of the SA (Polish Court of Appeal) in Łódź from 20.12.2016, I ACa 769/16, Legalis.

extraordinary change in economic and social relations as a result of this pandemic (lockdown).[17] At the margin, it ought be noted that the case would perhaps be different in e.g. December 2022, as currently both cyclical outbreaks of various coronaviruses and their effects in the form of paralysis of socio-economic life are to be expected. This means that even if the application of Article 357^1 of the Polish Civil Code is allowed for rental agreements under the conditions of the CoVid-19 pandemic, the possibility for tenants to invoke this regulation is temporarily limited.

Article 357^1 of the Polish Civil Code requires the occurrence—as a result of an extraordinary change in relations—of an excessive hardship in the performance of the obligation, which is to be of a pecuniary nature, or the threat of a gross loss. In the first case, it is a situation where the debtor's inputs are out of proportion to the inputs assumed by the debtor at the time the obligation came into existence.[18] On the other hand, when it comes to the term "threat of gross loss", it is to be understood through the prism of effect. It is argued that a gross loss will occur when the performance of the obligation has lost economic significance for the party to such an extent that the continuation of the obligation in an unchanged form will threaten the party with adverse consequences.[19]

The threat of gross loss is not understood too strictly. The idea of equating this concept with the ruin in which the debtor could find himself if he fulfilled his obligation in an unchanged form has been widely rejected. It has been noted that the requirement of the occurrence of a threat of financial ruin would have the drawback that Article 357^1 of the Polish Civil Code could only be used by one who is threatened with insolvency or bankruptcy.[20] Therefore, the case law accepts that a "simple gross transactional loss" is sufficient, on condition that it nullifies the original calculation made by the contracting party.[21]

It is argued that the concepts of undue hardship and gross loss relate to a specific contractual relationship and do not refer to the general financial or economic situation of the debtor. This position— though enigmatic at first glance —has serious consequences. As a result even entities in a good financial position can benefit from the rebus sic stantibus clause as long as they are exposed to an undue hardship or may suffer a gross loss within the framework of a specific legal relationship that has been affected by an extraordinary change in relations. A different—restrictive—interpretation would make the rebus sic stantibus clause a kind of 'poor man's law'—which is not its function. It protects the contractual balance of the parties in a specific contract.[22]

---

[17] Kowalów-Ziułkowska and Stasiewicz (2022), p. 2; Mataczyński and Saczywko (2021), Commentary to art. 357^1, Rn 38.

[18] Kowalów-Ziułkowska and Stasiewicz (2022), p. 2.

[19] Kowalów-Ziułkowska and Stasiewicz (2022), p. 3.

[20] Kowalów-Ziułkowska and Stasiewicz (2022), p. 3.

[21] Judgment of the SN (Supreme Court of Poland) from 5.12.2013, V CSK 2/13, Legalis.

[22] Kowalów-Ziułkowska and Stasiewicz (2022), p. 4.

In the case of rental agreements for the use of commercial space—decreases in tenants' turnover by several tens of per cent, caused by the Covid-19 pandemic, may be qualified as a gross loss. Such a view may, however, raise some doubts. Therefore, it should first be noted that a different—restrictive—understanding of the extraordinary change of relations clause would make this provision practically inoperative. In fact, it would be necessary to force the debtor to bear the loss (paying rent for a rented commercial premises in a closed building) for the entire duration of the obligation, reckoning that perhaps in the future circumstances will change and in a multi-year context the loss incurred, e.g. in a pandemic period, will not be gross.[23] Secondly, it may be argued that decreases in turnover are not protected by the rental agreement. Such a view makes little sense as Article 357^1 of the Polish Civil Code is not a provision which allows modification of only rental agreements, but rather is a general regulation. It allows for the consideration of various circumstances affecting the stability of every obligation.

When it comes to the causal link between undue hardship or the threat of a gross loss and an extraordinary change in relations both legal doctrine[24] and the jurisprudence[25] require a conditio sine qua non link. As it is well known—the standard set by a causal connection of this type is not very high. Therefore, in the case of rental agreements concluded prior to the CoVid-19 pandemic, this premise will also generally be fulfilled. This is because, had the pandemic and its associated negative effects (primarily lockdown) not occurred, the tenant would have continued to use the leased office or retail space undisturbed and without causing gross losses.

Taking the above into account, under such conditions, it would be most reasonable—on the basis of Article 357^1 of the Polish Civil Code—for the court to significantly reduce the rent. In light of the negative socio-economic effects of the Covid-19 pandemic and the associated blockade, it has become pointless for the tenants to use the office or business rental space under the previous (pre-pandemic) conditions. Such shaping of the legal relationship is also the fairest solution, as it takes into account the interests of both parties to the rental agreement—the tenant and the landlord.

The other measure provided for by Article 357^1 of the Polish Civil Code, i.e. termination of the legal relationship, is considered in the legal doctrine to be the most intrusive way of distributing the contractual risk between the parties, and for this reason it is recommended to apply it with a considerable degree of caution.[26] In particular, it is argued that the court—when ruling on the basis of Article 357^1 of the Polish Civil Code—should seek to maintain an existing legal relationship.[27] Extensive application of this provision is also excluded.[28] The key to the

---

[23] Kowalów-Ziułkowska and Stasiewicz (2022), p. 4.

[24] See Brzozowski (2019), p. 325.

[25] Judgment of the SN (Supreme Court of Poland) from 7.12.2007, III CSK 172/07, Legalis.

[26] Brzozowski (2014), p. 49.

[27] Morek (2022), Commentary to art. 357^1, Rn 38.

[28] Judgment of the SA (Polish Court of Appeal) in Szczecin from 19.11.2019, I AGa 99/19, Legalis.

interpretation of Article 357^1 of the Polish Civil Code is to pursue a balance as well as and an adequate weighing of the interests of the parties.

At the same time, it should be borne in mind that it is accepted in case law that court interference on the basis of Article 357^1 of the Polish Civil Code may only relate to existing obligations,[29] and not, for example, those already fulfilled or time-barred. This view—although correct—should, however, be further clarified by pointing out that the exercise of rights under Article 357^1 of the Polish Civil Code should be possible as long as it is possible to enforce a claim for the performance in kind.[30]

However, the question arises as to what criteria should be taken into account when there is a judicial change in the amount of obligations of the parties to the rental agreement. Since it is necessary to adhere to the directive to keep the contract in force, the effects of the extraordinary change in relations caused by the pandemic should be distributed equally to both parties. It must be emphasized that it is not possible to shift the burden of the loss either solely to the landlord or solely to the tenant. The general criteria for modifying the content of a contract under Article 357^1 of the Polish Civil Code are the interests of the parties and the principles of social co-existence, which speak in favour of treating both parties equally. Such treatment means that the burden of the consequences of a change in relations is distributed between both parties. It is surely difficult to point out all possible constellations depicting the configuration of all mutual interests of the parties. Nevertheless, the question of the impact of state aid on the scope of a court decision shaping the legal relationship play a major role in the practice of applying this provision.

It is necessary to start from the fact that the financial aid received by tenants from the state, from the so-called anti-CoVid-19 shield, was not a benefit whose purpose was defined by the legislator as aid directed, for example, to satisfy the claims of landlords. Article 2a of the Act on Special Solutions Relating to the Prevention, Counteracting and Combating of Covid-19, Other Infectious Diseases and Crisis Situations Caused by Them merely states that the government's programmes for providing financial support are intended to counteract the Covid-19 pandemic. There is no suggestion that the government's aid serves to regulate the private-law relationship between the parties to the rental agreement. At the same time, it should be borne in mind that landlords could also have received public help. This also applies—as often happens in Poland in the case of renting an office or business space—if such a landlord has acted as a branch of a foreign entrepreneur.[31]

On the other hand, when it comes to the reference to the principles of social co-existence, it is assumed in the legal doctrine that they prescribe taking into account the constitutional axiology and the principles of law. In this respect, the principle of

29 Judgment of the SA (Polish Court of Appeal) in Gdańsk from 15.12.2015, V ACa 579/15, Legalis. Otherwise: Judgment of the SA (Polish Court of Appeal) in Warsaw from 25.9.2013, VI ACa 71/13, Legalis.

30 Lackoroński (2012), pp. 65 et seq.

31 SKO.OG-COVID/41.12/1/2021/218 (Polish Local Government Board of Appeal).

social justice, which finds expression in Article 2 of the Constitution of the Republic of Poland, would be of significant importance. The jurisprudence of the Polish Constitutional Tribunal recognises it as an expression of striving to maintain a balance in social relations.[32] This justifies a modification of the rental agreement, the continuation of which in its unchanged form would lead to gross losses for the tenant. In accordance with the case-law of the Polish Constitutional Tribunal, the principle of social justice is also relevant at the stage of application of the law.[33] In practice, this means that the most appropriate solution would first require determining what state aid the contracting parties have received. This support must then be translated into the situation of the parties to the rental agreement. It is not an easy task, but a manageable one, at least with some approximation.

The specific extent of the court's intervention in a rental agreement should result from a detailed evidentiary investigation and be the effect of a careful analysis of the factual and economic situation of the parties. It should also be borne in mind that, in certain circumstances, a doubt may arise as to whether the debtor's performance is not unreasonably difficult but impossible, which raises the question of whether the impossibility under Article 475 § 1 of the Civil Code should be invoked.[34] This would, however, give rise to the need for mutual reimbursement of obligations by both parties to the rental agreement.

3 Possibility to Reduce Rent from a Rental Agreement Under German Law

However, how are the factual situations discussed above assessed under German law? Are there any differences? In the case law, it was relatively soon that rulings began to appear and not only from the courts of first or second instance, but also from the Federal Supreme Court. They comprehensively addressed the issue of rent modification under the conditions of CoVid-19 pandemic. Therefore, it can be said that a relatively consistent judicial practice is already taking shape in Germany.

The German judiciary in principle rejects the possibility of amending the contract when tenants allege a defect in the rented property. This defect is supposed to arise from lockdown. In other words, German courts are reluctant to recognise that the inability to use the rented premises as a result of lockdown amounts to a defect in the property. This is because it is difficult to prove that the rental object was defective under such conditions. Lockdown does not mean that the landlord did not fulfil his contractual obligations under § 535 (1) sentence 2 BGB.[35] According to

---

[32] Judgment of the TK (Polish Constitutional Tribunal) from 12 4.2000, K 8/98, Legalis.

[33] Judgment of the TK (Polish Constitutional Tribunal) from 12.12.2001, SK 26/01, Legalis.

[34] Nowak-Górski et al. (2020), p. 7.

[35] Judgement of the OLG Dresden (Provincial High Court of Dresden) from 24.2.2021, 5 U 1782/20, Judgement of the OLG Karlsruhe (Provincial High Court of Karlsruhe), 7U 109/20,

this provision, the rental agreement obliges the landlord to give the tenant the use of the rented property during the rental period. However, for the Higher Regional Court of Dresden, the defect in the form of a public-law obstacle existed. Nevertheless, the distribution of risk between the contracting parties was decisive and it was therefore assumed that, within the scope of § 535 (1) sentence 2 BGB, the effects of the lockdown could not be attributed to the landlord's sphere of risk.[36] In the opinion of the Higher Regional Courts of Frankfurt, Karlsruhe and Munich, on the other hand, there was no defect under the conditions of the CoVid-19 pandemic because the restrictions ordered by the authorities were not of a material nature, i.e. not related to the condition, quality or location of the rental property.[37]

It is therefore necessary to seek another basis for the distribution of contractual risk within the rental agreement. Article 240 §7 of the Introductory Act to the German Civil Code (EGBGB), which came into force on 1.1.2021, provides some guidance here. According to this provision, a circumstance within the meaning of § 313 (1) BGB is presumed to have arisen in the event of a pandemic-related closure or reduction of business activities. Section 313 (1) BGB provides that if the circumstances giving rise to the contract have changed seriously after the conclusion of the contract and if the parties would not have entered into the contract or would have entered into it with a different content if they had foreseen the change, an adjustment of the contract may be demanded unless one of the parties can reasonably be expected to adhere to the unchanged contract, taking into account all the circumstances of the case, in particular the contractual or statutory allocation of risks.

Section 313 BGB refers to cases in which it is unreasonable for one of the parties to comply with the contract in its original form because the relevant circumstances have changed after the conclusion of the contract or did not exist as they were assumed at the time of the conclusion of the contract. If the requirements of Section 313 BGB are fulfilled, a party may demand an adjustment of the contract or withdraw from it.[38] The details of this provision create controversy in the literature. Nevertheless, it is the vagueness of § 313 BGB that is considered to be the strength of this legal institution, as it is supposed to allow for the unproblematic establishment of justice in individual cases.[39]

The prerequisites for the application of this institution are as follows. Firstly, there must be a basis for the legal act whose essence is to be modified in some way. This term is not defined in § 313 BGB. According to the case law, subjective criteria

---

Judgement of the OLG München (Provincial High Court of Munich) from 17.2.2021, 32 U 6358/20, Judgement of the OLG Frankfurt (Provincial High Court of Frankfurt) from 19.3.2021, 2 U 143/20.

[36] Judgement of the OLG Dresden (Provincial High Court of Dresden) from 24.2.2021, 5 U 1782/20.

[37] Judgement of the OLG Karlsruhe (Provincial High Court of Karlsruhe), 7 U 109/20, Judgement of the OLG München (Provincial High Court of Munich) from 17.2.2021, 32 U 6358/20, Judgement of the OLG Frankfurt (Provincial High Court of Frankfurt) from 19.3.2021, 2 U 143/20.

[38] Looschelders (2018), p. 279.

[39] Fikentscher and Heinemann (2017), p. 149.

(subjective basis of the contract) are primarily decisive for its interpretation. This refers to the ideas of one of the contractual parties which were apparent at the time of conclusion, recognisable to the other party and to which the latter did not object, or the common ideas of both contractual parties on which the intention to conclude the act is based (German: *Geschäftswille).* Within the framework of § 313 BGB, the basis of the action may also be determined according to purely objective criteria, independent of the subjective views of the parties (objective basis of the action).[40]

Secondly, a major change in circumstances or a significant error is required. As far as the effects of Covid-19 are concerned, the main significance will be attributed to changes in political, economic or social conditions (war, inflation, revolution, natural disasters, etc.). At the same time, it must be borne in mind that such an event must have a direct impact on the contractual relationship, e.g. it must lead to a disturbance of equivalence or to the end of the usefulness of the object of obligation.[41]

Thirdly, it is necessary that such a circumstance is relevant to the formation of the contract. It must therefore be established that the contract would not have been concluded or would have been concluded with a different content if the parties had correctly assessed the situation or foreseen the change of circumstances.[42]

Fourthly, the aforementioned is to lead to the unreasonableness of keeping the contract unchanged. The point is that the disruption of the basis of the contract is only relevant if one of the parties cannot reasonably be expected to comply with the unchanged contract. This rationale is present if the continuation of the contract unchanged due to the changed situation would lead to a result that is irreconcilable with law and justice and constitutes an unbearable hardship.[43] This is an issue that is a subject to a complex assessment. According to § 313 I BGB, it should be determined on the basis of all the circumstances of the specific case, whilst balancing the interests of both parties. When determining unreasonableness, the contractual and juridical distribution of risk is of particular importance. At the same time, unreasonableness shall be denied if the investigated circumstance falls within the sphere of the risk of the injured party. It is therefore necessary to examine whether a party has expressly or impliedly assumed a particular risk.[44]

In the legal doctrine, the prerequisites indicated above are also put somewhat more synthetically. Therefore, it is assumed that § 313 BGB will be applicable if the following elements are present: **(a)** a factual element, which consists in the fact that certain circumstances formed the basis of the contract. These circumstances have seriously changed after the conclusion of the contract; **(b)** a hypothetical element: the parties would not have entered into the contract or would have entered into it with a different content if they had foreseen the change of circumstances; **(c)** a normative element: taking into account all the circumstances of the individual case

---

[40] Looschelders (2018), p. 281.

[41] Looschelders (2018), p. 282.

[42] Looschelders (2018), p. 282.

[43] Looschelders (2018), p. 282.

[44] Looschelders (2018), p. 283.

(in particular, the contractual or legal distribution of risks), it cannot reasonably be expected that one of the parties would adhere to the unchanged contract.[45]

So much for the theory. As far as practice is concerned, one must start by noting that German case law refers to § 313(1) BGB in order to adapt the rental agreement to the new, changed conditions. At the same time, this provision is applied with extreme caution. The Provincial High Court (OLG) of Frankfurt (2U 13/21) ruled that the effects of CoVid-19 pandemic can seriously disrupt the economic basis of the rental relationship if the contracting parties did not take them into account when concluding the agreement. The question of whether and how this prerequisite leads to an adjustment of the rental agreement must take into account all the circumstances of the specific case. Therefore, despite the willingness of the German judicature to apply § 313 BGB in the case of CoVid-19 restrictions, this does not at all mean that German courts always agree to adjust the rent based on this provision.

However, on contrary to the BGH's rather cautious approach, reference should also be made to the ruling of the Provincial High Court (OLG) of Dresden (5U 1782/20), which found a rent reduction of 50% for a period of 2 months to be justified, as neither party to the contract agreed on or foresaw the cause of the disruption of the basis of the contract. It was therefore reasonable to share the associated burden equally between the two parties. In the court's view, such a solution was at the same time in line with the former case law on similar cases.[46] Moreover, the OLG Dresden left open the question of whether the payment of state aid to one of the parties to a rental agreement allows for a change in rent. This view leads to a great simplification and acceleration of the proceedings.

Nevertheless, the above approach was rejected by the German Federal Supreme Court (BGH) in a ruling from 12 January 2022.[47] This judgment confirms the prevailing view that in the case of lockdown, there is no case of impossibility as well as a defect in the rental object. As a rule, the risk of changes occurred during the duration of the rental agreement is borne by the tenant. However, the BGH accepted that losses or burdens on the tenant result from decisions taken by the state to combat pandemic CoVid-19, such as the temporary closure of commercial activities, go beyond the tenant's normal risk.[48] Especially since the economic losses suffered by a commercial tenant due to a pandemic-related closure are not the result of decisions made by him. They are the consequence of extensive state intervention in economic and social life to combat the CoVid-19 pandemic, for which none of the parties to the rental agreement can be held responsible.

In such a case, it is possible to distribute the contractual risk between the parties to the rental agreement by allowing the tenant's claim for an adjustment of the rent

[45] Fikentscher and Heinemann (2017), p. 150.

[46] Judgment of BGH from 23.11.1989, VII ZR 60/89, NJW 1990, 572, 573; Likewise Judgment of OLG Karlsruhe (Provincial High Court of Kalrsuhe) from 15.5.1992, 15 U 297/91, NJW 1992, 3176, 3177, concerning expiry of mutual obligations from a contract for musicians to perform at a carnival event that was cancelled due to the war in the Persian Gulf.

[47] Judgment of BGH from 12.1.2022, XII ZR 8/21.

[48] See: judgment of OLG Munich, NJW 2021, 948, 951.

due to the disruption of the basis of the contract (§ 313 BGB). At the same time, the BGH rejects blanket solutions based on automaticity of adjudication, which do not take into account the circumstances of the specific facts, e.g. based on a 50/50 risk distribution between the parties. This is because the prerequisite for an adjustment is that the tenant cannot reasonably be expected to comply with the unchanged contract. Even if the restrictions concerning the use of the rented premises related to the closure of the business due to a pandemic cannot be attributed solely to the tenant's risk, this does not mean that the tenant can always claim an adjustment of the rent for the period of closure.

Whether it is unreasonable for the tenant to adhere to the unchanged agreement also requires a comprehensive consideration. All the circumstances of the individual case must be taken into account. The tenant must explain and, if necessary, prove what losses he has suffered as a result of the closure and what reasonable efforts he has made to compensate for the upcoming losses. In doing so, only the object of the rental agreement must be taken into account. With one important exception. The financial benefits that the tenant has obtained from state funds in order to compensate for these pandemic disadvantages must, as a rule, also be taken into account when examining unreasonableness. However, ordinary loans from the government should not be taken into consideration, as the tenant does not achieve final compensation for the loss of turnover incurred thanks to them. A threat to the tenant's maintenance is not required. However, if this is the case and can be demonstrated, this is another circumstance to be considered in the balancing of interests. Finally, the interests of the landlord must also be kept in mind, for example the extent to which the landlord is economically dependent on the rent.

4 Summary

A comparison between the two legal orders—Poland and Germany—in terms of the reaction concerning the amount of rent from a rental agreement under the conditions of the CoVid-19 pandemic allows for the conclusion that—despite differences at the systemic level—similar solutions are generally applied. In fact, both countries reject automatic rulings leading to the burdening of only one of the parties to the rental agreement with the consequences of the CoVid-19 pandemic, or being more specifically—the lockdown.

The prevailing view is that in the exceptional conditions related to the virus and its impact on socio-economic life, the key importance should be attributed to flexible instruments, applied by the courts, on the basis of their reasonableness and assessment of the individual circumstances of a specific case. Therefore, in the case of Polish law, the application of Article 357[1] of the Polish Civil Code is proposed, while in German law, the application of Section 313 of the BGB is recommended.

Although the view has been expressed about the two institutions that they are different—as Article 357[1] of the Polish Civil Code is supposed to prescribe taking into account the economic hardship of the parties, whereas § 313 BGB also demands taking into account other circumstances, it should be noted that in practice the application of both provisions is very similar. At the same time, it must be borne in mind that the applicability of both provisions is never automatic and practice of law—very cautiously—requires that they are not applied in an entirely thoughtless manner.

References

Brzozowski A (2014) Wpływ zmiany okoliczności na zobowiązania. Klauzula rebus sic stantibus. Legalis, Warszawa

Brzozowski A (2019) Wykonanie zobowiązań. In: Brzozowski A, Jastrzębski J, Kaliński M, Skowrońska-Bocian E (eds) Zobowiązania. Część ogólna, Warszawa

Fikentscher W, Heinemann A (2017) Schuldrecht Allgemeiner und Besonderer Teil. Berlin

Kadner-Graziano T (2019) Comparative contract law. Cases, materials and exercises. Cheltenham

Kaliński M (2022) Nadzwyczajność zmian jako przesłanka zastosowania klauzuli rebus sic stantibus (polemika z Adamem Brzozowskim). Państwo i Prawo (9):129–139

Kowalów-Ziułkowska J, Stasiewicz M (2022) Stosowanie klauzuli rebus sic stantibus w trakcie pandemii Covid-19. Monitor Prawniczy (1):21–26

Lackoroński B (2012) Klauzula rebus sic stantibus a odpowiedzialność ex contractu. Państwo i Prawo (3):65–74

Looschelders D (2018) Schuldrecht. Allgemeiner Teil, Düsseldorf

Mataczyński M, Saczywko M (2021) In: Gutowski M (ed) Kodeks cywilny. Tom II. Komentarz. Art. 353 – 626. Legalis

Morek (2022) In: Osajda K (ed) Kodeks cywilny. Komentarz, Legalis

Nowak-Górski B, Mróz D, Olszak K (2020) Stosowanie klauzuli rebus sic stantibus w dobie epidemii wirusa SARS-CoV-2. Monitor Prawniczy (10):507–514

Piotr Ratusznik Doctoral student at Warsaw University, author of many publications concerning tort law, contract law as well as law of new technologies.

Socio-Economic Implications of Covid-19 and the Imposition of Contractual Penalties upon Contractors Performing Public Procurement

Izabella Gil

Abstract This study conducts a comprehensive examination of the effectiveness of Polish legal regulations implemented during the COVID-19 pandemic in safeguarding entrepreneurs from the detrimental effects of the global crisis. The research delves into the specific issue of the impact of the pandemic on the imposition of contractual penalties upon contractors engaged in public procurement and examines the adequacy of legal protections for actors in such extraordinary, global situations.

1 The Purpose of Regulations Introduced in the Event of a State of Epidemic or State of Epidemic Threat

The socio-economic implications of COVID-19 are and will continue to be experienced by various people, especially those conducting business activities, despite the formal revocation of the epidemic state in the territory of the Republic of Poland, since the state of epidemic emergency remains maintained.[1] In that regard, measures

[1]As a result of the outbreak of SARS-CoV-2 virus infections in the territory of the Republic of Poland, an epidemic threat state was first introduced, which was turned into a state of the epidemic, subsequently also lifted and once again replaced by an epidemic threat state. Under § 1 of the Regulation of the Minister of Health of 13.3.2020 on declaring an epidemic threat state in the area of the Republic of Poland [Regulation of the Minister of Health of 13.3.2020 on Declaring an Epidemic Threat in the Area of the Republic of Poland (Journal of Laws, item 433, as amended); https://sip.lex.pl/#/act/18969933?unitId=par(1)&cm=DOCUMENT; a state of epidemic threat was introduced, which was in effect from 14 March 2020 until 20 March 2020, following the entry into force of the regulations of § 1 of the § 1 of the Regulation of the Minister of Health of 20.3.2022 on lifting an epidemic threat state in the area of the Republic of Poland [Regulation of

I. Gil (✉)
University of Wrocław, Wrocław, Poland
e-mail: izabella.gil@uwr.edu.pl

E. Hadrowicz (ed.), *Polish Entrepreneurial Law in the Era of the COVID-19 Pandemic*, Ius Gentium: Comparative Perspectives on Law and Justice 114,
https://doi.org/10.1007/978-3-031-57480-1_8

adopted by individual countries to mitigate the negative socio-economic consequences, not only for the duration but also after the cessation of all kinds of sudden, unpredictable events, especially those having global implications, should be assessed positively. The conceptual scope of an epidemic is very broad, which is why it has been proposed to be modified by the doctrine.[2]

Depending on the socio-economic system, as well as the economic potential of a given country, various types of legal measures and other forms of aid are being put in place to mitigate the consequences resulting from the wide range of negative effects that have occurred due to the spread of the SARS-CoV-2 virus. The appearance of an epidemic threat of such a large scale was the basis for implementing legal solutions also within the Polish legal framework, involving the adoption of legal instruments intended to minimize the consequences of challenging for many entities situation, which was brought about by the pandemic and associated with the emergence of the infectious disease COVID-19, caused by the SARS-CoV-2 virus. The steadily deteriorating economic condition of many Polish entities during COVID-19 caused the state authorities to undertake measures aimed at supporting these entities also in financial terms. In view of this phenomenon, questions have been raised in the literature as to whether current regulations sufficiently protect entrepreneurs from the adverse effects of COVID-19. It has been pointed out that in regard to the existing pandemic situation, in order to mitigate its consequences, it is necessary to take legislative action and introduce special legal provisions that provide adequate legal protection for economic entities.[3] The literature on the subject holds the view that it is necessary to distinguish the unpredictability of the consequences of a change in relations from the unpredictability of a change in relations themselves[4] since unpredictable can be the change itself (including the cause of the change, such as war, plague, economic crisis, etc.), as well as the effect on the circumstances relating to the fulfillment of legal relations, and consequently the effect on the ability of the parties to perform the contract.[5] It has been considered, among other things, whether the state of epidemic threat may also be covered by the concept of force majeure. Doubts have arisen in the literature[6] regarding the suspension or withholding of the run of prescription periods in connection with entering into force

the Minister of Health of 13.3.2020 on Lifting an Epidemic Threat in the Area of the Republic of Poland (Journal of Laws, item 490, as amended); https://sip.lex.pl/#/act/18972566?unitId=par(1)&cm=DOCUMENT. As of 20.3.2020, an epidemic state was in force in the territory of the Republic of Poland, which was subsequently lifted as of 16.5.2022, following the entry into force of the Ordinance of the Minister of Health of 12 May 2022 on the revocation of an epidemic state in the territory of the Republic of Poland [Resolution of the Minister of Health of 12.5.2022 on the revocation of an epidemic state in the territory of the Republic of Poland (Journal of Laws, item 1027); https://sip.lex.pl/#/act/19240388?cm=DOCUMENT.

[2] Bosek (2022), p. 182.

[3] Reasoning of the bill Parliamentary form of the ninth parliamentary term, No. 299.

[4] Kondek (2021), p. 77.

[5] Bagińska (2010), p. 183.

[6] Kondek (2021), pp. 34–37.

of regulation contained in Article 15zzr of the Act of 2.3.2020 on Special Solutions for Preventing, Counteracting and Combating COVID-19, Other Infectious Diseases and Crisis They Caused,[7] which has been repealed.[8] The pandemic situation was analyzed in the context of the performance of obligations under civil law contracts, and in particular as to whether the pandemic can be recognized as a situation that may exempt the debtor from liability for failure to meet contractual deadlines since the Article 354 § 1 of the Polish Civil Code[9] (introducing the requirement to perform the obligation in compliance with its content and in a manner consistent with its socio-economic purpose and the principles of social coexistence, and if established customs exist in this regard—also in a manner corresponding to these customs) pertains to the ordinary state of affairs, where the debtor, while exercising due diligence, may perform the obligation arising from the concluded contract.[10] Whereas regulation mitigating consequences of inability to perform the contract contained in the Article 357[1] § of the Polish Civil Code (according to which—if, due to an extraordinary change of circumstances, the performance of the obligation would be connected with excessive difficulties or would threaten one of the parties with substantial loss, which the parties did not foresee at the time of the conclusion of the contract, the court may, after considering the interests of the parties, in accordance with the principles of social coexistence, determine the manner of performance of the obligation, the amount of the payment or even adjudicate on the termination of the contract) may be insufficient to mitigate the consequences of extraordinary states and events, such as a pandemic This is particularly true given the view expressed in the case law that "The essence of the extraordinary change in circumstances referred to in Article 357[1] §1 of the Polish Civil Code is specifically a change in external relations which has an extraordinary effect on the possibility or manner of performance of an obligation, most typically by one of the parties. The *rebus sic stantibus* clause, however, will not apply in the event of circumstances, including extraordinary ones, arising on the part of any of the parties to a given contractual relationship. Therefore, it will not apply in the case of non-performance or improper performance of an obligation by one of the parties, including the situation where the cause for this is attributed to third parties".[11]

The consequences of the pandemic were experienced to various extents and intensities in all sectors of manufacturing, tourism, catering, and construction, which often also entailed the inability to properly execute contracts because of the

[7] Act of 2.3.2020 on special solutions related to the prevention, counteraction, and combating of COVID-19, other infectious diseases, and emergencies caused by them (Journal of Laws of 2020, item 695 as amended).

[8] Under Article 46 of the Act of 14.5.2020 on amending certain laws with regard to protective measures in connection with the spread of the SARS-CoV-2 virus (Journal of Laws of 2020, item 875).

[9] Article 354 § 1 of Act of 23.4.1964. The Polish Civil Code (i.e. Journal of Laws of 2022, item 1360, as amended).

[10] Kondek (2021), pp. 38, 42.

[11] Judgment of Court of Appeals in Warsaw of 9.5.2022, VII AGa 965/21, LEX No. 3425394.

disrupted delivery dates of goods on the international market. The result of the deteriorating economic-commercial situation was difficulty in liquidity, which was reflected in the deterioration of the liquidity of other entities and considerable complications in acquiring external funding. Besides taking measures to overcome economic problems, entrepreneurs have also met social difficulties brought by illness, their own quarantine, or of those who cooperate with them, as well as their employees and entities cooperating with them. The epidemic made it necessary to restrict personal interactions in larger gatherings of people. As an example may serve the regulation of 13.3.2020 issued by the Minister of Health on the declaration of a state of epidemic threat in the territory of the Republic of Poland, and the regulation of 20.3.2020 on the declaration of a state of the epidemic in the territory of the Republic of Poland, which imposed a temporary restriction on the running of certain activities, reflected in a total or partial ban on such activities.

These unfavorable social, economic, and commercial phenomena have in many cases led to the withholding of orders, the rescission or termination of concluded contracts, or the emergence of claims for delays or nonperformance of concluded contracts. Subsequently, the inability to meet public law and civil law obligations typically results in a state of insolvency, which gives grounds for the implementation of restructuring proceedings or even the declaration of bankruptcy of the entity. Declaration of bankruptcy triggers the initiation of a procedure involving the sale of the bankrupt's assets, in order to evenly satisfy creditors, but it also leads to redundancies, which negatively affect the county's economy, resulting in widespread social consequences.

Such negative socio-economic consequences, therefore, require stimulating negative state interference and introduction of legal regulations ensuring the maintenance of financial liquidity of entrepreneurs, enabling the preservation of jobs also during the state of epidemic or epidemic threat, for it is this sector of state functioning that significantly affects the stability of the economy.

2 State of Emergency vs. State of Epidemic or Epidemic Threat

It should be agreed that it will not always be possible to identify a state of emergency as a special situation occurring when there is a high likelihood of the rapid and uncontrolled spread of a disease that requires taking measures to simultaneously ensure the protection of public health. For the above mentioned reasons, a special regulation was introduced under the anti-crisis Act of 2.3.2020. Article 1(1) of this act determines the subject matter, pursuant to which the act provides for:

1. the methods and mode of prevention and combating the infection with SARS-CoV-2 virus and the spread of the infectious disease in humans caused by this virus, including the methods and mode of taking anti-epidemic and preventive measures in order to neutralize the sources of infection and cut the pathways of spread of this infectious disease;

2. the obligations of public administration bodies in preventing and combating the infection or infectious disease specified in point 1;
3. rights and obligations of healthcare providers and recipients as well as other persons residing in the territory of the Republic of Poland in the prevention and combating of the infection or contagious disease referred to in point 1;
4. the terms of financial coverage for carrying out the tasks referred to in points 1–3, in particular procedure for financing health care services for persons with suspected infection or infectious disease referred to in point 1, in order to ensure proper access to diagnostics and treatment for these persons.

Due to dynamic changes caused by the pandemic, the analyzed act has been amended numerous times (69 times), including changes resulting from lifting the state of epidemic and the state of epidemic threat.[12] The primary purpose of the act in question was "counteracting COVID-19," which, according to Article 2(2) of the act, means "all activities related to the combating of infection, prevention of its spread, precaution, and control of the consequences, including socio-economic consequences, of the disease, referred to in section 1 thereof."

3 Special Legislation Relating to the Performance of Public Procurement in the Event of an Epidemic or State of Epidemic Threat

The period of the pandemic caused by the COVID-19 virus has adversely affected the performance of contracts, including those carried out under public procurement. A number of entities that carried out construction contracts faced difficulties in performing them or were forced to stop the performance altogether for reasons outside of their control. The above situation, resulting from the pandemic, was acknowledged by the legislature, and legal instruments were introduced to limit the adverse consequences in the public procurement sector. The measures implemented included "solutions to assist participants in the public procurement market, including measures preventing loss of liquidity for contractors, as well as those designed to increase the participation of SME sector in the public procurement market. On the one hand, the possibility of, i.a., offsetting contractual penalties from the salaries of contractors carrying out public procurement during the COVID-19 epidemic state and for 3 months after its lift was restricted. On the other hand, regulations for part payments, advance payments, and performance bonds have been introduced".[13]

Initially, Article 6 of the anti-crisis act (i.e., in its original version) stipulated that the provisions of the Public Procurement Act do not apply to contracts for goods or

[12] Some of the provisions contained in the anti-crisis act no longer apply. The last amendment to this act was made under Article 217 of the Act of 1.2022 on the profession of a paramedic and the self-government of paramedics (Journal of Laws of 2022, item 2705).

[13] Reasoning for project No. 382, p. 3.

services necessary to combat COVID-19 where there is a high likelihood of rapid and uncontrolled spread of the disease, or where the protection of public health requires it. The wording of this provision raised interpretation doubts with respect to the regulation contained in Article 2(2) and Article 2(10) of the Public Procurement Act, and in particular in the context of the definition of "supply" understood as the acquisition of things and other goods, in particular under a contract of sale, delivery, tenancy with no right to collect fruits, tenancy with the right to collect fruits, and leasing with or without a purchase option, which may additionally include placement or installation. The term "goods" also raised interpretation questions, as it is not defined in the Public Procurement Act. It was considered, in particular, "whether this is a legislator's mistake or a deliberate attempt to narrow the scope of the exclusion. Regardless of the reason, the use of the term "goods" by the legislator means that it should not be synonymous with the term "supply".[14] Doubts were also raised regarding the very construction of the introduced exclusion involving the phrase "the provisions of the Public Procurement Act do not apply", as a result of which "the legislator decided a priori not to apply Public Procurement Act, leaving no discretion in this regard on the part of the contracting party, (…) the discussed provision does not authorize the contracting party to decide on the subject of exclusion but explicitly excludes the application of the provisions of Public Procurement Act.[15]" Subsequently, under Article 1(5) of the Act of 31 March 2020 amending the Act on Special Solutions Related to the Prevention, Counteraction and Combating of COVID-19, Other Infectious Diseases and Crisis Situations Caused by Them, and Certain Other Acts, it was amended as of 31 March 2020, by adding that the act of 29 January 2004—The Public Procurement Act shall not apply to contracts awarded by Bank Gospodarstwa Krajowego, Polski Fundusz Rozwoju Spółka Akcyjna or regional development funds referred to in Article 13 (1a) of the Act of 5 of June 1998 on voivodeship self-government (Journal of Laws of 2019, item 512, 1571 and 1851), related to carrying out:

1. tasks related to the operation of funds established, entrusted or transferred under separate provisions and related to the carrying out of government programs or other programs performed financed with public funds, or
2. tasks relating to the use of resources from such funds—which concern support instruments necessary to counteract the adverse economic consequences of the occurrence of COVID-19 (Article 6(2) of the COVID-19 impact act).

Pursuant to Article 15r (1) of the COVID-19 Act additional obligations have also been imposed on the parties to a public procurement contract, in the sense of in the Act of 11 September 2019—Public Procurement Law, to immediately inform each other of the influence of the occurrence of COVID-19 on the proper performance of this contract, insofar as such influence has occurred or is likely to occur. The parties to the contract should prove this influence by enclosing to the information mentioned in the first sentence statements or documents, which may relate in particular to:

---

[14] Falkowska (2020), Rn 3 and 4.

[15] Falkowska (2020), Rn 8 and 9.

1. absence of employees or persons performing work in return for remuneration on basis other than employment relationship, who participate or could participate in the performance of the contract;
2. decisions issued in connection with the counteraction of COVID-19 by the Chief Sanitary Inspector or the national voivodeship sanitary inspector acting on his authorization, which impose an obligation on the contractor to take certain preventive or monitoring actions;
3. instructions or decisions issued by voivodes, the minister competent for health or the Prime Minister, related to counteracting COVID-19, as provided for in Article 11(1–3);
4. suspension of deliveries of products, product components or materials, difficul ties in access to equipment or difficulties in transportation services;
5. other circumstances that preclude or considerably limit the ability to perform the contract;
6. the circumstances referred to in points 1–5, to the extent that they concern the subcontractor or further subcontractor.

Either party to the contract specified in Section 1 may request additional representations or documents confirming the influence of circumstances related to the occurrence of COVID-19 on the proper performance of this contract (Article 15r(2) of the COVID-19 act). A party to the agreement, on the basis of the received representations or documents specified in sections 1 and 2, shall, within 14 days from the date of their receipt, inform the other party about their position, along with a reasoning regarding the influence of the circumstances referred to in section 1 on the proper performance of the contract. If the party to the agreement has received further representations or documents, the time limit is calculated from the date of their receipt (Article 15r(3) of the COVID-19 act). Significant is the regulation contained in Article 15r(4) of the COVID-19 act, according to which—the contracting authority, upon determining that the circumstances related to the occurrence of COVID-19, referred to in section 1, influence the proper performance of the contract referred to in section 1, shall, upon consultation with the contractor, amend the contract referred to in Article 455(1)(4) of the Act of 11 September 2019—Public Procurement Law, in particular by:

1. changing the date of performance of the contract or its part, or temporarily suspending the performance of the contract or its part,
2. changing the manner of supply, services or construction works,
3. changing the scope of the contractor's performance and accordingly, the remuneration or the manner of settlement of the contractor's remuneration—insofar as the increase in remuneration caused by each subsequent change does not exceed 50% of the value of the initial contract. Should it be determined that circumstances related to the occurrence of COVID-19 may influence the proper performance of the contract, the contracting authority, after consultation with the contractor, may amend the contract (Article 15r(4a) of the COVID-19 act).

However, if the public procurement contract contains provisions more favorable to the contractor than those provided by section 4, those provisions shall apply when amending the contract, provided that the circumstances related to the occurrence of COVID-19 referred to in section 1 may not constitute an independent basis for exercising the contractual right to rescind the contract (Article 15r(5) of the COVID-19 act). The contractor and the subcontractor, upon determining that the circumstances related to the occurrence of COVID-19, may influence or influence the proper performance of their contract related to carrying out the public procurement or its part, shall agree upon an appropriate amendment to this contract, in particular, they may change the time limit for the performance of the contract or its part, temporarily suspend the performance of the contract or its part, change the manner of performance of the contract or change the scope of mutual obligations (Article 15r(7) of the COVID-19 act). Should the contract be amended, if such amendment applies to the part of the contract to be carried out by a subcontractor, the contractor and the subcontractor shall agree on an appropriate amendment to their contract, in a manner that ensures that the terms of the subcontractor's performance of that contract are not less favorable than those of the amended contract (Article 15r(8) of the COVID-19 act).

During a state of epidemic threat or a state of epidemic and consequential movement restrictions, public procurement contracts shall, under pain of nullity, be concluded in writing, or, upon the consent of the contracting authority, in an electronic form signed with a qualified electronic signature (Article 15r(10) of the anti-crisis act). Article 15r(11) of the anti-crisis act further specified that the provisions of sections (1)–(9) also apply respectively to public procurement contracts excluded from the application of the act of 11 September 2019—Public Procurement Law.

4 Imposition of Contractual Penalties on Contractors Carrying Out a Public Procurement in the Event of an Epidemic or a State of Epidemic Threat

The possibility of imposing contractual penalties is governed by the provision of Article 483 §1 of the Polish Civil Code, pursuant to which the parties may specify in the contract that redress of damage resulting from non-performance or improper performance of a non-monetary obligation shall take place by payment of a specified sum. In the case of the non-performance or improper performance of the obligation, the contractual penalty shall be due to the creditor in the amount stipulated for that case regardless of the damage suffered.[16] The Supreme Court has held that a contractual penalty is an extra-contractual provision introduced into a contract under freedom of contract.[17] The opinion should be supported that "The contractual penalty, as means of redressing damages by a contractual stipulation that redress of damages resulting from non-performance or improper performance of a non-monetary obligation shall be made by payment of a specified sum, takes the place

[16] Article 484 § 1 of the Polish Civil Code.

[17] Supreme Court judgment from 8.8.2008, ref. V CSK 85/08, LEX No. 457785.

of compensation (Article 361 § 2 in conjunction with Article 471 of the Polish Civil Code). However, even though the occurrence of damage and its value is irrelevant for the emergence of a claim for payment of contractual penalties, the prerequisites for liability must correspond to those upon satisfaction of which damages can be claimed *ex contractu*".[18] The contractual penalty is a type of "surrogate for compensation" for the improper performance of a contractual non-monetary obligation in the sense that the parties upon the conclusion of the contract specify in advance a contractual penalty in the event of non-performance or improper performance of the obligation by the debtor, and this penalty compensates for all negative consequences arising for the creditor as a result of the breach of the obligation.[19] Given that the contractual penalty is subject to the regime of liability for non-performance or improper performance of an obligation, it is the duty of the entitled party to prove the existence of prerequisites for imposing a contractual penalty, and the challenge of this presumption shall be achieved by proving that it occurred for reasons that are not attributable for the party obliged to pay contractual penalties and rests with this party.[20]

Should the public procurement contract, as defined by the act of 11 September 2019—Public Procurement Law, contain provisions regarding contractual penalties or damages for its non-performance or improper performance due to specified circumstances, the party to the public procurement contract shall demonstrate the influence of the circumstances related to the occurrence of COVID-19 on its due performance and the influence of the circumstances related to the occurrence of COVID-19, on the validity of establishment and claiming of these penalties or compensations, or on their amount (Art. 15r(6) of the anti-crisis act).

Another solution temporarily ensuring the inability to pursue claims by public procurers towards contractors was the regulation introduced under Article 15r[1] of the Act of 19 June 2020 on subsidies to the interest rate of bank loans granted to entrepreneurs affected by the effects of COVID-19 and on a simplified procedure for approval of the arrangement due to the occurrence of COVID-19 (entered into force on 24 June 2020). Under the provision in question, during the state of epidemic threat or state of epidemic announced in connection with COVID-19, and for 90 days from the date of the lifting of the state that was last in force, the contracting authority may not offset the contractual penalty reserved for non-performance or improper performance of the contract referred to in Article 15r (1), from the contractor's remuneration or from their other receivables, and may not seek satisfaction from the performance bond for this contract, should the event for which the penalty was reserved occurred during the state of epidemic threat or state of epidemic. The above mentioned provision has been regarded by the doctrine as a supplement to the regulation contained in the provision of Article 15r by limiting the possibility of offsetting contractual penalties against the contractor's salary or other receivables, as well as seeking satisfaction from the

[18] Judgment of the Court of Appeals in Warsaw from 22.9.2022, V ACa 109/22, LEX No. 3433736.
[19] Reasoning of the judgment of the Court of Appeals in Warsaw from 24.5.2019, VII AGa 1195/18.
[20] Judgment of the Court of Appeals in Katowice from 29.1.2015, I ACa 680/14, LEX No. 1661150.

performance bond.[21] The case law established that "it clearly follows from this regulation that if, during the state of epidemic threat or an epidemic state declared in connection with COVID-19, circumstances causing the contractor's liability for damages occur, the ordering party may not deduct the contractual penalty reserved for non-performance or improper performance of the contract from the contractor's remuneration or from other receivables".[22]

Whereas, provision of Article 15s of the anti-crisis act provides that the failure to establish or recover from a party to the contract referred to in Art. 15r (1) receivables arising in connection with non-performance or improper performance of the public procurement contract as a result of circumstances related to the occurrence of COVID-19, referred to in Article 15r (1) of the anti-crisis act, does not constitute a violation of public finance discipline, referred to in Article 5(1)(1) and (2) and Article 17(6) of the Act of 17 December 2004 on Responsibility for Violation of Public Finance Discipline.

The above regulation, limiting the offset of the contractual penalty reserved for non-performance or improper performance of the contract and the possibility of seeking satisfaction from the performance bond during the period of the state of epidemic threat or the state of epidemic declared in connection with COVID-19, and additionally for 90 days from the date of cancellation of the state that was last in force, has expired.[23] The reasoning for this amendment states that "The maintenance of the current regulations would have negative consequences for contractors, guarantors, as well as for contracting authorities, which may face difficulties in enforcing aggregated contractual penalties. The proposed regulations are in line with the postulates of contracting authorities and banks, that from the beginning pointed out issues arising from the application of Article $15r^1$ of the Act and advocated for its amendment or repeal".[24]

However, it was reserved[25] that in the case of claims for which recovery was limited under Article 15r1(1) of the COVID-19 effects act, which related to events that occurred:

1. before 31 December 2020, the contracting authority may offset from the contractor's remuneration or from his other receivables, as well as claim satisfaction from the performance bond, but not earlier than from 1 October 2022;
2. from 1 January 2021 to 31 December 2021, the contracting authority may offset the contractor's remuneration or its other receivables, as well as claim satisfaction from the performance bond, but not earlier than from 1 January 2023;

---

[21] Falkowska (2020), Rn 6.

[22] Judgment of the District Court in Bydgoszcz—VIII Commercial Division from 912.2021, VIII GC 74/21, Legalis.

[23] Pursuant to Article 10 of the Act from 5.8.2022 amending the Act on the Government Road Development Fund and certain other laws, Journal of Laws item 1768.

[24] Reasoning for the governmental bill amending the Act on the Government Road Development Fund and certain other acts Form No. 2398, https://www.sejm.gov.pl/Sejm9.nsf/druk.xsp?nr=2398.

[25] Article 32(1) of the aforementioned Act of 5 August 2022 amending the Act on the Government Road Development Fund and Certain Other Laws.

3. from 1 January 2022 to the date of entering into force of this act, the contracting authority may offset from the contractor's remuneration or from his other receivables, as well as claim satisfaction from the performance bond, but not earlier than from 1 April 2023.

The prescription periods of those claims the course of which had not begun by the date of entry into force of the aforementioned law, and for those which begun and have been suspended until that date, shall respectively begin to run or continue to run from 1.10.2022 from 1.1.2023, from 1.4.2023—provided that the prescription period may not expire earlier than 30 days from the date on which the suspended period began to run.[26]

Furthermore, should the performance bond expire in the period from the date of entry into force of this Act until 13.10.2022, 13.1.2023, 13.4.2023, respectively—the contracting authority may seek satisfaction from this security before the expiration of the periods indicated in paragraph 1 point 1–3, respectively, unless the contractor, 14 days prior to the expiration of the bond, each time extends it or submits a new bond, the terms of which will be accepted by the contracting authority.[27]

The provision of the Article $15r^1$ of the anti-crisis act regulated time limits on the admissibility of set-offs and satisfaction from the performance bonds by the public contracting authority, therefore, with its repeal, an appropriate postponement of the periods for pursuing claims by contracting authorities and adjustment of the validity dates of contract performance bonds needed to be applied.[28]

The aforesaid legislative procedure confirms that the separate qualification of unforeseen circumstances enables a more flexible response in terms of the forms of support provided by the state. Though the contracting authority was legally able to impose contractual penalties on the contractor for the duration of the epidemic on the basis of the public procurement contract, it was temporarily unable to exercise this right. The restoration under the abovementioned regulation of the contracting authorities' right to pursue claims and to make a set-off of the contractual penalty after the lift of the epidemic state complies with the so-called "necessity clause", which is one of the constitutional measurements of the power of the state authorities to limit the freedoms and rights of its citizens.[29]

It is the view to be shared that Polish legal regulations pertaining to civil law relations do not provide sufficient legal protection for the so-called "unsettled, crisis times", for the duration of which "norms are needed either to adapt the content of the obligation to the circumstances or to constitute safety vents justifying the non-performance or improper performance of the obligation".[30] It has been criticized in

---

[26] Article 32(2) of the aforementioned Act from 5.8.2022 amending the Act on the Government Road Development Fund and certain other acts.

[27] Article 32(3) of the aforementioned Act from 5.8.2022 amending the Act on the Government Road Development Fund and certain other acts.

[28] Reasoning of bill 61–62, Sejm of the 9th term, as well as, Falkowska (2020), Legalis.

[29] Machnikowska (2022), p. 81.

[30] Kondek (2021), pp. 42–43.

the doctrine that most of the restrictions introduced in connection with the COVID-19 pandemic lacked a sufficient legal basis,[31] and the regulations failed to meet the standards of proper legislation,[32] often limiting fundamental rights of individuals,[33] did not always reflect the purpose of the restrictions[34] were chaotically and vaguely regulated, or that contained issues unrelated directly to the pandemic itself.[35] This calls for the enactment of more universal legal solutions of statutory rank,[36] which will allow for the legal protection of the actors in such extraordinary situations of a global nature.

References

Bagińska E (2010) Klauzula rebus sic stantibus – współczesne zastosowania. GSP (24):183

Bosek L (2022) Stan epidemii. Konstrukcja prawna, Warszawa

Czarnow S (2021) Między stanem epidemii a stanem klęski żywiołowej - COVID-19 a niektóre prawa człowieka. Radca Prawny. Zeszyty Naukowe (3):13

Kondek JM (2021) Wpływ sytuacji kryzysowych na stosunki cywilnoprawne. Warszawa

Falkowska M (2020) In: Szmid K (ed) Ustawa o szczególnych rozwiązaniach związanych z zapobieganiem, przeciwdziałaniem i zwalczaniem covid-19, innych chorób zakaźnych oraz wywołanych nimi sytuacji kryzysowych. Komentarz do art. 6 Rn 3 i 4. Warszawa

Florczak-Wątor M (2020) Niekonstytucyjność ograniczeń praw i wolności jednostki wprowadzonych w związku z epidemią COVID-19 jako przesłanka odpowiedzialności odszkodowawczej państwa. Państwo i Prawo (12):17

Izdebski H (2020) In: Gardocka T, Jagiełło D (eds) Pandemia COVID-19 a prawa i wolności obywatela, Warszawa

Machnikowska A (2022) Zasada jawności w postępowaniu procesowym – modernizacja czy marginalizacja? Wybrane zagadnienia, Polski Proces Cywilny (1):81

Radajewski M (2021) Stan zagrożenia epidemicznego oraz stan epidemii jako formy prawne ochrony zdrowia publicznego. Przegląd Legislacyjny (4):74–75

Roszkiewicz J (2022) Granice ograniczeń wolności gospodarczej wprowadzonych w celu przeciwdziałania epidemii (uwagi na tle orzecznictwa sądów administracyjnych). Zeszyty Naukowe Sądownictwa Administracyjnego (2):43

Trociuk S (2021) Prawa i wolności w stanie epidemii, Warszawa

Izabella Gil Professor at the University of Wroclaw; attorney-at-law with many years of experience in representing entrepreneurs; lecturer at trainings for trainees, legal advisers, attorneys-at-law, judges, and prosecutors; specializes in broadly understood civil proceedings, as well as bankruptcy, restructuring and economic proceedings; author of many studies (monographs, comments, articles) devoted to these fields.

[31] Radajewski (2021), pp. 74–75.

[32] Czarnow (2021), p. 13.

[33] Trociuk (2021), pp. 15–16.

[34] Florczak-Wątor (2020), p. 17.

[35] Izdebski (2020), p. 32.

[36] Roszkiewicz (2022), p. 43.

Epidemic-Related Protection of the Indebted Employee, and the Impact on Circumstances of the Entrepreneur Employer Regarding Salary Attachment

Tadeusz Zembrzuski

Abstract The right to collect debt effectively in judicial enforcement proceedings has been significantly curtailed during the COVID-19 epidemic. Outcomes of reducing employees' livelihood income have been temporarily moderated by increasing the garnishment-exempt amount. Not only does this regulation have significant influence over the debtor's (employee's) procedural circumstances—it also indirectly affects businesses (entrepreneurs) who are also employers, i.e. entities obliged to provide benefits to the enforcement debtor.

Legal provisions have opened up the regulation wide to potential abuse in application, encouraging dishonest and disloyal behaviour and fuelling claimant attitudes. They clearly boost and favour the debtor's procedural position at the expense of creditor rights. The statutory mechanism does not differentiate between individual debtors, failing to account for confirmed family or asset property circumstances. It further undermines the assumption that enforcement proceedings under civil law should serve the purpose of securing efficiency and true effectiveness of benefits arising from final judicial rulings. Procedural regulations ought to be assessed in view of values underpinning the principle of proportionality, and the related need to ensure equality for all participants in legal proceedings.

1 Introduction

Regardless of whether businessmen or consumers, all debtors should voluntarily pay their civil law claims. In practice, however, debtors frequently avoid payment, or lack the capacity to cover claims. Hence the need to develop a legal protection

---

T. Zembrzuski (✉)
Faculty of Law and Administration, University of Warsaw, Warsaw, Poland
e-mail: zembrzuski@wpia.uw.edu.pl

E. Hadrowicz (ed.), *Polish Entrepreneurial Law in the Era of the COVID-19 Pandemic*, Ius Gentium: Comparative Perspectives on Law and Justice 114,
https://doi.org/10.1007/978-3-031-57480-1_9

system allowing forced claim collection.[1] A normative civil law enforcement mechanism,[2] the process has to comprise an enforcement stage. Writ of execution enforcement remains an essential operational component of broadly defined justice. Enforcement bodies, the lead role among them conferred upon the bailiff,[3] are obliged to perform duties stipulated in legal acts classified as writs of execution, their characteristics including enforceability.[4]

Effective and inescapable procedural instruments necessitate delivery under civil law obligations, offering a sense of legal security. All legal transactions benefit from the capacity to implement realisable norms. In combination with the principle of swift judicial enforcement,[5] effective enforcement remains an immanent component of the right to fair trial, and a prerequisite for economic development—the capacity to secure enforcement recognisable as swift and effective is essential.[6] Nonetheless, the effectiveness of judicial enforcement in practice is not particularly high, the debtor's position progressively reinforced over the years at the creditor's expense one of the reasons.[7]

2 Enforcement Proceedings in the COVID-19 Epidemic Context

The right to collect debt effectively in judicial enforcement proceedings has been significantly curtailed during the COVID-19 epidemic. From the year 2020 onward, multiple processual regulations have been introduced pursuant to the so-called COVID Law of March 2nd 2020[8] as well as other legislation. Attempts were made to influence the way courts of law functioned in emergency crisis conditions,[9] particularly in terms of the open justice principle[10]; the course of judicial proceedings with regard to so-called urgent case category was interfered with[11]; and judicial deadlines were tampered with.[12]

---

[1] Gaul (2003), p. 34.

[2] Zembrzuski (2017), p. 152.

[3] Bomba (2020), p. 22.

[4] Zembrzuski (2022b), p. 7.

[5] Derlatka (2017), p. 119.

[6] Łazarska (2012), p. 308.

[7] Romańska (2021), p. 502; Cieślak (2022), p. 21.

[8] The Law of March 2nd 2020 on special-purpose solutions linked to the prevention, deterrence and control of COVID-19, other infectious diseases and emergencies caused by the same (uniform text: *Journal of Laws* 2021, item 2095). Hereinafter referred to as *"the COVID-19 Law"*.

[9] Kulski (2020), p. 441.

[10] Kościółek (2021), p. 22; Litowski (2021), p. 68; Machnikowska (2021), p. 80.

[11] Gapska (2020), p. 949.

[12] Gołaczyński (2020), p. 396.

Regulations were hastily designed and amended in the early phase of the pandemic in particular, the incoherence and inconsistency of extensive legal regulations occasionally glaring.[13] Their typical features would include punctiliousness combined with attempts at introducing *ad hoc* solutions to crisis emergencies and ever-increasing doubts through hurried patching.[14] Legislative action taken at the time might well be considered a manifestation of the rightly stigmatised phenomenon of *"bypassing standards of proper legislation and deviating from good legal norms"*.[15] The functioning of assorted mechanisms introducing special-purpose legal circumstances for the epidemic period increasingly prompts critical reflection[16] and analysis.[17] The above becomes even more significant in view of the fact that the state of epidemic threat has not been formally revoked until this day.[18] In consequence, the judiciary in Poland shall continue operating in altered social and procedural reality for months to come.

With regard to regulations introduced in connection with the epidemic, controversial solutions regarding property (real estate) execution were pointed to most frequently.[19] Noted and analysed less often, not only are amendments to salary garnishment (Articles 880-888 of the Code of Civil Procedure)[20] significant in determining the indebted employee's procedural circumstances—they also, albeit indirectly, affect employers (most usually businesses) as entities obliged to provide benefits to the enforcement debtor.

Pieces of legislation commonly referred to as the "protective shield" or "shield legislation" have included the Law of May 14th 2020 amending selected acts of law with regard to protective measures taken in conjunction with the spread of the SARS-CoV-2 virus.[21] In Article 52, it references salary attachment, expanding debtor protection[22] through awarding additional enforcement waiver rights. The provision concerns amounts listed under Article 87[1] §1 of the Labour Code,[23] thus

---

[13] Zembrzuski (2022d), *Przeciwdziałanie*, p. 59.

[14] Zembrzuski (2022c), *Ograniczenia*, p. 4.

[15] Izdebski (2021), p. 29.

[16] In something of a counterbalance, it ought to be pointed out that legal regulations and institutions which had seen daylight at the time do include favourable solutions, primarily including the dynamically evolving computerisation of judicial proceedings and bold moves to introduce state-of-the-art technologies. See Gołaczyński, Kotecka-Kral (2020), p. 637; Gołaczyński (2022), p. 145; Gołaczyński and Dymitruk (2021), p. 685; Zembrzuski (2023), (in press).

[17] See e.g. the special edition of *Polski Proces Cywilny* 2022/1, *Wymiar sprawiedliwości w czasach pandemii COVID-19* (*Justice in Times of the COVID-19 Pandemic*).

[18] January 15th 2023.

[19] Kulski (2022), p. 149; Łyszczek (2022), p. 150; Ged (2022), p. 291.

[20] Code of Civil Procedure of November 17th 1964 (uniform text: *Journal of Laws* 2021, item 1805, as amended).

[21] Journal of Laws 2022, item 875. Hereinafter referred as "Shield Law".

[22] The provision came into force as of May 16th 2020.

[23] Labour Code Law of June 26th 1974 (uniform text: *Journal of Laws* 2022, item 1510, as amended). Hereinafter referred to as *"the LC"*.

interfering with principles stipulated in the Code of Civil Procedure. A special-purpose norm, it should therefore not be interpreted in an extending manner (*exceptiones non sunt extendendae*). Yet it also applies to enforcement against other recurrent benefits provided as subsistence or constituting the only source of income for private individual (natural person) debtors.[24]

3 Increases to Garnishment-Exempt Salary Attachment Amounts

Pursuant to Article 833 of the Code of Civil Procedure, employee salaries may be subject to enforcement to the extent stipulated in Labour Code provisions.[25] Consequently, employee salaries[26] are subject to collection for alimony purposes up to three-fifths, salary amount notwithstanding (Article 87 §3 item 1 of the LC), and up to one-half for purposes of other payables (Article 87 §3 item 2 of the LC). Yet the salary amount equal to the minimum wage full-time employees are eligible for shall be garnishment-exempt, said wage determined pursuant to separate legal provisions.[27,28]

Article 52 of the Shield Law mitigates the outcomes of reducing employees' livelihood income. Should an employee's pay be cut *"for reasons of measures taken by sanitary-and-epidemiological services on the territory of the Republic of Poland with intent to prevent SARS-CoV-2 viral infection"*, the garnishment-exempt amount shall be increased, the debtor's family circumstances taken into account as well. Consequently, limitations on enforcement have been introduced[29] through restrictions to the interest of one of the participants of proceedings to collect (the creditor) to the benefit of another participant (the debtor).

The application of the mechanism stipulated under Article 52 of the Shield Law has been linked to the subjective aspect of a household shared with family members of the indebted employee. The garnishment-exempt amount has been increased by 25% per each of the employee's non-earning dependents, albeit only until the end of the COVID-19 epidemic. Notwithstanding the above, a proviso has been

---

[24] Proper application of Article 87^1 of the LC arises from Article 833 $§1^1$, 2 and 2^1 of the Code of Civil Procedure.

[25] Kamieński (2022), p. 68.

[26] After social security premiums, Personal Income withholding Tax and Employee Equity Plan payments, had the contribution schedule not been cancelled.

[27] Pursuant to the Council of Ministers ordinance of September 13th 2022 regarding the minimum salary and minimum hourly wage in the year 2023 (*Journal of Laws* 2022, item 1952), the minimum salary shall amount to PLN 3,490,00 and PLN 3,600,00 as of January 1st 2023 and July 1st 2023, respectively.

[28] Should the employee be employed part-time, amounts stipulated under Article 871 §1 of the LC shall be reduced in proportion to the contract worktime.

[29] Romańska (2022), p. 173.

introduced,[30] reducing the exemption threshold to 50% of the amount stipulated under Article 87[1] §1 of the LC.

The Law lists a catalogue of family members defined as dependents the protective regulation shall apply to. These include spouses and/or co-parents, minor children, children younger than 25 years of age if in the education system, or any older children if with disabilities. With regard to the aforesaid catalogue, the Law stipulates that the above shall apply to the employee's own children, and/or children of the spouse or co-parent, provided that the employee had been the children's provider. The legislator acted upon the assumption that the formerly garnishment-exempt minimum wage amount will be insufficient to provide for the family of an employee with family dependents (non-earning spouse or children), especially if some employees find themselves unemployed or with pay reductions as a result of protective measures taken.[31]

4 Application Scope for Article 52 of the Shield Law

The standard arising from Shield Law Article 52 shall apply in three cases: (1) of the debtor employee's salary being cut by the employer; (2) of a family member of the debtor employee losing his/her source of income; (3) of the two aforesaid reasons coinciding. The aforementioned shall apply to occurrences tying in with measures stipulated in the COVID-19 Law, the act specifying i.a. the principles, procedures and public administration bodies' responsibilities in the area of preventing and deterring SARS-CoV-2 viral infections and the spread of the infectious disease caused by the said virus in the human population, including principles and procedures to be observed when taking anti-epidemic and preventive measures with a view to neutralise sources of infection and cutting the infectious disease spread pathways. The law further regulates rights and responsibilities of benefit providers, beneficiaries and other persons present on the territory of the Republic of Poland as concerns measures to prevent and/or deter infections and/or the infectious disease.

Rationale for applying Shield Law Article 52 may include termination of employment and/or remuneration conditions (the so-called amending notice) arising from the need to take measures to prevent SARS-CoV-2 viral infection, or the employer entering into[32] a collective agreement with trade union organisations and/or the in-house trade union organisation with regard to conditions and procedures of work to be performed in times of economic standstill or reduced working hours.[33]

---

[30] As of July 7th 2022.

[31] Justification to the governmental draft of the Law amending selected acts of law with regard to protective measures taken in conjunction with the spread of the SARS-CoV-2 virus, *Sejm* (Lower House) in the 9th term of office, Sejm publication No. 344, p. 78.

[32] Written form of the agreement shall be of consequence to evidence collection (*ad probationem*).

[33] Or with employee representatives, should there be no in-house trade union organisation.

Proportional pay cuts as a result of working hours having been reduced for the employee may be a factor as well.[34] Consequently, a reduction to the debtor employee's salary (or a family member losing his/her job) for any other reason shall not make the debtor eligible for applying the otherwise favourable Shield Law Article 52 solution.[35] Statutory and non-statutory factors[36] may occasionally coincide.

The effort to define and delineate aforementioned circumstances raises the occasional doubt – and may prove impossible under some circumstances. Reference sources argue that *"provisions increasing the garnishment-exempt salary amount have been based on sufficiently vague legislative prerequisites to merit extreme criticism, having offered vast space for potential creditor abuse with intent to harm."*[37] Greatest objections have been raised with regard to the failure to differentiate between debtor circumstances, and setting up a mechanism without heed for the debtor's true family and asset situation. The provision offers equal protection to persons in poor and sound financial condition.

The legislator has failed to specify the amount of salary reduction making employees eligible for an increase in the minimum garnishment-exempt remuneration amount. Article 52 of the Shield Law shall apply not only when the employee takes a considerable pay cut, but also if the reduction is symbolic. It goes without saying that any—however token—reduction in salary gives rise to a considerable increase in the garnishment-exempt amount. The interpretation doctrine accentuates that once remuneration is reduced by PLN 0.01 pursuant to the employee's agreement with the employer (entrepreneur), the minimum garnishment-exempt remuneration amount grows by 25%, a development easily classifiable as a manifestation of abusing the law.[38]

The rationale of the debtor employee's family member *"losing his/her source of income"* is equally vague in nature. The term cannot ostensibly be considered tantamount to *"loss of income"*[39] as stipulated in the COVID-19 Law.[40] This means that prerequisites for applying Shield Law Article 52 should not involve a reduction in salary or other earnings, but rather and exclusively their complete loss[41] pursuant to the employer terminating the employee's contract or failing to enter into a successive employment contract, the latter in case of fixed-term or trial period agreements. Furthermore, employment contract termination in an ordinary procedure (Article 30 *et seq.* of the LC) rather than on grounds of temporary epidemic provisions renders the use of preferences arising from Article 52 of the Shield Law unjustified as well.

---

[34] Pursuant to Article 5zzzzzq clause 1 item 3 and Article 15zzzzzs clause 1 of the COVID-19 Law.

[35] Marciniak (2020), p. 667.

[36] E.g. the employee losing his/her capacity or eligibility to perform work.

[37] Łyszczek (2022), p. 153.

[38] Rydel (2023), p. 434.

[39] Defined as a reduction in salary or wages earned under an employment or other job contract.

[40] Marciniak (2020), p. 669.

[41] Kulski (2022), p. 155.

One might also express doubt with regard to the aforesaid regulation's applicability should the employee's family member lose only one of many sources of income.

In light of the above, one might well conclude that Article 52 of the Shield Law is imprecise, opening the regulation wide to application-related abuse. The above arises from an assumption that the minimum salary as defined under Article 87^1 §1 of the Code of Civil Procedure is unconditional in nature, whereas the minimum salary increased pursuant to the Shield Law depends on specific conditions having been met, which makes it a relative (conditional) category.[42] Unwarranted use of increased debtor protection may arise from difficulties in verifying the presence of statutory prerequisites for the regulation under analysis, as well as from the variability of the amount of remuneration payable to the employee. An employee who had taken advantage of the Shield Law Article 52 standard cannot in all likelihood be expected to file a statement to confirm occurrences duly eliminating the prerequisites for an increase the garnishment-exempt amount under changed circumstances, such statement blatantly to his/her disadvantage. Furthermore, one cannot reasonably expect employers (entrepreneurs) to immediately redefine amounts to be collected and transferred to a bailiff once having obtained new and relevant information.

5 Proceedings Required to Increase the Garnishment-Exempt Amount

The procedure of determining the form of applying Article 52 of the Shield Law may trigger reasonable doubt as well. It remains unclear whether and to what extent due modification ought to arise from action taken by the employer (entrepreneur) or—conversely—by the bailiff handling the enforcement procedure and salary attachment.[43]

Choosing legislative phrasing of the garnishment-exempt amount to read *"being subject to an increase"* means that the outcome takes place by law, once one of the statutory prerequisites have been met. As an entity concerned with securing greater protection when under enforcement, the employee should file a respective demand listing justifying facts and evidence to support them.[44]

Notably, the court bailiff—when serving the employer with a demand to refrain from paying the debtor employee his/her remuneration in the amount of the benefit under enforcement and until the claim has been covered in full[45]—does not specify the amount of the part of the salary to be transferred to the enforcement body.[46]

[42] Marciniak (2020), p. 674.

[43] Kulski (2022), p. 156.

[44] Marciniak (2020), p. 673.

[45] Excepting the garnishment-exempt salary amount.

[46] Or to the creditor.

Respective calculations are then prepared by the employer,[47] their correctness only verifiable by the bailiff. This means that requests for increased garnishment-exempt amounts pursuant to Article 52 of the Shield Law should not be filed with the enforcement body then duly charged with assessing their admissibility and/or justifiability. Such requests should be addressed to the employer (most usually a business) responsible for handling the salary attachment.[48] The burden of proving circumstances justifying any increase in the garnishment-exempt salary amount rests with the employee, the employer charged with verifying all documents attached to the application. Request approval gives rise to an obligation to notify the court bailiff and creditor as appropriate without undue delay.

When in doubt, the bailiff may serve the employer with a demand to submit clarification with regard to applying Article 52 of the Shield Law.[49] The creditor is also authorised to seek and secure respective knowledge.[50] Should the employer refuse to provide clarification without justification, provide incomplete clarification, or knowingly submit false information, he/she may be penalised with a fine[51] or face criminal charges for failing to meet or abusing his/her professional duties.[52] The employer may be also held responsible for damages to the creditor (Article 886 §3 of the Code of Civil Procedure). It is, however, doubtful, whether creditor protection will be sufficient under such circumstances.

The legislator is responsible for designing rules and mechanisms of judicial enforcement in a form and manner rendering all measures taken as part of proceedings to seek claim coverage specific, non-arbitrary, and subject to no extension interpretation or analogy.[53] The introduction of any execution-related prerogatives should involve a detailed delineation of their nature, prerequisites and time restrictions. None of the above have been met in the case in point. Once interpreted, Shield Law Article 52 gives rise to grave doubts, indirectly encourages dishonest and disloyal behaviour, and fuels claimant attitudes. It can further cause disorientation in the business employer community.

Negative consequences of greater employee protection from the viewpoint of salary attachment effectiveness are already visible in practice,[54] frequently making it completely impossible for creditors to seek redress or enforce claims due to them.[55] The current circumstances generate something akin to an enforcement

---

[47] In consideration of Article 87 *et seq.* of the LC in conjunction with Article 833 of the Code of Civil Procedure. For details, see Marciniak (1986), p. 5; Jackowiak and Dalka (1992), p. 58; Antkiewicz (2010), p. 59.

[48] Once filed with the court bailiff, the request should also be served to the employer.

[49] Pursuant to Article 761 §1 of the Code of Civil Procedure.

[50] Borek, Wisłocki (2017), p. 173; Flaga-Gieruszyńska (2018), p. 317.

[51] Up to and including PLN 2,000.00.

[52] Marciniak (2002), p. 5.

[53] Zembrzuski (2022), *Kilka uwag*, p. 13.

[54] See statistical data in: Łyszczek (2022), p. 151.

[55] Marciniak (2020), p. 676.

immunity for the employee,[56] its presence destabilising business relations and breaching the principle of equality before the law.

6 Overprotection of the Debtor

The purpose and subject matter of any enforcement procedure turn it into a forum where creditor and debtor interests—contradictory to the core—tend to clash.[57] Protecting debtors against parties interfering with their rights and freedoms rests upon powerful axiological foundations, an expression of humane proceedings, respect for human dignity, and need to provide the debtor with a modicum of sustenance.[58] Yet whether directly or not, such protection usually occurs at the expense of the creditor. Debtors are gaining ever more extensive protection, the phenomenon giving rise to the following question: where should the line be drawn in terms of regulating measures to deliver under the rule of refraining from burdening the debtor beyond reasonable need when collecting financial claims?[59] Enforcement procedure effectiveness should be the fundamental point of reference. The need to protect the debtor should not occasion enforcement distortion caused by failing to respect the principle of equality for all parties concerned, or any other applicable rules of civil law proceedings.[60] Enforcement should remain a coherent system, a resultant of private and public interest protection to the extent required.[61] Failing that, one would be hard-pressed to imagine processes of building or boosting any sense of legal security.

Satisfying claims under private law in judicial enforcement proceedings is the fundamental purpose of judicial enforcement,[62] any procedural regulations duly assessed in consideration of values from beyond the processual system: the principle of proportionality, and the related need to secure equality for all parties to legal proceedings.[63] The regulation under analysis is in glaring breach of the principle of proportionality, grounded in Article 31 clause 3 of the Polish Constitution[64]—the meta-principle determining the use of other rules.[65] It engenders unjustified depletion in—if not deprivation of—the creditor's right to collect any due claims. It contravenes the thesis pursuant to which enforcement rules should *"primarily and*

---

[56] Łyszczek (2022), p. 149.

[57] Zembrzuski (2022b), *Kilka uwag*, p. 12.

[58] Cieślak (2022), p. 40.

[59] Muliński (2022), p. 81.

[60] Gudowski (2005), p. 1015.

[61] Rosmarin (1935), p. 434.

[62] Zembrzuski (2022a), *Funkcje i cele*, p. 830.

[63] Cieślak (2020), p. 13.

[64] Marciniak (2020), p. 677; Rydel (2023), p. 434.

[65] Śledzińska-Simon (2019), p. 23.

predominantly focus on his/hers (the creditor's) interest".[66] While debtor protection boosting tendencies are reflected in the centuries-old evolution of enforcement proceedings,[67] they have contemporarily become overprotective.[68] The standard behind Article 52 of the Law is an undesirable manifestation of "fetishising the debtor protection principle"[69] or "exorbitant debtor protection",[70] an expression of legislative action blatantly strengthening and favouritising the procedural position of the debtor,[71] as a result of which one might well doubt whether contemporary enforcement proceedings are truly effective from the creditor's perspective,[72] or rational as seen by a third party—an employer in an entrepreneur's hat.

The right to fair trial comprises the exploratory—or evidence collecting—stage as well as the capacity for enforcing the judicial sentence. Delivering the function of repressive judicial enforcement requires that the adequacy of processual *ad casum* instruments and enforcement measures be preserved. It shall be indispensable to reach a *communis opinio* to the effect of enforcement proceedings targeting the purpose of securing efficiency and true effectiveness of benefits laid out in final judicial rulings. The aforementioned applies to the legislator and enforcement bodies as well as to parties to enforcement proceedings, obliged to observe all applicable legal regulations. Only such an approach makes for a stabilising factor offering protection against undesirable and rash legislative changes.

Current conditions—including those caused by intricate epidemic-related factors—notwithstanding, the legislator should be expected to implement institutions in no contradiction to fundamental principles prevailing in the given field of law. Solutions involving salary attachment as described in the Shield Law of May 14th 2020 merit immediate elimination, without any grace period of awaiting comprehensive revocation of temporary epidemic-related regulations. Otherwise, the process of salary attachment effectiveness plummeting will only become more profound.[73]

References

Antkiewicz A (2010) Ograniczenia egzekucji sądowej ze świadczeń pomocy społecznej w ujęciu czasowym (*Restrictions to Judicial Enforcement Proceedings against Social Welfare Benefits*). Przegląd Prawa Egzekucyjnego 5:59–63

66 Korzonek (1936), p. 462.

67 Cieślak (2022), p. 38.

68 Strus-Wołos (2022), p. 142.

69 Korzan (1995), p. 10; Zembrzuski (2020), p. 163.

70 Rylski (2022), p. 131.

71 Jabłoński (2020), p. 55; Zembrzuski (2022a), *Funkcje i cele*, p. 835.

72 Białek (2022), p. 125.

73 Łyszczek (2022), p. 154.

Białek T (2022) Systematyczne pogarszanie się sytuacji prawnej wierzycieli – perspektywa sektora bankowego (*Regular Deterioration of the Creditors' Legal Situation – Banking Sector Perspective*). In: Bednorz-Godyń H, Marciniak A (eds) Prawa wierzyciela a ochrona dłużnika (*Creditor Rights v. Debtor Protection*). C.H. Beck, Warsaw, pp 125–132

Bomba K (2020) Konstytucyjne uwarunkowania pracy komornika sądowego (*Constitutional Conditons for Court Bailiffs and their Professional Obligations*). Wolters Kluwer, Warsaw

Borek M, Wisłocki KR (2017) Dostęp do informacji o postępowaniu egzekucyjnym i egzekucji – wybrane zagadnienia (*Access to Enforcement Proceedings- and Enforcement-related Information – Selected Issues*). In: Jabłoński M, Flaga-Gieruszyńska K, Wygoda K (eds) Reforma ochrony danych osobowych a jawność dostępu do informacji sądowej (*Personal Data Protection Reform in the Context of Judicial Information Access*), Wrocław, pp 173–197. https://www.bibliotekacyfrowa.pl/dlibra/publication/92803/edition/89093/content

Cieślak S (2020) Założenia aksjologiczne postępowania cywilnego – propozycja sformułowania kryteriów aksjologicznej oceny regulacji procesowej (*Axiological Assumptions to Civil Law Proceedings – Postulated Criteria for an Axiological Evaluation of Procedural Regulation*). In: Cieślak S (ed) Założenia aksjologiczne nowelizacji KPC z 4 lipca 2019 r. (*Axiological Assumptions for Code of Civil Procedure Amendments of July 4th 2019*). Wydawnictwo Uniwersytetu Łódzkiego, Łódź, pp 13–37

Cieślak S (2022) Zakres ochrony prawnej udzielanej stronom i innym uczestnikom sądowego postępowania egzekucyjnego a wymagania sprawiedliwości proceduralnej (*Scope of Legal Protection Extended to Parties and other Participants to Judicial Enforcement Proceedings in the Procedural Justice Context*). In: Cieślak S (ed) Aksjologia egzekucji sądowej. W poszukiwaniu optymalnego poziomu ochrony praw wierzyciela i dłużnika w postępowaniu egzekucyjnym i upadłościowym (*The Axiology of Judicial Enforcement. A Quest for the Optimum Measure of Creditor and Debtor Rights Protection in Enforcement and Bankruptcy Proceedings*). Currenda, Sopot, pp 21–57

Derlatka J (2017) Zasada sprawnej egzekucji sądowej (*Principle of Swift Judicial Enforcement*). Res Bull Catholic Univ Lublin 3:119–138

Flaga-Gieruszyńska K (2018), Realizacja obowiązku informacyjnego wobec stron w postępowaniu egzekucyjnym (*Delivering under the Information Obligation to Parties in Enforcement Proceedings*). In: Barańska A, Cieślak S (eds) Ars in vita. Ars in iure. Księga jubileuszowa dedykowana Profesorowi Januszowi Jankowskiemu (*Ars in vita. Ars in iure. Anniversary Volume Dedicated to Professor Janusz Jankowski*). C.H. Beck, Warsaw, pp 317–330

Gapska E (2020) Bieg postępowania w sprawach cywilnych w czasie epidemii. Cz. I – sprawy pilne (*The Course of Civil Law Proceedings during the Pandemic. Part One – Urgent Cases*). Monitor Prawniczy 17:892–897

Gaul HF (2003) Ochrona prawna w egzekucji w świetle podstaw konstytucyjnych i dogmatycznych (*Legal Protection in Enforcement Proceedings in Light of Constitutional and Dogmatic Foundations*). *Przegląd Prawa Egzekucyjnego* 1:30–101

Ged M (2022) Dylematy wokół prawa do wykonania orzeczenia – rozważania na tle art. 952[1] KPC (*Dilemmas Regarding the Right to Enforce Rulings*). In: Ciapała J, Piszko R, Pyrzyńska A (eds) Dylematy wokół prawa do sądu (*Right to Fair Trial Dilemmas*). C.H. Beck, Warsaw, pp 291–302

Gołaczyński J (2020) Przedawnienie roszczeń majątkowych i terminy zawite w okresie po ogłoszeniu stanu epidemii związanej z Covid-19 (*Statutory Limitations for Property Claims and Time Limits after the Proclamation of the COVID-19-related State of Epidemic*). Monitor Prawniczy 8:397–402

Gołaczyński J (2022) Informatyzacja postępowania cywilnego. Od odrębności do modelu podstawowego (*Computerisation of Civil Law Proceedings. Separateness to the Basic Model*). *Gdańskie Studia Prawnicze* 5:145–179

Gołaczyński J, Dymitruk M (2021) Rozprawa zdalna i doręczenia elektroniczne w dobie pandemii COVID-19 po wejściu w życie nowelizacji z 28.5.2021 r. (*Remote Judicial Hearings and*

Documents Served Electronically during the COVID-19 Pandemic in the Wake of Legislative Amendments of May 28th 2021). Monitor Prawniczy 13:685–697

Gołaczyński J, Kotecka-Kral S (2020) Elektronizacja pism procesowych, doręczeń i posiedzeń jawnych w postępowaniu cywilnym w okresie pandemii COVID-19 (*Computerisation of Pleadings, Documents Served and Open Judicial Hearings in Civil Law Proceedings during the COVID-19 Pandemic*). Polski Proces Cywilny 4:637–664

Gudowski J (2005) O kilku naczelnych zasadach procesu cywilnego – wczoraj, dziś, jutro (*On Several Prime Principles of Civil Law Proceedings – Yesterday, Today, Tomorrow*). In: Nowicka A (ed) Prawo prywatne czasu przemian, księga pamiątkowa dedykowana profesorowi Stanisławowi Sołtysińskiemu (*Private Law in Times of Change, Commemorative Volume Dedicated to Professor Stanisław Sołtysiński*). Wydawnictwo Naukowe UAM, Poznań, pp 1015–1033

Izdebski H (2021) Legislacja dotycząca COVID-19 i ustawowy nihilizm prawny (*COVID-19-related Legislation and Legislative Legal Nihilism*). In: Gardocka T, Jagiełło D (eds) Pandemia COVID-19 a prawa i wolności obywatela (*The COVID-19 Pandemic in the Civic Rights and Freedoms Context*). C.H. Beck, Warsaw, pp 29–58

Jabłoński M (2020) Konstytucyjność zmian w przepisach Kodeksu postępowania cywilnego wprowadzonych ustawą z 22.3.2018 r. o komornikach sądowych (*Constitutionality of Change in Code of Civil Procedure Provisions Introduced Pursuant to the Court Bailiffs Law of March 22nd 2018*). In: Jagieła J (ed) Sądowe postępowanie egzekucyjne. Nowe wyzwania i perspektywy (*Judicial Enforcement Proceedings. New Challenges and Perspectives*). C.H. Beck, Warsaw, pp 33–82

Jackowiak U, Dalka S (1992) Dopuszczalność egzekucji z zasiłków dla bezrobotnych (*Admissibility of Enforcement against Unemployment Benefits*). *Praca i Zabezpieczenie Społeczne* 7:58–64

Kamieński G (2022) Egzekucja sądowa z wynagrodzenia za pracę (*Judicial Enforcement against Salary Earnings*), Sopot

Korzan K (1995) Status prawny komornika w ujęciu historycznym oraz jego odpowiedzialność za powstałą szkodę na tle celu postępowania egzekucyjnego oraz krytycznego spojrzenia na wyrok Sądu Najwyższego z dnia 22 grudnia 1993 r. (*A Historical Perspective of the Legal Status of Court Bailiffs, and their Accountability for Damages against the Backdrop of Enforcement Proceedings and a Critical Take on the Supreme Court Ruling of December 22nd 1993*). *Problemy Egzekucji Sądowej* (XIV):5–44

Korzonek K (1936) Ochrona dłużnika przeciw egzekucji (*Protecting the Debtor from Enforcement*). Głos Prawa 10–12:462–468

Kościółek A (2021) Jawność posiedzeń sądowych w postępowaniu cywilnym w dobie pandemii COVID-19 (*Open Judicial Hearings in Civil Law Proceedings in Times of the COVID-19 Pandemic*). Przegląd Sądowy 5:22–40

Kulski R (2020) Wpływ stanu zagrożenia epidemicznego lub stanu epidemii ogłoszonego z powodu COVID-19 na postępowanie cywilne (*Impact of the State of Epidemic Threat or State of Epidemic Emergency Proclaimed for Reasons of COVID-19 on Proceedings under Civil Law*). Monitor Prawniczy 9:442–449

Kulski R (2022) Wpływ regulacji anty-covidowych na sprawność egzekucji sądowej (*Impact of Anti-COVID Regulations on Judicial Enforcement Effectiveness*). Polski Proces Cywilny 1:149–162

Łazarska A (2012) Rzetelny proces cywilny (*Fair Civil Law Trial*). Wolters Kluwer, Warsaw

Litowski J (2021) Ograniczenie jawności postępowania cywilnego z uwagi na stan epidemii wywołany wirusem COVID-19 (*Restrictions to the Principle of Open Judicial Hearings in Civil Law Proceedings for Reasons of the COVID-19-caused State of Epidemic Emergency*). Monitor Prawniczy 2:68–79

Łyszczek R (2022) Wpływ ustawodawstwa antycovidowego na efektywność i skuteczność egzekucji sądowej (*Impact of Anti-COVID Legislation on the Effectiveness and Efficiency of Judicial Enforcement*). In: Bednorz-Godyń H, Marciniak A (eds) *Prawa wierzyciela a ochrona dłużnika*. C.H. Beck, Warsaw, pp 149–154

Machnikowska A (2021) Zasada jawności w postępowaniu procesowym – modernizacja czy marginalizacja? Wybrane zagadnienia (*Principle of Open Judicial Proceedings – Modernisation or Marginalisation? - Selected Issues*). Polski Proces Cywilny 1:80–124

Marciniak A (1986) Ograniczenia egzekucji sądowej (*Limitations to Judicial Enforcement*). Acta Universitatis Lodziensis Folia Iuridica 26:1–168

Marciniak A (2002) Pojęcie i system środków przymusu w sądowym postępowaniu egzekucyjnym (*Notion and System of Enforcement Measures in Judicial Enforcement Proceedings*). Problemy Egzekucji Sądowej 21:5–39

Marciniak A (2020) Ograniczenia egzekucji z wynagrodzenia za pracę w świetle postanowień ustawy z 14.05.2020 r. o zmianie niektórych ustaw w zakresie działań osłonowych w związku z rozprzestrzenianiem się wirusa SARS-CoV-2 (*Limitations to Salary Attachment in Light of the Law of May 14th 2020 amending selected acts of law with regard to protective measures taken in conjunction with the spread of the SARS-CoV-2 virus*). Polski Proces Cywilny 4:665–678

Muliński M (2022) Zasada nieobciążania ponad potrzebę strony biernej postępowania zabezpieczającego i egzekucyjnego (*The Principle of Refraining from Burdening the Passive Party to Pledge and/or Enforcement Proceedings beyond Reasonable Need*). In: Cieślak S (ed) Aksjologia egzekucji sądowej, W poszukiwaniu optymalnego poziomu ochrony praw wierzyciela i dłużnika w postępowaniu egzekucyjnym i upadłościowym, Currenda, Sopot, pp 81–105

Romańska M (2021) Badanie okoliczności materialnoprawnych w postępowaniu klauzulowym i egzekucyjnym (*An Examination of Property Law Circumstances in Enforcement and Warrant Proceedings*). In: Dziurda M, Zembrzuski T (eds) Praktyka wobec nowelizacji postępowania cywilnego – konsekwencje zmian (*Legal Practice in the Face of Amendments to Civil Law Proceedings – Consequences of Change*). Warsaw, Wolters Kluwer, pp 489–516

Romańska M (2022) Ograniczenia egzekucji sądowej – uporządkowany system odpowiadający warunkom społecznym czy anachroniczne rozwiązania? (*Limitations to Judicial Enforcement – an Orderly System Reflecting Social Conditions or a Set of Anachronic Solutions?*). In: Cieślak S (ed) Aksjologia egzekucji sądowej, W poszukiwaniu optymalnego poziomu ochrony praw wierzyciela i dłużnika w postępowaniu egzekucyjnym i upadłościowym. Wydawnictwo Uniwersytetu Łódzkiego, Sopot, pp 173–202

Rosmarin S (1935) Wadliwe czynności egzekucyjne (*Defective Enforcement Measures*). Polski Proces Cywilny 13–14:425–435

Rydel K (2023) Skuteczne postępowanie egzekucyjne jako element konstytucyjnego prawa do sądu w dobie pandemii (*Effective Enforcement Proceedings as a Component of the Constitutional Right to Trial in Times of the Pandemic*). In: Orzeł-Jakubowska A, Zembrzuski T (eds) Konstytucyjne aspekty procesu cywilnego (*Constitutional Aspects of Civil Law Proceedings*). Warsaw, Wolters Kluwer, pp 417–439

Rylski P (2022) Efektywna ochrona wierzycieli w sądowym postępowaniu egzekucyjnym (*Effective Creditor Protection in Judicial Enforcement Proceedings*). In: Cieślak S (ed) Aksjologia egzekucji sądowej, W poszukiwaniu optymalnego poziomu ochrony praw wierzyciela i dłużnika w postępowaniu egzekucyjnym i upadłościowym. Currenda, Sopot, pp 105–139

Śledzińska-Simon A (2019), Analiza proporcjonalności ograniczeń konstytucyjnych praw i wolności. Teoria i praktyka (*An Analysis of Proportionality in Limitaions to Constitutional Rights and Freedoms. Theory and Practice*), e-publication, Digital Library of Law and Economics, Wrocław. http://www.bibliotekacyfrowa.pl/publication/102713

Strus-Wołos M (2022) Skutki społeczne nadmiernej ochrony dłużnika w egzekucji sądowej i postępowaniu upadłościowym (*Social Consequences of Debtor Overprotection in Judicial Enforcement and Bankruptcy Proceedings*). In: Cieślak S (ed) Aksjologia egzekucji sądowej, W poszukiwaniu optymalnego poziomu ochrony praw wierzyciela i dłużnika w postępowaniu egzekucyjnym i upadłościowym. Currenda, Sopot, pp 141–170

Zembrzuski T (2017) Nieważność postępowania w procesie cywilnym (*Invalidity of Proceedings in Civil Law Trials*). Wolters Kluwer, Warsaw

Zembrzuski T (2020) Zarządzenia sądu z urzędu a odpowiedzialność odszkodowawcza komornika sądowego i Skarbu Państwa (*Ex Officio Judicial Orders in the Context of Liability for Damages of Court Bailiffs and the State Treasury*). In: Jagieła J (ed) Sądowe postępowanie egzekucyjne. Nowe wyzwania i perspektywy (*Judicial Enforcement Proceedings. New Challenges and Perspectives*). Wolters Kluwer, Warsaw

Zembrzuski T (2022a) Funkcje i cele egzekucji sądowej (*Functions and Purposes of Judicial Enforcement Proceedings*). In: Jagieła J, Kulski R (eds) *Symbolae Andreae Marciniak dedicatae*. C.H. Beck, Warsaw, pp 815–825

Zembrzuski T (2022b) Kilka uwag o funkcjach egzekucji sądowej (*Several Comments on the Functions of Judicial Enforcement Proceedings*). In: Bednorz-Godyń H, Marciniak A (eds) Prawa wierzyciela a ochrona dłużnika. C.H. Beck, Warsaw, pp 7–16

Zembrzuski T (2022c) Ograniczenia jawności postępowania w sprawach cywilnych w dobie pandemii – potrzeba chwili czy trwałe rozwiązania? Forum Prawnicze 3:3–18

Zembrzuski T (2022d) Przeciwdziałanie i zwalczanie epidemii COVID-19 w postępowaniu cywilnym, czyli pożegnanie z kolegialnością orzekania (*Preventing and Combatting the COVID-19 Epidemic in Proceedings under Civil Law, or Farewell to Collegiality in Judicial Ruling*). Polski Proces Cywilny 1:59–79

Zembrzuski T (2023) *Remote Court Hearings in Polish Judicial Civil Proceedings – Manifestation of Justice or Aftermath of the Epidemic?* In: *The State, Security and Human Rights in the Digital Era*, Chişinău 2023

Tadeusz Zembrzuski Professor at Warsaw University, Department of Civil Proceeding, Faculty of Law and Administration, Warsaw University; legal counsel; the Supreme Court Research and Analyses Office member. Author of over 150 scientific publications in the field of civil proceedings—fields of research: Appeal measures in civil cases, The Law of evidence, Enforcement proceedings, Legal representation, Costs of legal proceedings, Multi-stakeholder participation in proceedings under civil law.

Proceedings in Commercial Cases During Covid-19 Epidemic

Marcin Dziurda

Abstract Under Polish law, cases involving entrepreneurs are regulated in separate proceedings in commercial cases. During Covid-19 epidemic these cases were covered by the episodic provision of Articles 15zzs(1), 15zzs(2) and 15zzs(7) of the Covid-19 Act. Those articles introduce material changes to the civil proceedings. First of all, they exclude collegiality in common courts' decision-making. Secondly, they significantly limit the openness of the proceedings.

The experience gathered during the Covid-19 epidemic shows that separate proceedings in commercial cases which were implemented in 2019 have not fulfilled the expectations. They are considered to be too formalistic, which does not make the proceedings more effective.

1 Introduction

Under Polish law, legal disputes involving entrepreneurs are settled in separate proceedings in commercial cases—restored, after a seven-year break, on 7 November 2019.[1] A few months later, the Covid-19 pandemic started. Therefore, it requires an assessment to find out how the provisions on commercial proceedings worked during the period of restrictions aimed at limiting the spread of SARS-CoV-2. First, it is necessary to outline the legal framework, both in terms of the commercial proceedings and special episodic provisions implemented in Poland during the Covid-19 epidemic.

[1]Pursuant to Polish Civil Procedure Code's and Certain Other Acts' Amendment Act of 4.7.2019 (Polish Journal of Laws [Dz.U.], item 1469 as amended).

M. Dziurda (✉)
Faculty of Law and Administration, University of Warsaw, Warsaw, Poland
e-mail: m.dziurda@wpia.uw.edu.pl

E. Hadrowicz (ed.), *Polish Entrepreneurial Law in the Era of the COVID-19 Pandemic*, Ius Gentium: Comparative Perspectives on Law and Justice 114,
https://doi.org/10.1007/978-3-031-57480-1_10

2 Commercial Proceedings in Poland

Proceedings in commercial cases are regulated in Articles 458(1) to 458(13) of the Polish Civil Procedure Code[2] (CPC). It is one of about a dozen of the so-called separate proceedings which provide for different special regulations as compared with the general provisions governing a trial. The scope and the type of those special regulations depends on the reason why specific separate proceedings were implemented.

Sometimes separate proceedings are implemented due to the nature of cases heard—for example, marital cases (Articles 425 to 452 of the CPC) or cases relating to the parents-children relationship (Articles 453 to 458 of the CPC). Otherwise, the legislator has implemented separate proceedings in cases of a certain category in order to afford greater protection to the weaker party in the proceedings, for example, to the employee (Articles 460-477(7a) of the CPC).

Following the general trends in the majority of legal systems, Polish legislator implemented simplified procedure which is to ensure faster and cheaper review of the smallest claims—under Polish law, the simplified procedure covers cases if the value in dispute is under PLN 20,000 (Article 505(1) of the CPC). The need for introducing a cheaper and faster procedure governing minor cases is even stronger under Polish law, because Article 176 section 1 of the Polish Constitution[3] mandates that court proceedings be heard at least by courts of two instances. Therefore, the parties have the right to appeal in each case, regardless of its value. Unfortunately, the Polish regulation governing the simplified civil procedure is not a good one. It is too formalistic which is its main weakness as—instead of making the proceedings easier—it complicates them in the smallest cases.

Separate proceedings in commercial cases are also aimed at expediating the proceedings. Those were the assumptions of the legislator whose starting point was that cases involving entrepreneurs should be handled faster than cases involving other entities. The lawmaker concluded that it was necessary for ensuring proper commercial trade, and in particular to prevent payment backlogs and thus provide the entrepreneurs with financial liquidity.[4]

The lawmaker decided that formalising commercial proceedings would be the best way to make them faster. A strict regulation was introduced, whereby—as a rule—the claimant is required to disclose all pleadings and evidence in the statement of claim, and the defendant is required to do so in the statement of defence (Article 458^5 § 1 of the CPC). The admissibility of bringing a counterclaim was excluded. The possibility of making subject-related changes, including the extension of the lawsuit, was significantly limited. All that certainly increases the

[2] Civil Procedure Code Act of 17.11.1964 (Polish Journal of Laws [Dz.U.] of 2023, item 1550 as amended).

[3] Constitution of the Republic of Poland of 2.4.1997 (Polish Journal of Laws No. 78, item 483 as amended).

[4] Print of the Polish Sejm of the 8th term, No. 3137, p. 95.

chances for a faster outcome of specific commercial proceedings. However, critics point out that the restrictions will have a negative influence on the overall efficiency of the judicature. By eliminating the admissibility of bringing a counterclaim, the court will have to review two cases rather than one. Eliminating the possibility of entity transformations and limiting the admissibility of subject-related transformations will have the same consequences.

The assumption that commercial proceedings should cover all entrepreneurs, including private individuals running their own business,[5] is also criticised. There are nearly 3 million private individuals running their own businesses in Poland, not to mention legal entities and other organisational units running business operations, particularly companies. In keeping with Article 458(2)§ 1.1 of the CPC, as a rule, all cases under civil relationships between entrepreneurs within the scope of their business operations are reviewed in commercial proceedings. What is more, pursuant to Article 458(2) § 1.2 of the CPC, the case remains a commercial one even if either party, or even both parties, ceases to operate their business.

Article 458(2) § 1.5 of the CPC, whereby cases under contracts for construction works are reviewed as part of commercial proceedings, whether or not both parties are professionals, are particularly controversial. It does not seem right to submit cases concerning construction works (such as, renovating a residential building) ordered by a consumer, to be reviewed as part of formalised commercial proceedings.

As a rule, separate proceedings in commercial cases are more complicated and require greater legal expertise. Meanwhile, an individual entrepreneur may be a professional plumber or a shoemaker but does not necessarily have to be well-versed in the intricacies of the law. Running commercial cases for those entrepreneurs may be too complicated, but Polish provisions do not provide for mandatory representation of the parties by professional legal representatives—advocates or attorneys-at-law.[6]

Being aware of that, the legislator envisaged the possibility of avoiding the review of a case in formalistic commercial proceedings. In keeping with Article 458(6) § 1 of the CPC, upon the application of an entrepreneur who is a private individual, the court will hear the case in disregard of provisions governing commercial proceedings. Such an application may also be submitted by a person who is not an entrepreneur at all, for example, by a consumer who ordered the construction works.

The possibility of filing a binding application for the review of a case while omitting the provisions governing commercial proceedings as such is evaluated positively. At the same time, one may wonder about the need to implement separate proceedings regarding cases between entrepreneurs. If there are solutions adopted in the provisions governing separate proceedings in commercial cases that actually improve the effectiveness of the proceedings, then such solutions should be

[5] Dziurda, Szrajer (2020), p. 12.

[6] Ereciński(2002), p. 61.

implemented to general provisions governing a trial.[7] Rather than isolate proceedings in commercial cases, legislator could allow entrepreneurs themselves to take part in resolving such cases as commercial judges (lay judges). It was permitted in Poland before World War 2 and similar regulations are still in place in certain European countries.

Even though the common opinion on the provisions on separate proceedings in commercial cases which were implemented in 2019 is negative, the provisions remain in effect and have been applied to hundreds of thousands of cases per year. The shape of the new commercial proceedings in practice was significantly influenced by the fact that Covid-19 epidemic broke out shortly after the effective date of the provisions governing those proceedings; as a consequence, special regulations were implemented to limit its spread. They had an essential influence on the shape and the course of the court proceedings, also in commercial cases.

3 Regulations Relating to Covid-19 Pandemic

Shortly after the epidemic outbreak, the Polish government implemented the Special Solutions to Prevent, Counteract and Combat Covid-19, Other Infectious Diseases and the Ensuing Crisis Situations Act of 2 March 2020[8] (the Covid-19 Act), also known as the "Shield 1". It was subject to multiple amendments. Among the many regulations contained in the Covid-19 Act, there are also provisions (which were episodical by design) concerning the course of court proceedings in civil cases.[9]

Initially, in keeping with Article 15zzs of the Covid-19 Act which was implemented on 31 March 2020, the legislator envisaged halting the procedural deadlines (arising from the statute) and court deadlines (set by the court or by the presiding judge) in court- and enforcement proceedings. It turned out, however, that the courts continued to function (with certain restrictions), despite the state of epidemic, and consequently, Article 15zzs of the Covid-19 Act was repealed as soon as 16 May 2020. Nevertheless, during its effective term, Article 14a sections 4 and 5 of the Covid-19 Act specified urgent cases which had to be reviewed even if courts ceased to operate. Those urgent cases did not include, however, cases reviewed as part of commercial proceedings, which means that those cases were not considered by legislator to be extremely urgent.

Commercial cases were covered by the episodic provision of Articles 15zzs(1), 15zzs(2) and 15zzs(7) of the Covid-19 Act. Those articles introduce essential changes to the civil proceedings. First of all, they exclude collegiality in common courts' decision-making (but not in Supreme Court). Secondly, they significantly

---

[7] Weitz (2008), p. 22.

[8] Ustawa z 2 marca 2020 r. o szczególnych rozwiązaniach związanych z zapobieganiem, przeciwdziałaniem i zwalczaniem Covid-19, innych chorób zakaźnych oraz wywołanych nimi sytuacji kryzysowych, Polish Journal of Laws [Dz.U.] of 2021, item 2095 as amended.

[9] Rylski (2021), p. 157.

limit the openness of the proceedings. As a rule, both of those modifications may be considered the right way of responding to threats relating to the spread of SARS-CoV-2. Both resigning from court hearings open to all parties concerned and decision-making by one judge rather than by a panel of three judges limits the risk of infection. However, there are concerns about the proportionality of the provisions implemented by the Polish legislator, and in particular, the late date of their implementation and a long effective period.[10]

In accordance with the preliminary part of Article 15zzs(1) section 1 of the Covid-19 Act, the restriction on the openness of the proceedings and collegiality in decision-making provided for in that article, are to be effective not only during the term of the state of epidemic or the state of epidemic threat announced because of Covid-19, but also for one year from the repeal of the latter one. Thus, even though the majority of restrictions related to the Covid-19 epidemic in other areas of life have already been repealed, they are to apply to the civil proceedings at courts for a long time. It needs to be kept in mind that, on 16 May 2022, the state of epidemic in Poland was changed to the state of the epidemic threat. It is hard to forecast how long the state of the epidemic threat will last, and the restrictions arising from Article 15zzs(1) section 1 of the Covid-19 Act will apply one year after it ends. That period must be considered as being much too long.

As regards the restrictions on collegiality in decision-making, pursuant to Article 15zzs(1) section 1.4 of the Covid-19 Act, cases are reviewed by one judge in first- and second-instance courts. As a consequence, lay judges may not make decisions in first-instance proceedings. It is of no significance for commercial cases because lay judges do not make decisions in those cases anyway (they are only involved in some family cases and labour law and employment law cases). In the first instance courts, commercial cases are heard as they used to be because decisions regarding those cases are made by one judge (also according to the general provisions).

It is different in case of second-instance proceedings. In keeping with general provisions, both appeals (Article 367 § 3 of the CPC), and complaints (Article 397 § 1 of the CPC) are reviewed by a panel of three judges. This applies to commercial cases, amongst others. However, due to the regulation in Article 15zzs(1) section 1.4 of the Covid-19 Act, collegial decision-making by second-instance courts was temporarily excluded.

That solution gives rise to serious concerns, particularly that, even though the provision of Article 15zzs(1) section 1.4 of the Covid-19 Act is episodic in formal terms, it will be effective for a long time. It needs to be pointed out that the solution was implemented relatively late (3 July 2021)—one and a half years after the epidemic outbreak when the epidemic visibly started to fade. Apart from that, Article 15zzs(1) section 1.1 of the Covid-19 Act (which will be elaborated on below) allows some members of the collegial panel of judges to take part in the proceedings on a remote basis which—it seems—provides sufficient safety guarantees. The reasons for excluding the collegial decision-making in second-instance proceedings is also

[10] Machnikowska (2022), p. 124.

controversial. The legislator groundlessly stated that "it doesn't matter whether a decision in a case is made by one judge or three judges".[11]

Elimination of the collegiality in second-instance decision-making gave rise to serious concerns, both in the literature,[12] and in case law. In the decision of 29 April 2022, Case III CZP 77/22,[13] the Supreme Court emphasised that collegiality of the adjudicating panel, which is an established rule in appeal proceedings, warrants a higher standard of appeal control as it allows for the decision to be made by way of a discourse and dispute, it reinforces impartiality and independence of decision-making, and increases the legitimacy of the court decision in the public opinion; hence, it is desirable in view of ensuring proper protection of the rights of the parties and participants in the proceedings. The exclusion of collegiality of common courts while reviewing appeals and complaints, which arises from Article 15zzs(1) section 1.4 of the Covid-19 Act, and particularly extending that exclusion for as long as one year after the end of the state of epidemic threat, is highly controversial (particularly that the rule of decision-making by a three-judge panel has not been excluded in the case of the Supreme Court). Nevertheless, the adjudicating panel in Case III PC 77/22 decided that the analysed exception to the collegiality principle is not tantamount to a breach (particularly a manifest breach) of Article 45 section 1 of the Polish Constitution which provides for the right to a fair trial.

However, that was not the end of the controversies. In Case III PZP 6/22, the enlarged panel of 7 Supreme Court judges was presented with two legal questions. Firstly, whether or not a one-judge adjudicating panel (due to the episodic regulation of Article 15zzs(1) section 1.4 of the Covid-19 Act) in cases relating to labour and employment law is a "tribunal established by law" within the meaning of Article 6 section 1 of the European Convention on Human Rights. Secondly, should the answer to the first question be negative (i.e. should the Supreme Court decide that a one-judge panel is not a "tribunal established by law"), is it legitimate—pursuant to Article 91 section 2 of the Polish Constitution, whereby a ratified international agreement takes precedence over a statute—to disregard Article 15zzs(1) section 1.4 of the Covid-19 Act and establish the adjudicating panel in complaint proceedings according to the general provisions of the CPC, which generally provide for a three-judge panel. The same view should be adopted in commercial proceedings in case of which the CPC provisions provide for a three-judge panel to review both appeals and complaints, and the episodic provision of Article 15zzs(1) section 1.4 of the Covid-19 Act excludes that principle.

The commercial proceedings are also subject to the restrictions on the proceedings openness implemented by the Covid-19 Act. It should be noted, at the very beginning, that Article 15zzs(1) section 1.1 of the Covid-19 Act is the first regulation under Polish law that provides for conducting civil proceedings on a remote basis, that is using online messengers (*verba legis*: "using technical devices that

[11] Print of the Polish Sejm of the 9th term, No. 899.

[12] Zembrzuski (2022), p. 59.

[13] www.sn.pl.

allow for conducting them [the proceedings] on a remote basis with simultaneous direct transmission of image and sound"). The general provision of Article 151 §2 of the CPC allows only for conducting open remote proceedings in such a way that the proceedings participants stay at the building of another courthouse, and the course of the procedural acts (for example, witness hearing) is transmitted using the internal technical devices of the court.[14] In the decision of 8 November 2019, Case III CZP 13/19,[15] which was rendered shortly before the outbreak of Covid-19 pandemic, the Supreme Court concluded that Article 151 §2 of the CPC does not allow for hearing a witness via an online messenger. There are no general regulations in the CPC that would allow for conducting remote hearings using online messengers or in any manner other than that provided for Article 151 §2 of the CPC.

The introduction of Article 15zzs(1) §1.1 of the Covid-19 Act, as early as 15 May 2020, was a revolutionary change for Polish courts. The provision leaves no room for speculation and makes it clear that a hearing may be conducted using technical devices that allow for conducting it on a remote basis with simultaneous direct transmission of image and sound (a remote hearing), and the persons participating in the hearing, including the members of the adjudicating panel, do not have to stay at the courthouse building. That means that online messengers may be used not only by the parties and other persons participating in the hearing (for example, attorneys and even witnesses) but also by the members of the adjudicating panel. Covid-19 epidemic provided an opportunity for implementing remote hearings on a broader scale and that opportunity was seized.

Unfortunately (in this case), the regulation of Article 15zzs(1) §1.1 of the Covid-19 Act is also episodic and will expire one year after the end of the state of epidemic threat. It would be highly desirable to keep the option of remote participation in a hearing under Polish law on a permanent basis. However, it would require specifying in more detail the technical solutions to be used for that purpose, and guaranteeing the security of information being transmitted, including but not limited to the protection of personal data.

It is a pity that the legislator did not take advantage of the Covid-19 epidemic to transition from filing pleadings in the paper form to filing them electronically. The only thing that was done was to implement a new solution, whereby court letters—rather than being sent by regular mail—are made available to professional legal representatives (advocates and attorneys-at-law) at the so-called court information portal (Article 15zzz(9) of the Covid-19 Act). However, that solution is limited for three reasons. Firstly, the regulation is episodic also (it will cease to apply one year after the end of the state of epidemic threat). Secondly, it applies only to the service of documents to the professional representatives. Thirdly, and most importantly, it provides only for the electronic delivery of outgoing letters from the court, primarily decisions and notices of hearing dates.

---

[14] Karolczyk (2019), p. 99.

[15] www.sn.pl.

Despite the fact that there are many proponents of such a solution, the legislator did not implement the duty for the parties to deliver their pleadings in the electronic form instead of paper form. Such a solution would generate considerable time- and cost savings, as pleadings currently must be served by regular mail. This would help protect the natural environment too. The opponents of that solution point out that not all parties to the proceedings have access to electronic mail; consequently, implementing a requirement of electronic service of documents would lead to the exclusion of those people. However, just as in the case of the court information panel, the duty to submit pleadings in the electronic form could be imposed on the professional legal representatives only.

On the other hand, Article 15zzs(1) §1.3 of the Covid-19 Act, whereby the presiding judge may order a closed session when a remote hearing cannot be held, and conducting a trial or an open hearing is unnecessary, definitely deserves a negative assessment. It allows for conducting and completing the proceedings, both in the first- and second instance, during a closed session basically based on an arbitrary decision of the presiding judge, which clearly violates the principle of open proceedings. It should be added that, prior to 3 July 2021, where the court intended to hear a case during a closed session, the parties were able to submit a binding request for a trial. Following the amendment which came into force on 3 July 2021, the parties were deprived of that right. The amendment is even harder to understand, given the fact that the additional restriction on openness was imposed during a period when Covid-19 epidemic in Poland started to fade.

The regulation in Article 15zzz(1) §1.3 of the Covid-19 Act should be repealed as soon as possible; the same comment applies to Article 15zzz(2) of that Act, whereby—where the evidentiary procedure in a case heard according to the CPC provisions has been fully completed—the court may close the hearing and give decision during a closed hearing (without hearing) out upon first collecting written standpoints from the parties or participants in the proceedings. The latter provision does not even contain a reservation that the restriction on openness it imposes will apply only for one year following the end of the state of epidemic threat.

The above comments fully apply to the commercial proceedings. While implementing the possibility of remote hearings during commercial proceedings is a step in the right direction, limiting the openness and the collegiality of decision-making in appeal proceedings is a dead end.

4 Specific Nature of Commercial Proceedings During Covid-19

The Covid-19 epidemic and connected legal regulations provided a convenient training ground for new solutions introduced to the CPC in 2019, including but not limited to separate proceedings in commercial cases. As for regulations effective only in the case of commercial proceedings, some of them have not been well-received in practice. This applies in particular to evidentiary agreements (which allow for contractual exclusion of certain means of evidence). Their regulation in Article 458(9) of the CPC has proved not to be specific enough. It is even unclear whether or not it is permissible to exclude all means of evidence, and if not, there is no regulation as to how much detail one should go into when specifying means of evidence that the parties agree not to take. Besides, the practical significance of evidentiary agreements is definitely limited by Article 458(9) §7 of the CPC, whereby the courts may use the assertions of the parties in view of all facts of the case, in order to determine facts that would have to be proved by evidence excluded under the evidentiary agreement.

As for general provisions, regulations which provide for the possibility of conducting a preparatory meeting (which the legislator intended to be a rule) have not been widely applied yet. The provisions that regulate the preparatory meeting (and the entire organisational phase of the proceedings) are so formalistic that they discourage users from taking advantage of this new procedural institution. The change of the case plan (the procedure schedule), which is regulated in Article 205(11) of the CPC and which requires setting subsequent preparatory meetings, has in particular made the preparatory meeting a goal in and of itself rather than a means to improve the proceedings. It is, therefore, no wonder that the judges *en masse* take advantage of the option not to set it. It is permitted under Article 205(4) §3 of the CPC, whereby where the facts of the case imply that conducting a preparatory meeting will not make the review of the case more efficient, the presiding judge may send it for hearing during a trial.

In case of the commercial proceedings, there is an additional reason against setting a preparatory meeting, notably the lack of application of Article 205(12) §1 of the CPC, whereby – when a preparatory meeting has been set—a party may offer evidence until the approval of the case plan. A special, more restrictive regulation of Article 458(5) §1 of the CPC applies in commercial cases, where the claimant is required to disclose all pleadings and evidence in the statement of claim, and the defendant is required to do so in the statement of defence. The lack of the possibility to submit new assertions and new evidence during the preparatory meeting as part of the commercial proceedings lowers its significance and usefulness in practice.

The regulations concerning witness testimony also are controversial. According to Article 458(10) of the CPC, that form of evidence is subsidiary in case of commercial proceedings—the court may allow evidence in the form of witness testimony only if, having exhausted means of evidence or due to lack thereof, certain facts have not been clarified which are crucial for the adjudication of the case.

That law seems to be overly restrictive, and evidence in the form of witness testimony may be of significant importance also in cases between entrepreneurs. It does not necessarily have to prolong the proceedings because the legislator added Article 271(1) of the CPC to the general provisions, which allows for taking evidence in the form of written witness testimony.

Article 271(1) of the CPC gives rise to serious reservations, particularly that there is no provision allowing for hearing a witness who has already submitted testimony in writing. Without that possibility there may be concerns as to the credibility of written testimony. There is even no certainty as to whether or not the testimony signed be the witness were written by him/her in person. There is also no way to ask additional questions to a witness who has already given written testimony.[16] For those reasons, the usefulness of written witness testimony in court proceedings is considerably lower than in arbitration proceedings.[17] Having those reservations in mind, the evidence in the form of written testimony may be considered to be useful, particularly in case of commercial proceedings where it may be taken without impairing the speed of the legal action.

5 Conclusion

The prevailing opinion is that the new provisions on separate proceedings in commercial cases which were implemented in 2019 have not fulfilled the expectations. They are considered to be too formalistic, which does not make the proceedings more effective. Limiting the role of witness testimony in commercial proceedings, particularly after receiving written witness testimony became common during the Covid-19 epidemic, does not seem to be the right solution. Evidentiary agreements which were supposed to be a novelty effective only during the commercial proceedings did not gain popularity either.

The institution of preparatory meeting is an opportunity that has not really been seized—it was supposed to be mandatory and it is set rarely, also due to the fact that the provisions governing the way of constructing and changing the case plan are too formalistic. In the case of commercial proceedings, the importance of the preparatory meeting is additionally increased by the fact that Article 205(12) section 1 of the CPC does not apply to it and that article would allow for submitting new assertions and new evidence until the case plan has been approved. In general, the mechanisms ensuring completeness of pleadings and evidence to be used in evidence for the purpose of commercial proceedings are too complicated; in addition, they induce the parties to "hide" the professional legal representatives, at least during the initial stage of the proceedings (pursuant to Article 458(5) §2 of the CPC, a party who acts without a professional legal representative is entitled to an extra week for submitting new pleadings and new evidence).

Therefore, the purposefulness of keeping the provisions on separate proceedings in commercial cases needs to be reconsidered. As they are now, those regulations do not provide an effective way to improve and expediate the procedure. The experience gathered during the Covid-19 epidemic shows that legislator should introducing the option of remote hearings on a permanent basis, and allowing parties (particularly those represented by professional representatives) to file pleadings in the electronic form (so that they may be delivered in that form to the opponent may

[16] Dziurda (2019), p. 103.

[17] Dziurda (2020), p. 175.

bring better results). Such a change could significantly improve the civil proceedings, not only in cases between entrepreneurs.

References

Dziurda M (2019) Dowód z zeznań świadka na piśmie [*Written witness testimony as evidence*]. Palestra 11/12:103–112

Dziurda M (2020) W sądzie jak w arbitrażu – czy to się może udać? [*The court procedure as an arbitration procedurę – can it work?]*. In: Dziurda M, Zembrzuski T (eds) Praktyka wobec nowelizacji postępowania cywilnego – konsekwencje zmian [*The practice in view of the amendments to the civil proceedings – consequences of the changes*], Warsaw

Dziurda M, Szrajer M (2020) Postępowanie gospodarcze według nowych przepisów [*Proceedings in Commercial Cases According to New Provisions*]. Przegląd Prawa Handlowego 1:12–23

Ereciński T (2002) Kilka refleksji o przymusie adwokacko-radcowskim *[Some reflections on mandatory representation by an attorney*]. In: Żuławski J (ed) XX lat samorządu radców prawnych 1982–2002. Księga jubileuszowa [*20 Years of Attorneys-at-Law Self-Government. Jubilee Book*]. Warsaw

Karolczyk B (2019) Informatization of the civil justice system in Poland. An overview of recent changes. In: Uzelac., van Rhee CH (eds) Transformation of civil justice unity and diversity, Springer, pp 99–117 https://doi.org/10.1007/978-3-319-97358-6_6

Machnikowska A (2022) Zasada jawności w postępowaniu procesowym – modernizacja czy marginalizacja? Wybrane zagadnienia [*The principle of openness in civil proceedings – modernization or marginalization? Selected issues*]. Polski Proces Cywilny 1:80–124

Rylski P (2021) Transformation of polish civil procedure in light of covid 19. In: Krans B, Nylund A (eds) Civil Courts Coping with Covid-19

Weitz K (2008) Czy potrzebne jest postępowanie w sprawach gospodarczych? [*Do we need separate proceedings in commercial cases*]. Przegląd Sądowy 7–8:22–35

Zembrzuski T (2022) Przeciwdziałanie i zwalczanie epidemii COVID-19 w postępowaniu cywilnym, czyli pożegnanie z kolegialnością orzekania [*Counteracting and combating COVID-19 pandemic in civil proceedings – the end of collegiality of adjudication*]. Polski Proces Cywilny 1:59–79

Marcin Dziurda Assistant Professor, Department of Civil Proceedings, Faculty of Law and Administration, University of Warsaw, Poland. Author of numerous academic publications, primarily in civil procedure law. Has vast experience in running and coordinating court and arbitration cases, which he acquired i.a. as the President of the State Treasury Solicitors' Office (Prokuratoria Generalna Skarbu Państwa).

Support for Entrepreneurs from Public Funds in the Era of the Covid-19 Pandemic

Dariusz Kowalski

Abstract The covid-19 pandemic has changed the perception of the role of the state in economic processes in an unprecedented way. This resulted primarily from the dynamics of economic processes during the pandemic. Previously, economic changes were evolutionary in nature, while the pandemic was a revolution for the state and entrepreneurs.

The subject of the article is an analysis of the regulations on financing entrepreneurs before and during the pandemic. From the current time perspective, it is reasonable to examine whether the state reacted correctly to this crisis? The main risk factors were the speed of reaction and the scope of the changes introduced. This generates a fundamental question whether the introduced changes in the mechanisms of financing enterprises were introduced correctly and, consequently, helped the entrepreneur?

As a result of analyzes based on non-reactive studies, it was found that observing in retrospect the activities related to counteracting the effects of the COVID-19 pandemic on entrepreneurs, it should first be noted that the legislator (both at the EU and Polish level) reacted quickly and effectively to the changing economic circumstances. This may be evidenced by, for example, radical changes in the area of state aid regulations. In the first weeks after the outbreak of the pandemic, completely new aid rules were created, which allowed many entrepreneurs to be saved.

It is also worth noting that in the subsequent stages of the pandemic, economic circumstances changed and entrepreneurs began to adapt to operating in the circumstances of the pandemic. It also required adapting the support tools. In this area, it is worth paying attention to the targeting of aid activities for enterprises from industries most affected by the effects of the pandemic. The aid was targeted in particular at enterprises from the tourism, recreation and transport industries.

D. Kowalski (✉)
SWPS University of Social Sciences and Humanities, Faculty of Law, Warsaw, Poland
e-mail: dkowalski2@swps.edu.pl

E. Hadrowicz (ed.), *Polish Entrepreneurial Law in the Era of the COVID-19 Pandemic*, Ius Gentium: Comparative Perspectives on Law and Justice 114,
https://doi.org/10.1007/978-3-031-57480-1_11

1 Introduction

The covid-19 pandemic has changed the perception of the role of the state in economic processes in an unprecedented way. This resulted primarily from the dynamics of economic processes during the pandemic. Previously, economic changes were evolutionary in nature, while the pandemic was a revolution for the state and entrepreneurs.

The subject of the article is an analysis of the regulations on financing entrepreneurs before and during the pandemic. From the current time perspective, it is reasonable to examine whether the state reacted correctly to this crisis? The main risk factors were the speed of reaction and the scope of the changes introduced. This generates a fundamental question whether the introduced changes in the mechanisms of financing enterprises were introduced correctly and, consequently, helped the entrepreneur? In order to achieve the assumed goal, the problem analysis was based on non-reactive research, consisting in evaluating the available information. It included studies of normative acts and official statistical data. The basic research method used in the work is the dogmatic and legal method. Its subject was an analysis of the content of normative acts, both at the national and EU level, regulating the principles of financing enterprises from public funds.

2 Financial Support for Entrepreneurs Before the Pandemic

Financing enterprises from public funds is an unobvious form of state activity. This is due to the fact that it is related to the intervention of the state apparatus in economic relations, which in the current socio-economic system are regulated by market forces. Therefore, both Polish and EU law precisely regulate the rules defining the relationship between the state and entrepreneurs.[1] In national law, these principles can be found in the Constitution of the Republic of Poland (in particular Articles 20 and 22). At the level of EU law—Art. 107 of the Treaty on the Functioning of the European Union according to which aid granted by a Member State or through state resources in any form which distorts or threatens to distort competition by favoring certain undertakings is in principle incompatible with the internal market insofar as it affects on trade between Member States.

Before 2020, exceptions to the above-mentioned rule of non-intervention of the state in market processes most often resulted from the legitimacy of supporting selected types of enterprises in connection with the occurrence of market failure. As an example, we can mention supporting enterprises from the micro, small and medium-sized enterprises sector (as those with limited access to capital due to limited creditworthiness resulting from the scale of their operations). Another example is aid for research, development and innovation activities (as particularly important

[1] Kowalski (2014), p. 104.

from the point of view of the economy of the European Union). The admissibility of this intervention was explicitly expressed in Articles 17–24 and 25–30 of Commission Regulation (EU) No 651/2014 of 17 June 2014 declaring certain types of aid compatible with the internal market pursuant to Art. 107 and 108 of the Treaty. Another exception to this rule is the admissibility of financial support which, due to its small scale, does not affect market mechanisms. This is the so-called de minimis aid regulated in Commission Regulation 1407/2013 (EU) No 1407/2013 of 18 December 2013 on the application of Articles 107 and 108 of the Treaty on the Functioning of the European Union to de minimis aid.[2]

It is also worth emphasizing that before the era of the COVID-19 pandemic, the legal framework for supporting enterprises from public funds in the aspect relating to state aid was very stable. This means that major revisions of the regulations were made once every few years. For example, Regulation 651/2014 replaced the earlier Regulation No. 800/2008 of 6 August 2008, declaring certain types of aid compatible with the common market pursuant to Art. 87 and 88 of the Treaty. This means that the legal framework for aid was stable almost throughout the entire period of the financial perspective. The argument for this position was the need for a stable implementation of the measures. Frequent changes in regulations could be perceived negatively by entrepreneurs, as they reduced the stability of investments. It was almost unimaginable for entrepreneurs to react quickly to changes in the economic environment. However, taking into account what happened in January 2020, the rules for providing assistance to entrepreneurs have completely changed.

3 The Covid-19 Pandemic and Its Impact on Financing Entrepreneurs

The COVID-19 pandemic had a fundamental impact on the change in the legal framework governing the admissibility of aid with the use of public funds. The decisions that were made to limit the spread of the coronavirus were aimed at protecting the lives and health of citizens. Their result was decrease in demand for goods and services, reduced mobility or reduced supply caused by disruption of supply chains and absence of employees at the workplace. Uncertainty as to the further development of the situation translated into a reduction in the investment plans of entrepreneurs and deterioration of their financial liquidity. In order to counteract the negative economic effects of the fight against the pandemic, extraordinary public aid solutions had to be introduced. These solutions, contrary to the previous priorities, differed in the purpose of financing. Before the pandemic, the primary goal was to finance investment projects, while the pandemic caused the need for liquidity financing, the purpose of which was to keep companies on an ongoing basis, e.g. those that employed employees and could not suspend business activity. This

---

[2] Säcker, Montag (2015), pp. 474–482.

problem has also been noticed at the level of EU law. The European Commission has noticed about shock is affecting the economy through different channels. There is a supply shock resulting from the disruption of supply chains, there is a demand shock caused by lower consumer demand and there is the negative effect of uncertainty on investment plans and the impact of liquidity constraints for undertakings. The various containment measures adopted by the Member States, such as social distancing measures, travel restrictions, quarantines and lock downs are intended to ensure that the shock is as short and limited as possible. These measures have an immediate impact on both demand and supply, and hit undertakings and employees, especially in the health, tourism, culture, retail and transport sectors. Beyond the immediate effects on mobility and trade, the COVID-19 outbreak is also increasingly affecting undertakings in all sectors and of all kinds, small and medium enterprises as well as large undertakings. The impact is also felt on global financial markets, in particular with concerns for liquidity. These effects will not be contained to one particular Member State and they will have a disruptive impact on the economy of the Union as a whole.

As a consequence, it was decided to quickly introduce legal changes regarding state aid the regulations by means of which specific solutions regarding state aid were introduced as part of counteracting the effects of the pandemic were: Communication from the commission of 20 March 2020 Temporary Framework for State aid measures to support the economy in the current COVID-19 outbreak. The introduction of detailed solutions regarding state aid also translated into the level of national law, the Act of 3 April 2020 on special solutions supporting the implementation of operational programs was passed, and new aid programs were introduced, including, for example:

- Regulation of the Minister of Development Funds and Regional Policy of 14 April 2020 on providing assistance from financial instruments under operational programs for 2014–2020 to support the Polish economy in connection with the COVID-19 pandemic;
- Regulation of the Minister of Development Funds and Regional Policy of 26 May 2020 on granting aid in a simplified form of repayable support from financial engineering instruments subject to reuse and from financial instruments under operational programs for 2014–2020 to support the Polish economy in connection with the occurrence of the COVID-19 pandemic;
- Regulation of the Minister of Development Funds and Regional Policy of 28 April 2020 on granting aid in the form of subsidies or repayable aid under operational programs for 2014–2020 to support the Polish economy in connection with the COVID-19 pandemic.

When analysing the changes introduced in detail, it should be noted that financing from public funds was allowed not only for the sector of small and medium-sized enterprises, but also for large enterprises. It is worth analysing whether such action is correct. As already noted, the most important effects of counteracting the pandemic that affected the performance of business by entrepreneurs are:

(1) decrease in demand for goods and services,
(2) limiting the mobility of the population,
(3) limitation of supply caused by the disruption of supply chains and the absence of employees at the workplace,
(4) deterioration of the financial liquidity of enterprises.

The decline in demand for goods and services is caused by several factors. The most important are administrative orders related to limiting the transmission of the virus and the state of uncertainty of consumers who, for fear of losing their source of income, do not decide to buy new goods and services. According to the data of the Central Statistical Office, retail sales in April 2020 fell by 22.9%. compared to the corresponding month of 2019. In April 2020, the largest decrease in sales was recorded in the "textiles, clothing, footwear" group (63.4%), a significant decrease in sales was also reported by entities trading in motor vehicles, motorcycles and their parts (by 54.4%) and solid, liquid and gaseous fuels (by 32.9%). On the other hand, a lower decrease in sales was observed in the group of "food, beverages and tobacco products" (by 14.9%).[3] Based on the data quoted, it can be assumed that the decrease in demand affected not only enterprises from the SME sector, it can even be assumed that the decrease in demand affected industries in which large enterprises have a significant share in production (e.g. companies producing motor vehicles or fuels). In addition, the pandemic contributed to changes in consumer behavior related to e.g. remote work.[4]

Another effect of fighting the pandemic was limiting the mobility of the population. Industries most affected in this respect were primarily passenger transport companies, such as airlines, travel agencies, and rail and road transport companies. According to the data of the Polish Air Navigation Services Agency, the decrease in the number of flights on individual days of April 2020 amounted to approx. 90% compared to the corresponding month of 2019.[5] It can be assumed that the limitation of population mobility had a similar impact on the functioning of both large enterprises and those from the SME sector. There are no objective reasons to assume that this effect of the pandemic was more severe for enterprises from the SME sector.

The third impact of the pandemic analyzed was a reduction in supply due to the disruption of supply chains and the absence of workers from the workplace. In this case, it is also difficult to find a link between the effect of the pandemic and the size of the company. Moreover, there is no doubt that the disruption of supply chains has a significant impact on large enterprises, which more often than SMEs operate in innovative and technologically advanced industries (e.g. production of drugs and pharmaceutical substances, production of computers, electronic and optical products), so that their activities often relies on processed goods and services.

The last analyzed effect of the pandemic is the deterioration of the financial liquidity of enterprises, understood as the ability to pay their liabilities on an

[3] Polish Air Navigation Services Agency (2019).
[4] Sadecki (2022), pp. 47–62.
[5] Statistics Poland (2020).

ongoing basis. The aforementioned effects of fighting the pandemic undoubtedly affected the financial flows of enterprises. Limited demand and supply meant that enterprises could have problems with settling previously contracted liabilities. In this case, the industry in which the company operated had an impact on financial liquidity, its multiplicity was of secondary importance. One can only assume that large enterprises, as they have better creditworthiness, could more easily obtain external financing. However, confirmation of this hypothesis would require an extended economic analysis.

It can therefore be concluded that the possibility of granting aid from public funds not only to small but also to large enterprises was rightly accepted. To sum up this part of the analysis. It should be emphasized that the response of the legislator to the COVID-19 pandemic was quick and intense. The regulations enabled state support for the enterprise sector.

4 The Legal Framework for Financing Enterprises in the Final Stage of the Pandemic

The analyses presented so far have related to the first stage of the COVID-19 pandemic and the effects of preventing its effects. It is worth noting, however, that the impact of the pandemic on the economy has changed over time. Enterprises began to adapt to functioning in new circumstances. New factors have also emerged. The war in Ukraine was also such a factor. Among the many consequences of Russia's military aggression against Ukraine was the imposition of economic sanctions on Russia and retaliatory measures by the Russian Federation. These actions have direct economic consequences. Polish enterprises also experience various effects of these activities, both direct and indirect: a decrease in demand, disruptions in contracts and projects, decrease in turnover, disruptions in supply chains, especially in the case of raw materials and semi-finished products, or unavailability or economic unprofitability of other means of production. The Russian military aggression against Ukraine has disrupted the supply chains of certain products, especially cereals and vegetable oils, imported from Ukraine, as well as supply chains for exports to Ukraine. High energy prices have a negative impact on the economy and reduce the purchasing power of citizens, especially the most vulnerable.

They also have an impact on the competitiveness of enterprises, in particular in energy-intensive industrial sectors. Some industries already affected by the COVID-19 pandemic, such as transport and tourism, are particularly affected. The increase in production costs experienced as a consequence of the aggression of the Russian Federation against Ukraine may in some cases threaten the continued operation of enterprises that would otherwise be profitable. Lowering the profitability of production also has a negative impact on the level of employment in enterprises. The crisis is also felt in the financial markets, in particular in terms of financial liquidity and fluctuations in the commodity trading market. The military aggression of the Russian Federation against Ukraine has also led to a massive forced migration of Ukrainian citizens, both within the country and to neighbouring countries. This unprecedented flow of refugees into the EU has serious humanitarian and economic consequences. Under Polish law, an example of an aid program enacted as a consequence of the war in Ukraine was the Regulation of the Minister of Development Funds and Regional Policy of August 4, 2022 on granting aid from financial instruments and financial engineering instruments subject to reuse to support the Polish economy in connection with the aggression of the Russian Federation against Ukraine.

A fact worth noting in the final period of the pandemic was the change in the rules for selecting enterprises that qualify for aid. In the original period, all enterprises were financed. The legislator did not distinguish in any way the legal situation of enterprises due to their size or the industry in which they operate. As already signaled before the pandemic, the factor justifying the support was the scale of the company's operations. However, the pandemic has affected businesses in a similar way. Its effects were felt by both small and large enterprises. It was only in the second phase of the pandemic that the legislator observed that the effects of the pandemic are varied depending on the industry in which the companies operate. For example, the effects of the pandemic have been felt by companies in the tourism, entertainment and communication industries. For example, in the case of e-commerce, the pandemic has even contributed to the development of this branch of the economy. Therefore, the legislator rightly differentiated aid instruments and focused on helping those enterprises that were most severely affected by the effects of the pandemic. The legislator decided to diversify the legal situation by including the PKD code (Polish Classification of Activities) which the entrepreneur is obliged to specify at the stage of registering business activity.

The above means that the legal situation of enterprises has changed significantly since the outbreak of the COVID-19 pandemic. Currently, most aid programs for enterprises related to counteracting the effects of the pandemic have expired, and entrepreneurs are facing completely new challenges related to high inflation, high prices of energy carriers or the economic crisis. Therefore, it is reasonable for the state to also notice these circumstances and (as it was during the crisis caused by the pandemic) work intensively for the enterprise sector. Such actions may include, for example, simplifying the normative system related to running a business or optimizing the tax system for entrepreneurs.

5 Controversies in the Field of Financing Enterprises in the Era of the COVID-19 Pandemic

Although the legislator's reaction to the COVID-19 pandemic should be assessed positively—in terms of adapting the rules on state aid. Many legal actions have been controversial. These include, for example, the mode of introducing administrative restrictions on running a business. Doubts were raised by the fact that the freedom to conduct business activity was restricted under regulations—whereby, according to the Constitution of the Republic of Poland, restriction of the freedom of business activity is allowed only by statute and only for reasons of important public interest.

Other doubts were raised by the state's support of only selected groups of enterprises.). Several instruments supporting enterprises have been adopted, in which aid is selective. The most important criterion for the recognition of aid is the size of the enterprise. Selected selective instruments implemented by the Act of March 2, 2020 on special solutions related to the prevention, counteraction and combating of COVID-19, other infectious diseases and crisis situations caused by them (Journal of Laws of 2020, item 374, as amended):

(1) co-financing of salary costs—in accordance with Art. 15 zzb sec. 1, the staroste may, on the basis of the concluded contract, grant the entrepreneur within the meaning of art. 4 sec. 1 or 2 of the Act of March 6, 2018—Entrepreneurs' Law, co-financing of part of the employee remuneration costs within the meaning of Art. 15g sec. 4, first sentence, and the social security contributions due from these salaries in the event of a decrease in economic turnover as a result of the occurrence of COVID-19; in accordance with sec. 5, the co-financing referred to in par. 1 may be granted to micro, small and medium-sized enterprises within the meaning of the Act of March 6, 2018—Entrepreneurs' Law;
(2) a loan to cover the current costs of running a business; in accordance with Art. 15 zzd para. 1, in order to counteract the negative effects of COVID-19, the staroste may, on the basis of an agreement, grant a one-time loan from the Labor Fund to cover the current costs of running a business by the micro-entrepreneur referred to in art. 7 sec. 1 point 1 of the Act of March 6, 2018—Entrepreneurs' Law;
(3) exemption from contributions; in accordance with Art. 31 z para. 1, at the request of the contribution payer, the obligation to pay unpaid social security contributions, health insurance contributions, contributions to the Labor Fund, Solidarity Fund, Guaranteed Employee Benefits Fund or Bridge Pension Fund, due for the period from 1 March 2020 to on May 31, 2020, shown in the settlement declarations submitted for this period, if he was reported as a contribution payer and (...)—he reported less than 10 insured persons to social insurance (micro-entrepreneurs). in accordance with sec. 1a, at the request of the contribution payer, shall be released from the obligation to pay unpaid social security contributions, health insurance contributions, contributions to the Labor Fund, Solidarity Fund, Guaranteed Employee Benefits Fund or Bridge Pension Fund, due for the period from 1 March 2020 to until May 31, 2020, in the amount of 50% of the total amount due for contributions shown in the settlement declaration submitted for a given month, if it was reported as a contribution payer and (...) reported to social insurance from 10 to 49 insured persons (small entrepreneurs) Exemption from contributions.

The problem of selectivity resulted from the fact that the effects of counteracting the pandemic, such as administrative restrictions on running a business or broken supply chains, affected not only enterprises from the SME sector, but also large enterprises to the same extent. Therefore, in the light of the constitutional principle of equality before the law, doubts have arisen whether some support tools can be dedicated only to selected groups of enterprises distinguished by size. It seems that a better solution is to create aid solutions relating to the industries most affected by COVID-19.

Given this controversy, it should also be noted that the scale of the pandemic was unprecedented and required unprecedented action. However, it is worth drawing conclusions for the future and being legally prepared for such non-standard events.

6 Summary

Observing in retrospect the activities related to counteracting the effects of the COVID-19 pandemic on entrepreneurs, it should first be noted that the legislator (both at the EU and Polish level) reacted quickly and effectively to the changing economic circumstances. This may be evidenced by, for example, radical changes in the area of state aid regulations. In the first weeks after the outbreak of the pandemic, completely new aid rules were created, which allowed many entrepreneurs to be saved.

It is also worth noting that in the subsequent stages of the pandemic, economic circumstances changed and entrepreneurs began to adapt to operating in the circumstances of the pandemic. It also required adapting the support tools. In this area, it is worth paying attention to the targeting of aid activities for enterprises from industries most affected by the effects of the pandemic. The aid was targeted in particular at enterprises from the tourism, recreation and transport industries.

It is also worth emphasizing that in the second stage of the pandemic, additional difficulties for entrepreneurs related to the outbreak of war in Ukraine or the economic crisis overlapped. This forced the legislator to take a whole series of additional aid measures.

In conclusion, it should be emphasized that the full scale of the impact of the pandemic on the economy will only be observable from the perspective of several years after the end of the pandemic. This is due to the fact that many aid measures have a multi-level nature and their effects are spread over time—an example of such effects are supply-demand problems, which are the main cause of high inflation. This effect occurred several dozen months after the outbreak of the pandemic. It is likely that other long-term effects will continue to emerge. Nevertheless, it is necessary to emphasize once again the quick and thorough reaction of the legislator in the field of public support for entrepreneurship in the era of a pandemic.

References

Kowalski D (2014) The legitimacy of state intervention in support of micro, small and medium-sized enterprises, public funds in Poland. Polityki Europejskie Finanse i Marketing.

Polish Air Navigation Services Agency (2019) Report on traffic in Polish airspace. Polish Air Navigation Services Agency, https://www.pansa.pl/raport-o-ruchu-w-polskiej-przestrzeni-powietrznej-stan-na-15-kwietnia-br/

Säcker FJ, Montag F (2015) European state aid law, Munchen

Sadecki W (2022) Wpływ pandemii COVID-19 na podróże służbowe w branży małych i średnich przedsiębiorstw. Studia Periegetica. https://doi.org/10.5604/01.3001.0015.9324

Statistics Poland (2020) Statistical bulletin. Warsaw

Dariusz Kowalski PhD of Law, economist, legal advisor. Scientifically he deals with economic and financial law, deputy director of the Financial Ombudsman, expert at Bank Gospodarstwa Krajowego, member of the council at the SME Ombudsman, participant in many working groups at the Polish Bank Association, ministries, and industry organizations. Author of scientific articles in the field of entrepreneurship and financial law.

Printed in the USA
CPSIA information can be obtained
at www.ICGtesting.com
CBHW081737190724
11856CB00003B/214